*T*estifying and *R*escuing *A*frican *M*inds *W*orldwide With *T*raditional *Y*oruba *P*hilosophy

Adetokunbo Knowles Borishade, Ph.D.

Sankofa International Press

Tampa, Florida

SANKOFA PRESS
Tampa, Florida
borishade@gmail.com

Copyright © 2007 By
Adetokunbo Knowles Borishade, Ph.D.

All rights reserved.
No part of this book may be reproduced in any form, by photostat, microfilm, xerography information retrieval system, electronic or mechanical, without the prior written permission of the copyright owner.

ISBN #0-9654009-2-1 (pbk.)

1. African Values
2. Traditional Yoruba Philosophy
3. Yoruba Enculturation and Socialization
4. African Belief System
5. Yoruba Philosophy
6. Africentric Psychology
7. African Culture
8. FBI and COINTELPRO
9. African Spirituality
10. African American Intervention Strategies
11. African Character Development
12. African Religious Concepts
13. Racial Oppression and Mental Illness
14. African History
15. African American History
16. 1960s U.S. Progressive Movements
17. African Cultural Identity
18. African Identity Crisis

OTHER WORKS BY AUTHOR

Publications:

*Re-Aligning African Heads:
Yoruba Curatives for Maafa-Related Ailments*

*The Maafa Ritual of Healing,
Remembrance, and Transcendence*

*Classical African Values and Yoruba Philosophy for
African American Intervention and Personality
Development*

Audiotape or CD Series:
(Including Study Guides & References)

African History & Culture in Review:
Segment 1. Africa: The Birthplace of Humanity

Segment 2. African Contributions to Philosophy,
Religion, and Science

Segment 3. African Origins of Judaism,
Christianity, and Islam

Segment 4. African Matriarchy
and the Divine Feminine

DEDICATION

This book is dedicated to my son Mario. Thank you for being in my life. The decision to be your pathway into the world was the best one I ever made. Always remember your mother's undying love for you, and never forget what the Orishas have done for you.

It is also dedicated to my parents, James Washington Knowles and Julia Ann Liamon Knowles. The teachings you gave me since birth remain in the core of my soul, never to be erased from memory. I am who you were, and it shall ever be the same. Thank you for your continued guidance and support from across the veil. It is my hope that this book is true to your wisdom-whisperings that assisted me even as I ate and slept.

--Adetokunbo Knowles Borishade
(AKA Evelyn Louise Knowles)

ACKNOWLEDGMENTS

One tree does not make a forest.
--Yoruba Proverb

I offer heartfelt gratitude to the brilliant Dr. Kwasi Wiredu, whose friendship I honor in the highest degree. Your contributions have cut a clear path into the field of Western philosophy so that others like myself can set up our separate stalls along the roadsides. Likewise, I thank Dr. Roland Abiodun. Your excellent work in Yoruba art history and the philosophical bases of Yoruba art have enriched my knowledge and understanding since the days of my dissertation. Appreciation also goes out to Dr. Wande Abimbola, a veritable fountain of knowledge in Yoruba culture and religion. Exchanging ideas with these coleagues always brings new insights and understanding to this Diasporan neophyte in my quest for higher levels of knowledge in the religion and culture. I hope that my humble efforts do justice to your scholarship.

For my brother Mayo Ogedengbe, it is difficult to find words that adequately express my emotions. Your unflagging friendship over the years has inspired me to carry on, to push forward, and to make my scholarly voice heard despite obstacles and handicaps that stood to silence me. Neither the years nor the geographical distance between us ever affected our friendship, and for that I am grateful.

Thanks also go out to Bernice Parker Bell and Carlotta Williams, whose prayers and faith in my work were invisible yet tangible supports that assisted me in my determination to share my knowledge with the community. It has been a real joy working with you in ongoing community uplift programs over the past few years. Both of you provided cool waters of hope in seasons of drought and reminded me always to be true to myself. Thanks for being there.

May God's blessings rain down upon all of you mentioned above for being my friends, mentors, and colleagues. I believe it was a good decision made in Heaven when we chose to meet during this Incarnation.

My appreciation also goes out to Iyanla Vanzant and Julia Stewart for some of the proverbs that were quoted from their books, *Acts of Faith: Daily Meditations for People of Color,* and *African Proverbs and Wisdom: A collection for Every Day of the Year, from More than Forty African Nations,* respectively.

FOREWORD

This book began as an updated and sharpened second edition of *Classical African Values and Yoruba Philosophy* to improve upon the information presented in the first edition. It was out of print for a few years, but orders continued to arrive from as far away as England and Germany for about four years. When I finally decided to publish a second edition, the book took on a life of its own and evolved into an altogether new publication. I began with a seven-chapter outline. By the time I finished the book had expanded to twelve chapters.

One day before I was ready to submit the manuscript for publishing, it seems as if my distant Native American ancestors whom I *almost never* think about, began to speak. I had already directed included some Native American history in the book in appropriate places. I was directed first thing that morning to the very information I needed to end the book more meaningfully. That took me back into the manuscript one last time and provided information that will form the nucleus of the next book.

Eight years ago, with the publication of *Classical African Values and Yoruba Philosophy*, I expressed my dismay at the plight of African American moral and social decline. It is disturbing to note an even worse situation at the end of 2007.

Wholesome, pro-social values and cultural norms have not only been lost, but have been replaced by a self-destructive, self-deprecating counter-culture that is a reaction to the stress of racial oppression and a result of lost cultural values.

After eight years my spirit is even more troubled because of the continuing social decline in African American society due to the failure to teach our children from an Africa centered curriculum at all levels of education. There has followed a natural progression of cultural identity problems rippling out to create larger social, medical and legal issues. I acknowledge the many accomplishments of African American individuals to whom the medical and legal problems do not directly apply. However, many are indirect contributors to the escalating issues. A lack of cultural identity and cultural cohesion among the Black middle class is the basis for middle class abandonment of their people who were left in the inner cities to fend for themselves.

My concerns are focused on the masses of children and youth whose creativity and genius are being ignored, stifled, and misdirected by the design of hostile social and political forces, especially within the U.S. institution of education. It is important to read *The Miseducation of the Negro* by Carter G. Woodson, published in 1933. For more than 100 years, there have been essentially no positive changes in African American social conditions about which he commented!

My concern led me to investigate this stagnant situation by using models and jargons from various disciplines. I finally settled on medical concepts that are easily understood by laypersons like myself to explain how Western cultures, especially American culture, have a sickness of ego, greed, and power. If we take America, in particular, there is a pathological, uncontrolled drive for material power, force, and control that grossly contradicts all the lofty rhetoric about many of its leaders being "born again Christians." Even children have enough common sense to recognize that actions more accurately determine character and motives than words.

An understanding of America's contradiction lies in knowing the makeup and dynamics of **radical materialism** that is the **basis of the *Western cultural worldview.*** There are basically only two worldviews among all the various cultures on this earth. The view of the world that has been preserved by all the **ancient cultures** to date is the *Spiritual Worldview.* People with this mental image of the world believe in the **reality of a *Divine Spirit*** that gives life and value to all living things. This worldview is concerned with supporting life, preserving nature, and maintaining balance in the universe. The other is the **modern *Material Worldview*** held only by Western cultures. This image of the world claims that anything that cannot be experienced with the five senses is not real; thus, any belief in the reality of Divine Spirit is mere superstition. Humanity and nature are valued only as material objects that can be used or disposed of in order to turn a profit. This view of the world is an insane, radical interpretation of life that **values only material gains provided by wealth and power.** Thus, only those who hold wealth and power have value. Everyone and everything else in the universe are up for profit-producing grabs! Hearing this truth requires that we **stop listening to the propaganda and start analyzing the behavior!!!**

Radical Western materialism and aggression have reached the point of violent, out-of-control, anti-social, **anti-life pathology**, such that it aims to control all of life, living things, humanity, and even space. World nations are alarmed by America's aggressive behaviors and psychotic activities that threaten the balance and survival of the entire planet. Their illness is malignant, having the power to infect healthy societies worldwide. Strong **indicators of pathology and psychosis** also signal **terminal cultural sickness and lack of God's** *Spiritual Consciousness:*

- Overwhelming lust for power and control of life, living things, human beings, and even space;

- Compulsive drive to create hatred, division and conflict worldwide;

- Total disregard for life, living things, and humanity;

- Insatiable greed for material possessions;

- Inhuman compulsion to define the rest of the human family as mere non-human objects;

➢ Dynamics of raw aggressive personal, corporate, and political power;

➢ Fear of uncertainty and loss of control.

Corporate power mongers of America and other Western cultures habitually and pathologically oppose oversight and regulation of any kind. Corporations now own and control the power brokers in the U.S. Congress and all American institutions. For corporate profits our elementary school students are being socialized into and brought under the control of the American stock market, which is presently very unstable. A small number of corporations and international conglomerates now owns and controls most of America's mainstream media, preventing the general public from receiving any news that departs from the "official line" of propaganda.

Only a **pathological, inhuman lust** caused by **ego, greed, and power** compels nations to develop an imperialism that defines non-Caucasian people as less than human and reduces them to mere chattel objects. The huge, efficient Western imperialist mechanism of institutional racism indoctrinates and numbs the minds of non-Caucasians so that they lose the understanding that the godliness and humanity of individuals, groups, and nations are demonstrated by behavior. Undeniably, American and European history reveals the malignant mindset and motives of imperialistic leaders with their fat-cat corporate army invasions as they spread division, conflict, and death throughout the world. They are masters at setting local groups against each other then stepping back to criticize them when the programmed violence begins.

Only a spiritually dead form of psychosis causes people to have a gross disregard for life, living things, and humanity, such as that which impels European and American corporations to blatantly destroy life-supporting environments and to privatize God-given, free life-supporting elements such as water. American corporations privatized water in Bolivia, and then made it **illegal for poor people to collect rainwater for survival.** It is no surprise that the Bolivian people rose up *en mass* to protest.

Being **out of touch with reality** is a clear sign of **insanity** (as defined and described in the DSM-IV, published by the American Psychiatric Association), and causes those who suffer from the malady to deny the pervasive **personal and institutional malignancy of racism** that is embedded in their societies. The extent of the sickness even reaches Western religious institutions, where it is taught and preached that God sanctions this behavior. Victims are blamed for their victimization and called troublemakers or terrorists when they refuse to suffer in silence, and when they rise up to oppose racial tyranny.

The corporate-controlled politicians and leaders of the United States of America need to stop the Bible-thumping hypocrisy. They desperately need massive, long-term infusions of God's *Spiritual Consciousness* to cure their affliction. Diseased bodies cannot be a healing balm for healthy ones, and demented minds cannot advise balanced ones. All the political and religious **self-proclaimed "physicians"** first need to get themselves healed and "saved." The Rev. Martin Luther King, Jr. once spoke God's honest truth when he said that: "eleven o'clock on Sunday morning is the most segregated hour in Christian America." Once the sick ones get healed and "saved," they should begin working among Whites in America and Europe where it is critically needed. U.S. victims of hurricane Katrina stand as an outrageous affront to any talk about a concern for curing diseases and hunger abroad. Likewise, the recent election scandals neutralize the rhetoric about this being a democratic nation of laws.

The so-called leaders who claim to be the **"police of the world"** need to "arrest" their psychopathic behaviors that are recorded throughout their history. The entire global community needs relief from the unfathomable harm, suffering, and death caused by the **infectious psychosis of Western pathology** that goes so far as to construct legal arguments and precedents to support their violence. The diagnosis is a lack of *humanizing Spiritual Consciousness.* Spiritual Consciousness imparts a love for life, nature, and all humankind, and a lack of it brings death, destruction, and "double-speak" propaganda used as a weapon to dull and control the minds of the masses. Only massive infusions of God's *Spiritual Consciousness* can heal their hearts, cease their tyranny, and allow them to function as normal human beings in benign, civilized, stable socio-political environments.

Hundreds of years of Western history inform us that there is no collective will for Western cultures to seek healing. One might say that the cultural illness of the Caucasian majority makes them strongly predisposed to violence and the destruction of living things. It appears that this cultural predisposition is compounded by what seems to be an addiction to war, violence, and bloodshed.

Having said all the above, this book continues my efforts toward the cultural healing of my people. Black psychologists have told me over the years how much they appreciate my work in this area because of the effectiveness of the cultural information when integrated into clinical practice. During my nine years of community work within the Association of Black Psychologists I learned almost as much as I contributed.

This book is an act of love proffered to Caucasian government, corporate, and religious leaders who desperately need to hear the truth about their cultural behavior, rather than some slavish, grinning lie. Only a God-driven commitment of redeeming good will toward all humanity causes me to risk writing truth. However, it is not a completely altruistic act, because Caucasian self-assessment and healing will result in healing for the rest of humanity, at this juncture of world history.

For me, this book is an *ebo*, a sacrificial love offering to the Ancestors who ordered that time must be taken off so that it could be written. My concerns over the enormity of the African American identity crisis, the growing sense of hopelessness, and the alarming rate of social decline motivated me to obey the Ancestors and get it done. The work is presented with love to Africans who can discern the urgent voices and warnings of our Ancestors and elders through the cacophony of publicly mediated mass media appeals to participate in ignorance and madness.

The Ancestors who died on African soil fighting slavery and colonization are speaking to us. Those who chose to lie on the bottom of the Indian Ocean because of the Arabic-led slave trade, and those at the bottom of the Atlantic Ocean because of the Caucasian slave trade are calling out to us. The book is written for those of us who risk the anger and intimidation of the "establishment" by standing up, speaking out, and acting to save our children and youth. It is presented to those who know in their heart of hearts that our people are not being helped by the churches or the European social and psychological theories.

Hopefully, the book will provide parents, clinicians, and educators with substantive cultural information and source material. Rather than sitting by and idly bemoaning the darkness, I join the host of many other Africanist colleagues who are attempting to bring light.

There is no pretense of objectivity here. That is impossible, in view of the genocidal attacks on Africans everywhere. The language is set forth in a straightforward, conversational style to be used by parents, community programs, and clinical practitioners who are seeking effective Africa-centered alternatives to the culturally limited European theories that are imposed on African Americans and other non-Europeans. In that regard, this book is written for the common good of the world community.

--Adetokunbo Knowles Borishade, Ph.D.

LIST OF FIGURES

1. Attitude Hot Topics — 43
2. Strongly Held Concepts in American Belief System — 44
3. Value System Decision-Making Words — 45
4. Structure and Dynamics of Attitudes, Beliefs, Values — 46
5. Theories of African Personality — 57
6. Concordance of Traits Theory — 146
7. Culture-Biology-Environment Interaction — 153
8. African and Diasporan Spiritual Worldview and Belief System — 160
9. African Belief in Reincarnation: Original Concept Of Infinity — 161
10. European and American Material Worldview An Belief System — 163
11. Cultural Features — 164
12. Psycho-Behavioral Aspects — 164
13. Socio-Political System — 171

TABLE OF CONTENTS

	Page
ACKNOWLEDGMENTS............................	v
FOREWORD...	vii
LIST OF FIGURES.....................................	
INTRODUCTION..	1
CHAPTER 1... *Roles of Religion, Philosophy, and Culture*	32
CHAPTER 2... *Cultural Identity, Behavior, and Survival*	51
CHAPTER 3... *Post-1960s African American Identity Crisis*	65
CHAPTER 4 .... *COINTELPRO Versus 1960s Progressive Movements*	96
CHAPTER 5... *Two Models of History and Culture*	122

CHAPTER 6 144
Environment, Biology, Race and Culture

CHAPTER 7 155
Clash of Values, Beliefs, and Worldviews

CHAPTER 8 177
African Women Warriors

CHAPTER 9 205
Commonly Held African Values

CHAPTER 10 217
Significance of Yoruba Culture

CHAPTER 11 234
Yoruba Moral Concepts and Philosophy For Character Development

CHAPTER 12 260
Development from Childhood To Godhood

CHAPTER 13 269
From Mis-Education to Re-Education And Liberation

APPENDICES 299

BIBLIOGRAPHY 322

INDEX 338

INTRODUCTION

*Talk to them. If they do not listen
Let adversity teach them.*
-- West African proverb

*A time comes when silence is betrayal.
That time has come for us....*
--Martin L. King, Jr.

The primary purpose of this book is to serve as an *intervention,* as suggested in the title. The term "butting heads" has several interpretations here. On one hand, a headbutt is a strike with the most robust part of one's head against a vulnerable spot of someone else's head in order to make an impact. This book fits that definition; however, in this case the strike is delivered with a force intended to get attention without rendering harm. Headbutting can also refer to a clash of minds, mindsets, worldviews, and ideologies. This interpretation is quite apropos for the book, since it sharply challenges the existing negative, self-destructive ways in which Africans worldwide think about themselves and each other.

Some buffalos and rams lock horns when engaged in combative headbutting. With horns locked head-to-head, this book attempts to lock horns with the brutal, inhumane historical and cultural issues surrounding our planned, orchestrated social decline and physical demise. With unflagging determination, it head-wrestles vigorously in behalf of African people: the parents of all humanity; those who brought the gift of civilization to a world that was mired in barbarity. Accordingly, the book quite unflinchingly and unapologetically aims to give no quarter until the arteries of miseducation, misinformation, and racial oppression have been exposed and opened, however briefly, with this modest publication. It is not the size of the bully but the force, sharpness, and accuracy of his adversary's small stone that wins the day. I am grateful for the opportunity to add this humble missile to others that have been shot prior to mine.

In order to elevate the discussion to a spiritual dimension, a picture of the *"House of Head"* shrine is presented on the front cover. The picture symbolizes the Yoruba conceptualization of the spiritual *"inner head"* and *Divine Destiny* of an individual. However, I believe that *entire races and cultures* of people also have a Divine Destiny that can only be fulfilled through their *unified cultural activities and efforts*. Many African leaders apparently have completely overlooked this concept.

Africans worldwide have been programmed, brainwashed, manipulated, oppressed, and drained of energy to the point that we have had neither the time nor the motivation to entertain the critically important philosophical question: *"Why do we exist as a people with a distinct culture?"* Nor have we set our minds to the spiritual question: *"What is the Divine Destiny of our race and culture that Almighty God requires for us to fulfill?"* These ideas have nagged the back of our minds for some time, but no *Africa-centered, unified, organized* types of forums and discussions have taken place.

Apparently, these highly spiritual questions are not being raised in any concrete, substantive manner among most African Christians or Muslims. Thus, there are no concrete strategies, activities, or timelines formulated to save our people who are dying worldwide by the tens of thousands daily. God *must* have had *something* in mind at the time of our creation, considering the fact that *traditional Africans* were given the responsibility of: (a) bringing the entire human race through the evolutionary period successfully; and (b) establishing the first and greatest civilizations in the world. There is another glaring reality for us to consider, the scientific truth of which many people will find hellishly offensive. In the event of a nuclear holocaust, only African women have the genetic makeup to preserve humanity as we know it. How is that for having the "right stuff?" Was this also a part of God's plan that Black folks should consider?

Even now, it is *traditional Africans* who hold scientific, medical and mathematical knowledge of which Western cultures remain completely ignorant. In fact, the *indigenous priests* of *traditional religions* throughout the world have forgotten more knowledge about science, mathematics, medicine, and astronomy than the Western world will ever gain. It seems to me that the knowledge is not meant for them because they are apparently so locked into their material worldview and outlook on life that they lack the spiritual motivations and makeup to handle it.

This book is meant to be a *spiritual headbutt* that I hope will result in a *spiritual transformation* that will in turn motivate *physical action*. In my opinion, the act of sending forth abstract prayers are insufficient. Almighty God provided human beings with healthy brains, minds, and bodies with the expectation that we would use them. I am convinced that after giving us these gifts God refuses to do for us those things that we refuse to do for ourselves.

By self-admission, this publication is strongly idealistic. For this I make no apology, because the life-threatening issues involved require the articulation of the highest ideals imaginable to inspire our people and to motivate them in the direction of self-help. The French make no apologies when they romanticize and idealize France and French culture, and no one criticizes them for doing so. I claim the same right in regard to Africa, and it is irrelevant to me who disagrees.

African people worldwide stand at the juncture of a fork in our historical road. The road behind us represents our present history whereby we have adopted the worst elements in Western culture and rejected the best of our own. The road on the left represents a continuation of our present situation and leads to certain extinction, because our young are dying faster than the old. The road on the right represents positive, intelligent, unified cultural strategies that will lead to the re-establishment of our place in the center of world history and civilization. This publication presents source material and tools in the form of conceptual, historical, and cultural information that will assist people of African heritage in formulating strategies for a successful sojourn down the road on the right.

Indigenous descendants of *all* the ancient cultures and religions know that adherence to Western culture and its religion present a sure pathway to death and destruction. Native American nationalists know this. Native Americans, like traditional Africans, rely upon *social wisdom* and social/humanistic ethics when making decisions about what is best for the people. Native nationalists set forth four interpretive themes that they have found to be time-tested for strengthening and ensuring the survival of their people, culture, and religion: (a) tribalism; (b) nationalism; (c) relations to other life and land; and (d) religion. I suggest that Africans worldwide need to explore the highest ideals within these four themes to find our way back to some semblance of strength within and among ourselves.

Vine Deloria, Jr. (1989/1969) of the Sioux nations wrote a book entitled *Custer Died for Your Sins: An Indian Manifesto* that expresses the close parallels between "Red and Black" cultural and historical situations. In the book, Deloria offers social ethical "prescriptions" for African-Americans that are worth attention. He believes that the political philosophy of "Black Power" as developed by Stokely Carmichael (Kwame Toure) and others was taking us in the right direction, and remarked that Native people wondered in amazement why it took us so long to get to that point. For Deloria, "black power, black separatist and black nationalist aspirations are more righteous than the quest for civil rights, integration, and assimilation."

I wholeheartedly believe that the present serious decline in African American society began with the wholesale assimilation of Western cultural values after the 1960s Civil Rights Movement. It should be noted that the deplorable economic and ethnic strife seen today throughout Africa began with the 1960s African Independence Movement for the same reason. This book focuses on African Americans; however, the cultural messages and issues apply to a multitude of Africans on the Continent, as well as those throughout the Americas and the Caribbean. In other words, it is a book written by, for, and about people of African descent worldwide, irrespective of nationality. Despite that, the book expresses an understanding of, and is in sympathy with other world cultures that presently face devastating social strife and death tolls because of the same issues. It is up to individuals to decide which portions, if any, of the publication are useful to them.

Looking at the situation realistically, we tried integration and assimilation since the 1960s and failed. We failed because our leaders refused to give credence to the successful strategies taken by our African foreparents who were just emerging from slavery in the early 1800s. They were very successful in building all-African towns, complete with independent health, economic and educational institutions. This book suggests that we use time-honored knowledge gained by the *total African experience*, in the belief that those historical and cultural elements will assist us in healing ourselves and our communities worldwide.

We need to cease the self-deception that: (a) we can "change the hearts and minds of White people." If *Jesus Christ* has not changed them in the

45,000 or so years that they have been on this earth as a distinct race of people, Black folks stand little chance of doing so. Their *total history* on the planet demonstrates that it is impossible to get along with them in peace because peace is not in them. Anyone who denies this brutal, sledgehammer-bashing truth is truly living in a life-threatening fantasy world. A terrible price in human lives is being paid for going along with the "news in the market" rather than the dictates of conscience. We need to be aware that to participate in the market-driven insanity is to build "karmic debt" that will be paid by our children and grandchildren. It is impossible to change others. We can only change ourselves. In that respect, this book especially serves as a tool for African parents, educators, community leaders, clinical therapists, counselors, Christian pastors, Muslim imams, and community program facilitators who are ready to be "hearers and listeners" of the truth that can lead to positive change, survival, and advancement.

African American parents and grandparents who need to reconnect with their history, culture, and childrearing traditions are introduced to those positive healing elements in this book. Clinical therapists, counselors, community leaders, and program facilitators who seek Africa-centered information will hopefully find the historical, cultural, and philosophical source material, as well as the models in this book very useful in their efforts to strengthen children and youth and to rehabilitate wayward youth and ex-offenders. I only insist that you ask permission to use the material and give me credit as the source of the information, in accordance with standard copyright laws.

The book should be especially helpful to counselors and program facilitators dealing with ex-offenders who are attempting to re-enter society and the job market. The reality is that people who have been incarcerated for years have had to adopt a prison value system and behaviors that handicap them once they rejoin their families and re-enter society. Individuals of African heritage can use this book to strengthen, regain, and restructure the best aspects of their humanity and character to become fit as productive citizens of society. Many Continental Africans who reside in America and Europe send their children home to live with grandparents for one or two years because they recognize the serious problems that result from rearing their children in Western culture.

I contend that the core values within Western culture are antithetical to the wellbeing and healthy development of a balanced African personality. Especially in the case of America, Western culture holds that all values are baseless except those that result in profit and political control. Even the most perfunctory investigation of European and American behavior throughout Western history reveals features that are clearly pathological in nature, as defined in the *Diagnostic and Statistical Manual of Mental Disorders* (DSM-IV) that covers all mental health disorders, published by the American Psychiatric Association.

I refer particularly to the Caucasian "feelings of inadequacy and narcissistic need for admiration" as described in the DSM-IV, page 173. The clinical description and definition are consistent with studies conducted by noted psychiatrist Dr. Francis Cress

Welsing (1991:5-6). She presents an analysis of Caucasian personality, culture, and behavior in her book entitled *The Isis Papers: The Keys to the Colors*. In it Dr. Welsing argues that Caucasians' incessant reminder that they are superior in itself signals their deep-seated inferiority complex. According to her, their sense of inferiority is caused by two factors: (a) numerical inadequacy within world populations; and (b) genetic color inferiority among people of color worldwide. Dr. Welsing explains that since Whites were

> acutely aware of their inferior genetic ability to produce skin color, whites built the elaborate myth of white genetic superiority. . . and set about the huge task of evolving a social, political and economic structure that would support the myth of inferiority of Blacks and other non-whites.

Conventional wisdom indicates that when people are really superior in any manner they are recognized as such and do not have to talk about it all the time. Nor do they have to build massive institutional infrastructures and political strategies to ensure and uphold the false illusion of their superiority. True superiority has no need for such measures.

America's religious institutions operate under the same materialistic, profit-driven values and politic control motivations. Although they operate under the guise of helping the needy, they are actually helping themselves through fundraising efforts that bring dollars into their churches to support administrative salaries. The plethora of Christianizing campaigns helps the colonial/neocolonial powers to continue Western political control of foreign countries. Christian missionaries, even well-meaning Black ones, have always worked hand-in-glove with Western imperialism and slavery, and continue to do so knowingly or unknowingly, directly or indirectly. Again, historical investigation proves or disproves this claim. Researchers need to pay attention to parallels in church activities during the Dark Ages of Europe and activities in current American history. Many Black churches are participants in creating what I consider as the "Dark Ages of Modernity," explained later in the book.

Some will consider the positions taken in this book as an expression of hatred or as an attack on certain persons or classes. On the contrary, this publication is a work of love toward all people. It is the love of humanity and all living things that motivate me to expose hatred and oppression, because silence would render me as a participant in the worldwide death and destruction. Courts of law hold that maintaining silence when one has knowledge of wrongdoing means consent with and participation in the wrongdoing. In my case, speaking out is an act of love and healing for both the perpetrators and the victims of oppression.

My speaking out is also intended as a corrective for unsatisfactory and unsuccessful strategies and methods that have not worked in our favor. This, too, is an act of love. I am always spiritually moved when reading or listening to a speech delivered by The Rev. Martin Luther King in 1967, entitled "Beyond Vietnam: A Time to Break Silence." It is my fervent hope that our African religious leaders, Christian and Muslim, will follow Dr. King's suggestion to "move beyond the prophesying of smooth patriotism to the high grounds of a firm dissent based upon the mandates of conscience and the reading of history." This speech appears in its entirety in the **Appendix**.

The statements made about Western culture are directed toward leaders and self-proclaimed hate groups. These leading perpetrators desperately need healing more than their victims in this case where, in my opinion, we have an entire culture suffering from grossly antisocial and anti-life values. Anyone who studies America's progressive movements of the 1960s and listens to public radio today understands that these statements and sentiments do not apply to *all* Whites. However, because of a dark, deep-seated, pervasive culture-related illness, Western nations increasingly spread death and anguish in their own as well as every other culture with which it has contact. Embedded religious sanctions that justify their behaviors only go to further demonstrate that American and European leaders are clearly unbalanced, out of touch with reality, and unable to heal themselves. It is up to the rest of the world to somehow bring them into mental balance, if possible. Without that, I am convinced that the world will never experience peace, harmony, and wellbeing.

At the risk of being called an alarmist, let me state that my concerns are many because of the life-threatening health concerns and other issues among African Americans that are increasing at alarming rates. These concerns are shared by many people nationwide, and are discussed passionately in community meetings, in impromptu conversations within supermarkets and department stores, as well as during casual chats with friends and family members. These commonly known concerns need to be addressed as objectively, as intelligently, and as often as possible in the literature in order to elevate the urgent need for positive change to a higher level.

HIV/AIDS, as well as cervical and throat cancers are increasing at alarming rates throughout Black communities due to risky sexual activities. Many Black men released from prison are secretly engaging in bisexual behaviors, infecting the women in their lives with sexually transmitted diseases. Many young girls are engaging in dangerous alternative forms of intercourse, falsely believing that it preserves their virginity. Young mothers are no longer being taught the hygienic value of having their boy babies circumcised at birth so that they protect the health of their female sex partners later in life. Three generations of women often party together in the clubs, and sometimes experience men flirting with the grandmother, the mom, and the granddaughter simultaneously.

Some surprising religious beliefs are held by both Black and White southerners. Imagine my shock during some of my HIV/AIDS/STD workshops in the South to experience middle-aged women who believe it is a religious taboo to examine their own breasts for tumors. However, it is alright if their husbands examine their breasts even though he will have a different agenda while doing so. I met several women who, by self-report, had symptoms of

STD present in their genital areas, but considered it sinful to use a hand mirror to look at their own bodies. In a similar vein, I came across a number of women who did not know the names of their reproductive organs, and could not identify them when shown pictures.

In my anthropology class at the university a third-year nursing student stated that males have one less rib than females because one was removed from Adam to make Eve. Two male students joined the discussion by claiming that Adam was "created," while Eve was merely "made." All of them believed that a man originally gave birth to women. Common sense should inform them that this is impossible and should not be taken as fact. Still another student had been taught that men put the spirit of life and soul into a child at conception with his active sperm, while all women can do is to give it flesh because female eggs are "dormant." Had he done even lightweight reading on the subject of the female reproductive system, he would have learned about all the work the female's egg had already done by the time he shot his sperm. By then the female's egg has done its job and is in an *active resting phase*, alert and waiting to see if his sperm can do its job. Just as it is in life, the female does not need to run after a male. She is already prepared and only needs to sit and wait for him to pursue. If one male does not do his job by pursuing, she has only to wait for the next one who knows what to do and is willing to do it properly.

It is a common occurrence to find university students in the "Bible Belt" who are so heavily indoctrinated in biblical recitation that they are incapable of either thinking critically or engaging in intellectual discourse. They have been taught that every subject and question can be answered with a Bible verse in full, without question or further discussion. These students demonstrate an agitated pacing behavior when confronted with questions, ideas, and concepts that cannot be answered with a Bible verse.

Black folks in America are becoming extinct because we are killing each other. The critical nature of our situation is proven daily by the experience of the old burying the young. Several inner city funeral directors have told me that for the past 20 years they have been burying more young people and children than elderly people. We are burying too many babies and children because of physical assault, drive-by shootings, premature births, as well as congenital drug addiction and HIV infection. Visits to the hospital intensive care units reveal young people in their 20s and 30s connected to cardiac monitoring devices as a result of drug addiction. This means there is a decreasing number of young people available to take the place of the old as they die out. This phenomenon is against both nature as well as the Natural Order of the Universe, and demonstrates how the loss of historical knowledge, cultural values, and cultural traditions reduces one's ability to survive.

A critical issue deals with the small number of surviving young adults who will gain the education, status, wisdom, and survival strategies that their *offspring* will need to survive in a post-9/11 world. Many of them will not have the knowledge or even the will to ensure that legislation is in place to safeguard the rights and care of the elderly. The average ninth grader in America reads at the level of a fourth grader from three generations ago because the educational system had educators to stop teaching phonics and learning. In place of legitimate education schools began to emphasize memorization and high-stakes test-taking like the FCAT. The FCAT does not educate; it only trains students in test-taking skills.

The average age for grandmothers today is around 38 years old because of the significant number of mothers who gave birth during their teen years. Far too many teen mothers have insufficient knowledge, wisdom, values or survival skills to pass on to their children and grandchildren. Many of our middle-aged mothers and grandmothers suffer from arrested development and are trying to catch up on the years of their youth that were missed because of the responsibilities of single motherhood at a young age. The problems are compounded because young Black mothers have been instructed by White social workers that it is more important to be their children's friend than it is to assert the role of a parental authority figure that establishes and enforces rules and insists on maintaining a distance of respect between them.

Many African American males today continue to impregnate then abandon the mothers of their offspring. Such adult males are pitifully immature and lacking in basic human character development. They have succeeded where the White slave-master failed, by literally reducing themselves to stud animals lacking in human responsibility and the most basic of human relations skills. The females who tolerate this behavior likewise reduce themselves to mere breeding animals.

In place of the high regard and respect formerly given to women and elders, there is now a virulent disrespect. Black females now refer to themselves with debasing, disrespectful terms, popularized by the recording industry that expressly aims to denigrate Blacks. The importance of a good appearance and appropriate ways or modes of dressing is nonexistent. Completely gone is the understanding that pink hair, green contact lenses, provocative dresses, multiple gold tooth embellishments, and pants worn completely beneath the buttocks are not attractive and do not demonstrate civilized behavior. By traditional African standards, it demonstrates insanity.

Too many high-profile sports figures and rap artists arrogantly demonstrate the behavior of immature street thugs with no concept of what real manhood entails. They have money, but since they lack the knowledge and the will to do something socially significant with it, they have no power. The best they can muster at getting attention is to do something illegal that creates media attention but also destroys their lives and reputations. This is the behavior of untrained, out-of-control children. It is not the way thinking, responsible, disciplined adults act. With adults behaving in this manner, there is no wisdom or even common sense teachings available for their children.

The conscious connection between Black identity and Africa is almost nil since the 1960s push for integration and cultural assimilation. Assimilation is an anthropology term that explains how people give up the worldview, values, and identity provided by their mother culture and adopts those elements within a foreign culture. By the 1970s leading Black folks in the United States had stopped drawing from African history and culture for their identity and made a conscious decision to become more like Anglo Americans. They increasingly began to mimic Whites in the corporate world, academics, entertainment, and politics. It has become vogue for Blacks to boast membership in the very political party that has a tradition of being diametrically opposed to any significant Black social progress.

In view of these increasing problems, there is no way of convincing me that African Americans as a distinct social group have moved forward in the last fifty years. Some individuals have progressed financially in certain areas of American society. However, the progress of a few individuals becomes irrelevant when related to the fact that we have regressed *en masse* in those culture-related areas of life that support survival and advancement of the race.

The race problem in America's education system is as old as the United States itself. As far back as 1906 William E.B. DuBois delivered a speech entitled "The Hampton Idea" in which he advocated the critical need for Black colleges so that African Americans could strive for higher education and not just vocational schools. DuBois (1906) believed that a "great lack" in education existed that denied the race the energy, self-assertiveness, command, and use of its intellectual powers. He also spoke at length of a "great fear" among Anglo Americans and Europeans concerning people of

African descent and other people of color. DuBois used the metaphor of the sleeping giant who suddenly wakes and throws off the policies of harsh repression and gentle discouragement. The "great fear" is that people of color—especially Africans--will suddenly become conscious of their tremendous latent powers after being wakened by higher education. He understood the necessity of both vocational and liberal arts training for African Americans, but prioritized higher education.

In another essay entitled "Whither Now and Why" (1906), DuBois advocated for the formal teaching of African American history and culture courses in schools and universities. Otherwise, he argued, not only would knowledge of the history and culture be lost, but African Americans would completely lose their connection with the emerging African world. The most pressing problem that DuBois wrestled with was the possible loss of identity. He foresaw the danger of African Americans adopting the ideals of Anglo Americans to such an extent that we would be left with no ideals of our own. DuBois' fear is today's reality.

The problems faced by African Americans are not caused and perpetuated by Anglo-Americans alone, as noted by Carter G. Woodson. *Miseducation of the Negro,* published in 1933, became a literary landmark in African American history. Woodson approached the problems of education from an entirely different perspective from DuBois. Woodson's concerns about the race were centered on the fact that the accepted corrective strategies used by Black Americans to fight racism and segregation had not produced satisfactory results. His argument was that "educated Negroes" were the seat of the trouble because they held contempt for their own people. To Woodson it appeared that the more African Americans obtained higher education, the greater their disdain for anything concerning Africa, including their own people of African descent. After studying hundreds of African American high schools, Woodson reported that an expert in the U.S. Bureau of Education found only eighteen in the entire country that offered even one course in the history of African Americans.

Tones of despair were clearly evident in Woodson's (1933:56) writing as he noted that African Americans had lost ground in regard to racial progress two generations after DuBois. He compared the depth of vision held by his contemporaries with that of Africans who had recently emerged from slavery some fifty years earlier.

> In 1880 freed Africans went to school to prepare themselves for the uplift of a downtrodden people. In our time too many Negroes go to school to memorize certain facts to pass examinations for jobs.

Woodson (1933:97) continued to look to the past in tallying up the loss of Black American character, vision, identity, and sense of responsibility to each other:

> When the free Negroes were advised a hundred years ago [circa 1821] to go to Africa they replied that they would never separate themselves from the slave

population of this country as they were brethren by the "ties of consanguinity, of suffering, and of wrong."

Race-conscious Woodson argued that most African Americans in professional positions in the 1930s were lackeys and puppets who did no more than what they were told by White superiors. He claimed that most Black professionals were hand-picked for gate-keeping positions and merely served as tokens to give the appearance of liberal interracial cooperation. At the same time, their presence prevented other Blacks from charging businesses and government agencies with racial discrimination when race was clearly the issue in denial of employment and on-the-job racial discrimination and harassment. To their credit, many educators throughout the U.S. attempt to teach from an Africa-centered perspective. However, they are all under attack and often fired by Black and White administrators who don't want anyone under their supervision to teach anything that pushes against the racist nonsense in the "official curriculum."

Thus, African Americans in gate-keeping positions are full participants in strengthening racist barriers to any semblance of meaningful integration and justice. By upholding the racist interests of the White *status quo*, such Blacks sever connection with their own people. Woodson (1933:57) uttered the bitter complaint that "the Negro forgets the delinquents of his race and goes his way to feather his own nest...." The author lambasts politicians, ministers, teachers, directors of community centers, and heads of "social uplift agencies," and labels them as "racial racketeers" and "racial toadies."

This downward social and educational trend has continued, such that in 2007 inner city youth are virtually abandoned. I am sickened from witnessing years of endless research and meetings run by "poverty pimps": community stakeholders, university researchers, organization administrators, and sheriff's office representatives. The focus of all their activities revolves around how they who live outside of the Black community can profit from the misery of the people inside the community. The community never benefits from all the research, studies, and meetings. Actual positive change would translate to less grant money allotted to universities and community stakeholders. The community usually has no input or involvement in the studies being conducted about them.

The churches headed by "gospel pimps" are no better. Churches are springing up like mushrooms, sometimes ten to a city block, sucking money out of inner city residents like vacuum cleaners without giving anything back except the hope for salvation in Heaven. In the meantime, the pastors are "living large" in safe, beautiful gated communities.

I have always made a point of living within the African American community, much to the surprise of my colleagues. The sight of my people when I open my doors every morning is self-affirming. Thus located, the children, youth, and college students in the community get to know me. They come to visit, eat, watch TV documentaries, and have access to my considerably large personal research library. In this fashion my mere presence and accessibility makes it possible to bring some light back into urban communities, and is more acceptable to me than merely cursing the darkness of "ghetto ignorance." To some this may appear as a sacrifice. On the contrary, connection with my people brings mutual benefits and pleasure.

My soul is enriched each time I have an opportunity to reach out and expand the minds and lives of the young ones. Imagine the pleasure at being called "auntie" or "grandma" by children and youth, and the surprise at being introduced by a college student as someone who is "like a mother" to him. These are the relationships that I remember from growing up in Cleveland, Ohio. However, everything began to change in the 1960s and 1970s when the middle class abandoned those left behind in the inner cities of America.

In addition to my race conscious Nationalist upbringing, immersion into the study and practice of African religion and culture has had a profoundly positive effect on my philosophy of life and life itself. It is one thing to know that one's society is missing something vitally necessary for health, wellbeing, and advancement. It is another matter altogether when one can identify those missing components and pass them on to others. That is exactly what knowledge and practice of the religion, traditions, and culture of Africa have brought me. Once I became centered in the beliefs and culture of my own people I became a whole person. This healing knowledge is accompanied by a liberal understanding that geographic locations and cultures around the world created different spiritual dispensations. In that regard, whatever name someone calls God is irrelevant to me. God *is*, and there is only *one Creator God* called by different names by people in various cultures around the world.

Tolerance of and respect for religious differences in world cultures can lead to world peace. It is the use of religion as a tool for political power and material gain that presently has the world in turmoil. For the profit and power of a few, the United States' current practice of "disaster capitalism" has removed governance of the nation from the seats of government and has given it to multinational corporations. By the same token, the military has been given free reign to wage unprovoked wars and other "disasters" on other countries. The more the U.S. Government eliminates constitutional rights and protections, the more it appears that America is waging war with its own citizens. This appears abundantly clear to America's citizens of color who are increasingly targeted for arrest and abuse although they have committed no crimes.

There is no such thing in existence as a "one size fits all" worldwide religion, nor should there be. It mystifies me that ANY non-Caucasian—especially Africans— would continue to buy into it and pass it down to their children, when they know that it is used to enslave, colonize, and slaughter innocent people for political power and material gain. Do more than 500 years of participation in evil politics not teach something? It is amazing that people reject the beliefs of their own indigenous cultures and joyfully embrace those of their known enemy. I recognize that the crux of the problem is not the religion itself; it is those who control it. However, it is extremely difficult to separate the two, when those who control the religion use sermons, literature, and powerful electronic media messages to control the minds of believers.

History compels us to ask the question: **Does God advocate and support evil?** Did the Almighty smile down upon European immigrants and sanction the way they seized foreign lands and resources; murdered women and babies; enslaved and colonized people of color; and spread their diseases all over the world? What kind of God would do that? Yet Caucasians in America and Europe preach sermons from the pulpits and send messages through their media that God is on their side in these evil endeavors that destroy rather than support God-given life.

It is impossible to make me believe the hollow propaganda that Almighty God *requires* that people throughout the entire world *have* to accept the *new* religion of one tiny population of people. A lust for political power and material gain are the motivating forces behind such a false teaching, and those motives have already been revealed by examining Western history. In like manner, there is no reason to accept the idea that an even tinier group of people are God's chosen favorites just because they make that claim. If that is what they want to believe, it is their business. However, there is no need for anyone else to believe it. African Christians need to spend less time thinking about the Hebrews/Jews and more time thinking about Africans' chosen mission on this earth. Instead, most of us appear to have made slavery our comfort zone and are hesitant to move out of it. This is why we are still enslaved, and are happy slaves on the various types of plantations. All the energy spent on what others are doing just keeps us preoccupied and busy doing everything except discovering what God requires of *us* as a people.

Because of the devastating damage done to non-Caucasian minds worldwide, we have a planet filled with people who have identity problems. Black folks talk about the serious brainwashing job that has been conducted on us, but many are unsure of what are the best healing strategies for getting ourselves out of the debilitating condition. Reading Africa centered books on African history helps, but historical knowledge alone will not provide the strongest healing elements. The problem is that most Black folks are so deeply brainwashed that they immediately and vehemently reject the very Africa-centered healing potion they need.

The most powerful psychological and spiritual healing elements for people of African descent are found in African religion, philosophy, culture, and science. The same applies to all the other people of color around the world who are healing themselves by throwing off Western religion and culture and returning to their indigenous religions and cultural traditions. For example, the sociology literature and the news media report statistics on the positive ripple effects created when Native American groups returned to their indigenous religions and traditions. That one act of reclaiming their identity, *total* history, and spiritual traditions has the effect of solving all kinds of spiritual, psychological, social, and health problems.

It is our fault that we continue to be viewed as slaves, because we demonstrate slave thinking and behavior. It is 'way past time for African Americans to throw off the shackles of mental enslavement by embracing our own indigenous philosophy and traditions. We need to return to the African religious doctrines and traditions that we created as the first religion in the world that were carried and remembered by our children who developed as other racial types and cultures throughout the world. We should revisit the philosophical ideals of our own people, doctrines that are so spiritual and pro-social that they have the power to heal Africans and non-Africans alike. Our children should be reared with these doctrines and ideals from birth.

We need to begin talking, teaching and writing about the Divine Destiny of Africa and African people, and what *Africans* are chosen to accomplish on this earth. Every group of people has a Divine Mission, but Africans worldwide are so busy cozying up to our enemies and betraying our people for material gain that we haven't even dreamed about it. Why have the Black Ph.D.s in philosophy and religion not studied the philosophical ideals and religious doctrines of our own cultural heritage? Instead, most are contented to mouth European theories that do not fully relate to the reality of their own African heritage, history, and experience.

So-called Black theology is "high yellow" at best because it is based on the writings of European philosophers. I could not agree more with Dr. Yosef ben-Jochannon when he argues that our Black seminarians and Black clergy lack anything even close to Black Theology. Authors like The Rev. James H. Cone in his book *Black Theology and Black Power*, made a valiant attempt to Africanize Christianity for Africans, but fell short of the mark. The Rev. Henry Mitchell has revised his original 1975 text entitled *Black Belief: Folk Beliefs of Blacks in America and West Africa* so that the newer version is more relevant. Mitchell analyzed the transcripts of sermons by African American preachers to provide an emic (inside) understanding of traditional Black sermonics. He recognized similarities in religious beliefs between Yorubas and African Americans. In a book entitled *Conjuring Culture, Biblical Formations of Black America,* T.H. Smith brings "something new out of Africa" by combining biblical interpretation with magical transformation, as practiced by African Americans. He discusses the conjurational employment of biblical figures in African American religious folk traditions.

The debate in theological circles continues. However, scholars of Christian theology will remain locked into the worldview and perspective of early White philosophers and theologians in their articulation of Christian theology, hermeneutics, and revelation. In his collected essays, *Of National Characters: The Philosophical Works of David Hume,* the British philosopher wrote that the "capacities of non-whites, especially Indians and Africans, differed significantly from those of whites."

German philosopher Emmanuel Kant (1775) wrote in his book *Anthropology from a Pragmatic Point of View,* that "yellow Indians have a smaller amount of talent" and "Negroes are lower, and the lowest...of the American peoples." The writings of Hume and Kant are often included in theological discussions. Both of these eighteenth century philosophers were of the opinion that Africans are barbarians who never contributed anything to world civilization and that there was no reason to mention them in the literature. It was their influence that is most responsible for the removal of African history, culture, and civilization from world literature. Yet, both are considered philosophical heroes and direct or indirect contributors to Christian theological thought and discourse.

Chapter 1 defines and examines some of the fundamental roles of religion, philosophy, and culture and how these three disciplines are foundational elements with which we can examine African American cultural identity.

Chapter 2 discusses the importance of cultural identity and its direct connection to behavior, a sense of wholeness, health, wellbeing, and survival.

Chapter 3 discusses the destructive impact that cultural assimilation into Anglo-American culture has had on African Americans' sense of cultural identity. Current mental health and identity problems are discussed within the historical context of violent, oppressive U.S. government programs that targeted Black civil rights protesters during the 1960s civil unrest that included groups involved in the progressive movement.

Chapter 4 delves deeper into the violent measures taken by the FBI and their COINTELPRO Program in the 1960s to absolutely neutralize and eliminate any form of protest against its oppressive policies and practices. This includes measures to weaken and undermine African Americans' knowledge of their history, as well as their sense of race consciousness and race pride. A discussion of how other groups were similarly targeted increases the readers' understanding of the U.S. government's decision to use CIA strategies, formerly applied against foreign governments, against its own American citizens in its commitment to halt every group involved in the progressive movement.

Chapter 5 presents two models of history and culture: the Ancient Model and the Aryan Model. An explanation and historical development of each model is provided, along with the motivations behind the formulation of the Aryan Model.

Chapter 6 contains a detailed explanation of how the so-called distinguishable "races" developed over millions of years as environmental and biological adaptations in particular regions of the earth. It further explains development of the concept of race.

Chapter 7 discusses several defining features of African culture and presents contributions from several African scholars on the subject of values, beliefs and traditions that are commonly held by African societies across the continent of Africa. A cross-cultural view is presented to demonstrate some radical differences between African and European/American values, beliefs and traditions.

Chapter 8 takes the discussion of human adaptation to a higher level by analyzing the negative mental health effects suffered by African Americans in their attempts to adapt to the stresses of institutional racism in America. It investigates the current social decline and identity crisis among African Americans resulting from a loss of their cultural values, beliefs, and worldview. A cross-cultural analysis of differences between African American and European/American cultures is also presented.

Chapter 9 presents an explanation of why the Yoruba culture is selected for this book. A brief history of the Yoruba people traces them from the Nile River Valley civilization of Meroe into all three Americas and the Caribbean to demonstrate their central significance to this book and to African American identity and character development. The chapter argues that knowledge of African values and other cultural elements served as survival tool kits that African Americans gave away in the 1960s, making survival almost impossible in the overwhelming U.S. system of oppression in the twenty-first century.

Chapter 10 takes another step forward in the discussion of Yoruba culture by presenting Yoruba moral concepts and traditional philosophy, and how they are used in character development. The chapter continues the argument that African cultural features in general and Yoruba traditional philosophy in particular greatly assist in healing African American minds that are suffering due to losses in knowledge of African history and culture.

Chapter 11 presents a general outline of ideal traditional African expectations of human character development over the period of a lifetime and informs as to how social infrastructures, rites, and festivals provide formal structure to childrearing. Life stages of development are accompanied by an explanation of behaviors that must be demonstrated before the community declares that an individual has reached that level of personal and spiritual growth.

Chapter 12 summarizes the most important ideas presented in the previous chapters and expresses hope for positive change in the future.

1. ROLES OF RELIGION, PHILOSOPHY, AND CULTURE

*Set your heart on learning,
that you may direct the work of the world.*
--Ancient Egyptian proverb

Religion

Religion is a very real phenomenon that exists in every human society all over the world. It is central to the values, cultures, worldviews, and identity of the people. Every society in existence studied what they believed were the finest and highest attributes of humanity, then expanded those characteristics and attributes a thousand-fold to express what God must be like. Religion translates the highest ideals and concepts held by a group of people into doctrines that they believe are sanctioned and blessed by Almighty God. Such divine sanctioning gives ultimate authority to the lessons and themes within religious texts that are believed to be both *real and true.* The religion of a group presents their actual view or conception of society itself and sets forth an idealized interpretation of how life should be on earth. Every story within written and/or oral religious texts from culture to culture contains themes that set forth moral and ethical considerations that are expectations for human beings, human behavior, and human communities. The themes within these religious stories are powerful influences that become embedded within all of the society's institutions for the purpose of creating and maintaining social stability. Thus, the institutions of law, marriage, education, and medicine are a few examples of the social infrastructures that covertly reflect and overtly govern and enforce the themes within a society's religious text.

Religion expresses the group or collective consciousness of a society of people. As an ultimate authority it fuses together all of their individual consciousnesses into one large unified image which then creates a belief system and a reality of its own. This **perception of reality** is held by everyone in the religious group, and believed to be both **real and true**, although some individual variations will exist. The definition of **beliefs** within a culture are those things that the society considers real and true in an *unquestioning* manner because the beliefs are a part of the overall society's reality.

The power of religious mythology resides in its ability to shape and govern human behavior by setting forth a distinct **image of reality** in an extremely credible and authoritative manner. The most powerful **values** of a society are found within its religious themes. Social values provide an entire society with a more or less unified understanding of what is considered *godly or evil, good or bad, better or worse*. Serious problems arise when a dominant group claims that its oppressive acts are sanctioned by God but those acts are bitterly opposed by the oppressed.

Values are held by an entire society, even though every individual may or may not choose to adhere to them. They are stabilizing forces that provide a society with guidance when making judgment decisions. Values are powerful elements set forth as themes in literature and religious stories. Values are vital components needed for making individual and group decisions, as well as for administrative decision-making in organizations and institutions.

Politicians use commonly held values as a strategy to neutralize or minimize opposition by those whom they need to control. Religious leaders often deliver sermons that contain commonly held values so as to manipulate the thinking and opinions of the oppressed. Many pastors in traditional Black churches preach that slavery was a blessing for Africans because it introduced Christ into our lives so that our souls could be saved. On one hand, this is a way of saying that something good can come from something intended to be bad. On the other hand, it fails to hold Caucasians accountable for the wrongs they have committed. The message works best among people who strongly believe in the value and the "saving grace" of Christianity, and who fail to critically analyze such a statement within social and historical parameters. As a strategy such a message gets poorly educated, oppressed Blacks to agree with and participate in their own oppression.

Philosophy
Philosophy involves the exploration and understanding of the nature of reality, the meaning of life, and the governing principles of the universe.

It examines human evolution, culture, and history; knowledge and values; as well as social structure and development.

Philosophy has several important roles in human societies. First, it involves the investigation and discussion of wisdom, morality, ethics, and self-discipline, thereby enriching human life by setting forth ideals and principles toward which society is expected to strive. The enriching aspect of philosophy also addresses the questions and issues that confront individuals and societies. Philosophy transcends personal and social issues that are considered an ever-present reality and discusses alternative perspectives of problems. Philosophy demands positive change as it discusses social and political problems, because it moves from the *"isness"* of a present reality and presents the *"oughtness"*—the idealized alternative of what that social or political situation should be. In this manner, philosophy is drawn and constructed directly from a society's religious themes and values.

Second, philosophy conducts intellectual inquiries into the basic nature of things, subjects like the characteristics of God, as well as the makeup of human beings and their role in the divine scheme of things. Strongly held beliefs that are taken to be real and true are examined in the process of philosophical discourse. The scientific aspect of philosophy includes investigating such topics as:

➢ **Worldview.** An integrated, comprehensive interpretation or view of the world and the meaning of experiences;

- **Cosmogony.** Study of the evolution of the universe;

- **Cosmology.** Study of the beginning, process, dynamics, and structure of the universe;

- **Ontology.** Study of the nature and meaning of being or existence; Study of the place, role, and destiny of humanity and the rest of physical existence;

- **Epistemology.** Investigation and theories about the origin and nature of knowledge;

- **Metaphysics.** Investigation into the nature of first principles and ultimate reality—things that are considered *self-evident truths* that are passed on from one generation to another;

- **Aesthetics.** Presents theories concerning what is considered beautiful within a culture and its various artistic forms;

- **Reality.** A culture-based acceptance of things that are viewed and conceptualized as truly possessing existence or essence;

- **Logic.** A system of reasoning that enhances critical thinking and provides clarity.

Third, philosophy has a distinct place in education. The curriculum of every public school and every university discipline (major subject of study) is shaped and guided by a particular philosophy. Teachers, professors, and instructors are expected to adhere to the established theoretical guidelines within the official curriculum. Therefore, if a university department or a school maintains a **Europe centered philosophical theory** for educating its students, all research and analysis will be based on an assumption of White supremacy, and all pedagogy (teaching approach) will present information that is tailored to support the racist assumptions within the Eurocentric theory.

The Eurocentric philosophical guiding theories that are taught in educational systems generation after generation throughout America and Europe create a reality that is taken by students to be both real and true, but are actually fabrications. Study, research, and analysis using an **Africa centered philosophical theory** immediately expose the historical inaccuracies and overturns the falsehoods about African people, culture, and traditions. The Africa-centered teaching approach places Africans in the center of all discourse rather than at the outer periphery. It discusses what Africans accomplished and what they contributed to world civilizations.

Africa centered scholars like Kwasi Wiredu, V.Y. Mudimbe, and Wande Abimbola are born into, educated and experienced in traditional African philosophy, religion, and culture. Thus, they are able to teach from the center or heart of African culture in discussions that cut across every discipline: art, medicine, architecture, law, history, visual and performing arts, linguistics, archaeology, literature, etc. They present in-depth discussions of African thought, cosmology, and worldview rather than what Caucasians do and have done to and for Africans. African thoughts, traditions, and actions are analyzed within the context of African religious beliefs and philosophical principles. African behaviors are not presented as mere one-dimensional reactions in response to White oppression.

The Africa centered approach is a powerful educational tool that provides students with documented evidence and prevailing scientific studies to support its claims. It is extremely difficult for students to maintain belief in untruths when presented with ancient documents as well as contemporary studies written by Caucasians who recorded their amazement and gratitude after learning from Africans. Ancient Greeks themselves left written evidence about what they were taught by Africans who, at the time, were known worldwide as people with high levels of knowledge. The empirical evidence in the literature written by fifth century Greeks demonstrates that had it not been for Africans, what is known as Greek's classical period would not have been possible. If that is a falsehood, it is the Greeks themselves who told it. Ancient African men and women were highly regarded educators, scholars, medical doctors, high priests, political rulers, architects, surgeons, mathematicians, astronomers, warriors, and orators who held international reputations as great people of tremendous stature.

Contemporary anthropologists and scholars from various disciplines are writing books about how today's indigenous Africans are far in advance of the Western world in genetics, cosmology, astronomy, medicine, and science. Marcele Griaule, Shannon Dorey, Robert Temple, Laird Scranton, and Janheinz Jahn are just a few examples of Caucasian researchers who are writing the truth about the extent to which indigenous African scientific knowledge is far in advance of Western knowledge.

The reason why America's educational system kicks, screams, and devises barriers against the Africa centered approach being taught to students at all levels is because they lack the hard evidence to support what they are teaching. They cannot afford for this alternative information to be revealed to a world that has been hoodwinked into believing that Caucasians are the alpha and omega in scientific knowledge and civilization. White supremacy concepts are taken as *a priori truths*-- truths that are considered self-evident but are often not supported by empirical evidence. The White supremacy theme is embedded into every social institution as a means for creating a **"Matrix-like" false reality.** The claims and assumptions of these false, unsupported racist concepts collapse under the weight of Africa centered arguments that include empirical evidence in their presentation. As in the"Matrix" movie, people begin to see with new eyes.

The world is learning with accelerating speed that modern Western scientific knowledge is at a primary school level in comparison with thescientific knowledge held by ancient indigenous cultures. The problem is that the information is coded into highly spiritual mythological language that Western scientists are too limited to comprehend. The White supremacy model is tantamount to "modern" elementary schoolers convincing everyone that they have more knowledge than the indigenous people from all over the world who hold master and doctorate degrees. We have to admit that their ingenious methods to fool the world have worked for a long period of time. However, you cannot fool all the people all the time. At some point in one's history the truth emerges and rises even when crushed underfoot or buried. To borrow a well-known saying among architects, nothing stays buried forever.

Indigenous cultures all over the world have a profound respect and regard for the earth and for life itself in all its various forms. Western culture alone has a patent disregard for the earth, nature, and life. Apparently no one has been able to convince them that to fight with Nature is to wage a war that cannot be won. All the floods, fires, and earthquakes in the U.S. and Europe make it appear that "Mother Nature" is fighting back with freaky climate, weather, and flooding phenomena that cannot be controlled, defended against, or prevented.

Nature seems to be fighting back in another manner, as well. For at least fifty years Caucasians have been at a negative population growth rate, which accounts for all the panic and frenzy over aborting White babies. Europeans' and Americans' ability to reproduce grows weaker every generation. The *Stanford Review* (May 26, 2006) reports that Europe's death rate is higher than its fertility rate and that "Europe is in a demographic and cultural death spiral."

This information is very scientifically interesting, when we consider those persons who never cease to use the theories of Charles Darwin to claim the hardier fitness of Caucasians. Was it not Charles Darwin who taught that Nature always selects against (eliminates) the *weakest* of every living species? The sharp decline in Caucasian birth rates worldwide for the past fifty years is empirical evidence that sharply undermines the concept of White physical superiority. This discussion does not make me a racist. It is merely a scientific analysis and a comparison of the notions and claims that abound in Western literature with the facts of everyday life and experience.

It is also not a racist statement to mention that in case of any kind of a genetic-mutating nuclear accident, there is a strong probability that all humanity will once again be dependent upon African women for survival. The densely variable properties of African women's MtDNA, comprised of the largest number of dominant genetic traits on the planet, makes them the most hardily fit to carry forth humanity as we know it today. It will be extremely difficult for women with large numbers of recessive genes to carry out that role, especially if they already suffer from reproductive weakness. As I always advise my students, do not take my word for anything. Conduct some research; absorb and reflect on the information; perform your own critical analysis; then come back and we will discuss this further. The future of humanity itself depends upon our becoming serious about these issues.

All of the foregoing discussion demonstrates the critical importance of an Africa centered guiding philosophy for teaching children of African descent. The longer Black students remain in Western educational systems, the more deeply indoctrinated they become in the false notion that the claims of White supremacy in all aspects of life are, *a priori,* both real and true. This is the process by which the educational systems in America and Europe alienate people of color from themselves and turn students into walking, talking zombies filled with the poison of self-hatred and lacking in racial pride, cultural identity, and connection with their people.

Culture

Many people commonly mistake **expressions of culture** like music, dance, modes of dress, foods and styles of cooking as being culture itself. The most fundamental definition of culture deals with its role as a strategy for human survival. Culture is a social system of attitudes, beliefs, values, and ideals that **maximize and ensure survival, growth, and autonomy** for themselves and their children.

Attitudes are preconceived ideas about people, places, things, experiences, concepts, etc. that develop whether or not an individual experiences them personally. These ideas are initially passed on from parents to their children, and later are often reinforced by teachers when children begin attending school. *Figure-1* below lists some topics that are guaranteed to stir up lively discussions whenever they are mentioned. Some of the topics appear alone, some are diametrically

Figure-1

> **ATTITUDE "HOT TOPICS"**
> - Life / Death / Afterlife
> - Sin / Original sin
> - Freedom / Slavery
> - Science / Superstition
> - Racism
> - Sex / Celibacy / Marriage
> - Natural / Supernatural
> - Humanity / Animals / Nature
> - Normal /Paranormal, Natural / Supernatural
> - Spirituality / Materialism
> - Civilization / Barbarity
> - Justice / Law
> - Individualism / Communalism
> - Sexuality / Homosexuality
> - Resurrection / Reincarnation

opposed, and others are linked together because to discuss one automatically leads to a discussion of others.

Beliefs are notions of what is real and/or true. Religious stories and parables that are presented as lessons to strengthen morality, spirituality, and faith are sometimes taken to be both real and true. These are characterized as **religious beliefs**. Academic theories create a distinctive set of **scientific beliefs** about humanity, nature, and the universe. *Figure-2* contains subjects that are also certain to arouse heated discussions, and may even be political issues.

Figure-2

STRONGLY HELD CONCEPTS IN THE AMERICAN BELIEF SYSTEM

- Reality and power of Satan
- Reality of Heaven and Hell
- Creationist theory
- The curse of Ham
- Men gave birth to women
- The war in Iraq
- Jesus Christ as Almighty God
- White supremacy
- Virgin birth
- Evil nature of non-Christian religions
- Women as introducers of evil on earth
- African inferiority
- Male superiority
- Reality of angels

Values are principles used for making decisions and judgments—two extremely essential human activities. They are referred to as social anchors because of their role in stabilizing society. *Figure-3* presents a few values that are used for making decisions and judgments.

Attitudes are described as being structured in a shallow portion of the human psyche, which makes them easily changed. Think of experiencing a stirring sermon or a dynamic political speech during which one can be committed to a certain behavioral change or mode of action. If the message only reaches the shallow level of an individual's attitude,

Figure-3

VALUE SYSTEM DECISION-MAKING WORDS

- Good / Bad
- Right / Wrong
- Better / Worse
- Godly / Evil
- Moral / Immoral
- Ethical / Unethical
- Decent / Indecent
- Righteous / Unrighteous
- Sacred / Profane
- Justifiable / Unjustifiable

the commitment to action lasts for only a short period of time. Beliefs occupy a deeper level of the psyche. One belief has to be replaced with another in this case, much like replacing one brick with another so that the whole structure does not collapse. However, once that level of the psyche is reached, commitment to action or change lasts for a longer period than it does with attitudes.

Of all the cultural elements, values are the most powerful tools for creating long-term changes in human behavior. Values are said to occupy the deepest reservoir of the human psyche and they control attitudes, beliefs, and behavior. The puppet-master aspect of values is what creates a complex, integrated system whereby all three elements function interdependently. A change in someone's value system usually results in long-term behavioral change. *Figure-4* illustrates the structure and dynamics of attitudes, beliefs and values.

Ideals are closely identified with values because they set forth the highest, most honorable, most worthy principles used as social standards and models of near-perfection that are pursued as **goals** in a society. Ideals form the basis of social expectations and standards for **ethical behavior**, in accordance with a society's values.

Examination of these definitions and explanations provides an understanding of how human behavior is shaped and governed. Every human act directly or indirectly involves these cultural elements that influence the likelihood of an individual's survival, growth, and development or the opposite effect. In order to understand the meaning and motivations for particular individual and group behaviors, extrapolate inward from behavior to attitudes, to beliefs, and finally to the core values. As shown in *Figure-4*, the same process can be done in reverse by investigating core values first, and then by moving outward to arrive at an understanding of certain behaviors.

During the evolutionary period, human groups developed distinct cultural traits that **maximized survival** in particular geographic locations thousands of years ago. Those that developed in tropical regions created heat-adapted cultural features. The same is true for the groups whose cultures developed in temperate and arctic zones. Today's cultures continue to reflect the physical realities of prehistoric environmental influences.

It can be seen, then, that prehistoric societies developed their cultures to fit within particular geographic locations and physical environments. This means that culture is a practical, *adaptive response* to geographic and environmental stresses and conditions. Culture and environment are not independent phenomena. Rather, they are interdependent elements that mutually interact in such a way that they combine to create what becomes the human experience. Culture creates a context within which all experience gains meaning, and all learning occurs.

Figure-4

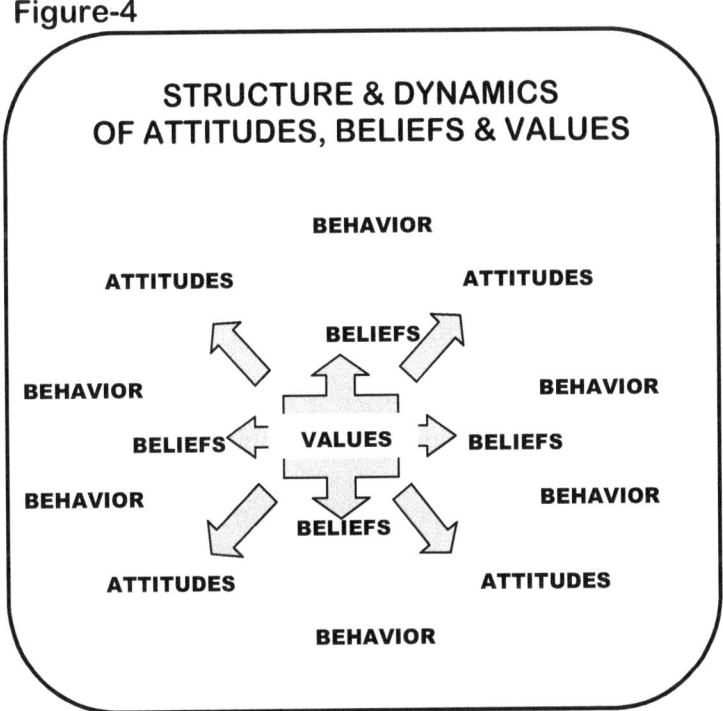

Culture maximizes survival because of its protective role in society. Dr. Cheikh Anta Diop (1990), in *The Cultural Unity of Black Africa, states*:

I consider culture as a rampart which protects a people, a collectivity. Culture must, above all, play a protective role: It must ensure the *cohesion* of the group. Following this line of thinking, the vital functions of a body of African human sciences is to develop this sense of collective belonging through a reinforcement of culture. This can be done by developing the linguistic factors, by re-establishing the historical consciousness of African people so as to arrive at a common feeling of belonging to the same cultural and historical past. Once this is attained, it will become difficult to "divide and rule" and to oppose African communities one against the other.

The protective aspect of culture was a natural development of societies designing and structuring their total way of life to fit within particular geographic locations and physical environments. This means that culture is a practical, **adaptive response** to support and protect human life within the stresses of geographic and environmental realities.

If we were to go back 40,000 years and then come forward in time, we would discover the process of adaptation to physical environments triggering both biological and cultural responses in early Homo sapiens. In the harsh, bitterly cold Arctic environments, human beings developed physical traits that make them physiologically superior for survival in that region. They developed relatively short, compact bodies with short extremities, and a heavy layer of subcutaneous fat under the skin. Light skin tones allowed for an easy absorption of the sun's rays that were in short supply. Some early cultural responses to the environment included a nomadic way of life; shelters in caves, or built from snow and sometimes animal skins; hunting, fishing and gathering; and clothing made from animal fur (Birdsell, J.B. (1981).

On the other hand, people in African tropical environments similarly developed physical traits that make them physiologically superior for survival in such regions. By comparison, they have taller, slimmer bodies with longer extremities and more muscle mass without the layer of subcutaneous fat. More sweat glands developed on their bodies to disperse heat, and dark skin tones protected against dangerous ultra-violet rays of the sun. Some African cultural responses include building houses from available vegetation or from earth, and wearing lightweight woven clothing. Depending upon the region, Africans created diets that may have included a greater variety of foods such as meat, fish, poultry, fruits, vegetables, roots, and dairy products. An agricultural, sedentary lifestyle developed earlier than in arctic regions that remained locked in the Ice Age for a longer period of time (Birdsell, J.B. (1981).

Culture is **shared** by all members of a society. It contains the shared commonalities that people in a society have developed, such that in general they hold the same values, norms, family lifestyles, social roles, and behaviors. Culture creates a context within which all learning occurs, and all experience gains meaning. Shared attitudes, beliefs, and values form the cultural context within which all experience is processed, and these elements are the mechanism by which interpretations of experience give meaning and richness to human life. All learning occurs within the context of a shared culture because all experiences and teachings are screened and examined through the society's shared system of attitudes, beliefs, values, and ideals. Thus, learning and knowledge are strongly influenced and shaped by the cultural elements that are commonly held by most people in the society.

When a small sub-group of people residing within a society has a radically different set of attitudes, beliefs, values and lifestyles, it creates a situation of cultural dissonance. Conflict develops as the smaller group struggles to maintain its indigenous cultural integrity that provide richness, meaning, and stability to their lives. The same holds true if a society becomes invaded by people from another culture. In both scenarios a bitter struggle ensues whereby the dominant group attempts to force its cultural norms and interpretations of experience upon people of another culture.

The above discussion about the roles of religion, philosophy, and culture form the groundwork for an examination of African American cultural identity, behavior, and wellbeing in the next chapter. The following chapter takes the next step in demonstrating how elements of religion, philosophy and culture play a critical role in shaping a healthy cultural identity, and how cultural identity influences behavior and supports survival.

2. CULTURAL IDENTITY, BEHAVIOR and SURVIVAL

*Take a day to heal from the lies you've told yourself
And the ones that have been told to you.*
--Maya Angelou

Cultural identity is based upon how well an individual identifies with and is centered within the cultural features of her or his mother culture. The more comfortable a person is with the vital core of the traditional philosophy, religion and culture, the stronger the individual's sense of cultural identity will be, and the greater ability the person will have for survival. Noted psychologist Amos N. Wilson (1990:27) is correct is his assessment of the critical connection between cultural identity and survival.

> The construction and organization of group and personal identity are of the utmost importance to individual, group functionality and survival. All groups or cultures, if they are to survive, autonomously exist and prosper, see the establishment of the identity of themselves and their constituents as their major role. This is accomplished through their controlling the nature of their environment, social experience, information, social interaction and symbols. Cultural symbols are utilized to help construct, maintain, and regulate the identity and behavior of the

constituents of a cultural group in such ways as to advance their individual group and cultural interests and successfully defend themselves against those who would exploit, dominate, abuse or destroy them....When the identity of the individual or group is manipulated by an alien entity, then that manipulated individual's or group's viability rests in hands other than its own. That individual's and/or the group's lot in life then moves beyond his or its self-control.

Cultural identity is the primary focus here, rather than racial identity. I agree with Dr. Asa Hilliard (1997:xix), that it is the cultural wealth of a community that serves as the basis for both individual and collective identity, since it overrides and is the highest order of identity.

Ethnic and cultural identity is that which grows out of the shared struggles and the collective heritage of a people. It is true that there are many aspects to a felt identity; however, ethnicity and culture are the core components of collective identity that compel and propel nationality, social class, and gender. These initiatives are important to be sure, however, none of them rise above the core identity.

In *The Cultural Unity of Black Africa,* Cheikh Anta Diop (1990:9) speaks of the importance for people of African descent to devote themselves to the investigation of their indigenous cultural origins.

For by doing this the people in question becomes aware of what is solid and valid in its own cultural and social structures and in its thought in general;

it becomes aware also of what is weak therein and consequently what has not been able to withstand the passage of time. It can discern the real extent of its borrowings from others and can now define itself in a positive fashion using not imaginary but real indigenous criteria. It will have a new consciousness of its worth and can now determine its cultural mission, not in a prejudiced, but in an objective manner; for it can better understand the cultural values which it is most fitted to develop and contribute to other peoples, allowances being made for its state of evolution.

Diop (1981:211-219) delves deeper into the subject of cultural identity by setting forth "three factors that contribute to its formation: (1) an historical factor; (2) a linguistic factor; and (3) a psychological factor." He sets forth the critical importance of the *historical factor*:

> The essential thing for people is to rediscover the thread that connects them to their most remote ancestral past. In the face of cultural aggression of all sorts, in the face of all disintegrating factors of the outside world, the most efficient cultural weapon with which a society of people can arm themselves is this feeling of historical continuity.

Diop (Op.cit.) refers the *linguistic factor* as a constituent element of cultural personality and, consequently, of cultural identity. He further stresses that language is the unique common denominator, the characteristic of cultural identity par excellence. In making this argument, Diop acknowledges that it is not practical for Africans to trace their languages back 5,300 years to the Nile Valley civilizations. He adds, however:

> The review of the historical and linguistic factors as constituent elements of cultural personality brings to light the necessity for a total recasting of the African program of education in the [African languages], and for a radical centering of these on Egypto-Nubian antiquity, in the same way that the Western educational system has its foundation in Greco-Latin antiquity, there is no way more certain, more radical, more scientific, more sane and salutary to reinforce the African cultural personality and, consequently, the cultural identity of Africans.

On one hand it might be argued that the linguistic bond is broken among Africans in the Diaspora. On the other, we can also note that the bond is not completely broken, evident in the retention of Niger Kordofanian grammatical/linguistic features in all Creole languages that formed throughout the Diaspora in all three Americas and the Caribbean (Borishade, 1994:1):

> Despite of the fact that Ebonics ("Black English") utilizes the English language, its phonological, morphological, syntactical, grammatical, and sometimes lexical features are such that it can historically and linguistically be considered as a Creole language deemed worthy of much deeper investigation. Historic and linguistic evidence support the theory that Ebonics among Africans in America is a bona fide language constructed from linguistic elements of Niger-Kongo languages in West Africa, i.e. Twi, Igbo, Ewe, Efik, etc.

Diop (Op.cit.) is at a loss in his attempt to define the features found within the African psychological factor. However, several African American psychologists have spent considerable time constructing theories about the core of the African personality. Although I am not a psychologist, my own culture-based theory of the African personality, published in *Psyche Discourse* (March-April 2000:4-11) is included below in **Figure-5**.

Culture represents a total way of life. All learned behaviors, attitudes, beliefs, values, language, customs, rules, and ways of doing things within a given population of people are characteristic of their particular culture as it developed tens of thousands of years ago. The same applies to the ancient religious beliefs of a people that have been maintained to date and continue to influence people in the various cultures today. The religious beliefs and sense of reality held to be real and true by one cultural group may be very different from those held by other groups, but **all are equally valid**.

Because human beings in the various cultures worldwide have maintained their ancient beliefs, values, worldview, and traditions, they are products of the original ancient geographical and ecological environments experienced during the tremendously long evolutionary period. Likewise, human beings are carriers of the ancient religious beliefs that have been passed down by our ancestors from generation to generation. Just as Diop suggests, when a belief system and way of life are practiced for that long, they form a reality so strong that individuals are not consciously aware of them unless something threatening happens. The more cultural elements come under attack, the greater the threat of breakdown to an individual's entire psychological and spiritual systems.

Culture is created by a society of people who share the same ideals and principles. Cultural thoughts and actions are those that are commonly shared within such a particular group or society. All human groups construct institutions to organize, stabilize, and govern their societies. In this respect, **all cultures and societies are equal**. Social institutions have a stabilizing role because their function is to enforce the ideals and principles found within the culture. Institutions are established to enforce and maintain society's cultural beliefs and values, and to regulate behaviors within the society. Institutions stabilize society by regulating and governing individual and group behaviors. Personal development from childhood to adulthood, and regulation from the cradle to the grave are overseen by social institutions such as marriage, education, health, medicine, labor, business, media, law, politics, etc. The worldview, beliefs, ideals, principles, and rules of the society are cultural resources with which institutional administrators make judgments, rulings, and decisions.

Religion and education are probably the two most important institutions for socializing people into a particular cultural reality. Both the religion and the educational institutions of America have been involved in the destruction of African American cultural identity. The educational system had to be forced to establish courses and departments for African American studies.

	STRUCTURE	**DYNAMICS**	**PERSONALITY**
Na'im Akbar	1. Three Components Of Being: -Physical; -Mental; -Spiritual (core)	Spirituality	Rhythm
Daudi Azibo:	1. Inner Core 2. Outer Core 3. I-Me-We Nexus of Selfhood	Spiritualistic energy	Cognitive Functioning Own-Race Bias Own-Race Preference & Maintenance
Joseph Baldwin	1. African Self-Extension Oriontation 2. African Self-Consciousness	Spirituality Melanin	Demonstration of African personality - - - -
Adetokunbo K. Borishade	1. Natural Order 2. Conceptual Order 3. Institutional Order 4. Soc-Behavioral Order	Divine Essence Spiritual Energies External & Internal spiritual energies Internal spiritual energy	African Consciousness Acceptance of adulthood Assertion of warriorhood Demonstration of godhood
Wade Nobles	1. Concrete Condition -Primary (Melanin) -Secondary (Envir't)	Spirituality	1. Harmonious relationships: -spiritual -material 2. Conceptual: -affective -connotative
Robert Williams	1. WEUSI Multi-Dimensional Blackness: -Collectiveness; Naturalness -Afrocentric Space &Time	Spirituality	Struggle for authenticity

Even now the schools and universities are only comfortable with educators who teach the courses from a European perspective that begin history lessons with events from 400 years ago. School boards appreciate Black teachers who use White authored textbooks, focus on what Whites did to and for Blacks, and whose lessons are based on notions of White supremacy.

The Christian Church has always played a significant role in upholding the lies, atrocities, and evils of White imperialism, such that terrible acts are committed in the name of God and are given biblical sanction. They give justification for African slavery by referring to the biblical story about a curse that was placed upon Ham and all his heirs. Ham was a dark-skinned Hebrew, so the story is stretched to the ninth dimension to claim that Africans are children of Ham. Cheikh Anta Diop (1974:7) probably put his finger right on the correct origin and motive of the so-called "curse" by placing the biblical passage into historical perspective. He claims that the curse was placed in Hebrew literature considerably later than the period of Israelite persecution and their exodus out of Egypt.

> Accordingly, Moses, in the Book of Genesis, attributed the following words to the Eternal God, addressed to Abraham in a dream: "Know for certain that your posterity will be strangers in a land not their own; they shall be subjected to slavery and shall be oppressed four hundred years.
> ....
> Here we have reached the historical background of the curse upon Ham. It is not by chance that

this curse on the father of Mesraim, Phut, Kush, and Canaan fell only on Canaan, who dwelt in a land that the Jews have coveted throughout their history.

Diop explains that the word *Kam* in Hebrew means heat, black, or burned. The Egyptians called their country Kemit or Kemet, designating the black soil of Egypt. By extension, Kemet was referred to by others as the black race of the country of the Blacks.

> That being so, all apparent contradictions disappear and the logic of facts appears in all its nudity. The inhabitants of Egypt, symbolized by their black color, Kemit or Ham of the Bible, would be accursed in the literature of the people they had oppressed.

Diop's argument makes sense historically and linguistically, when we consider the Israelites' role as collaborators with the Hyksos during their occupation of Egypt. Their betrayal caused persecution for themselves once the Egyptians regained control of their land and commenced to throw both Hyksos and Israelites out of Egypt. That well-known point of history is somehow rarely discussed in the literature.

> It is impossible to link the notion of Hamite, as we labor to understand it in official textbooks, with the slightest historical, geographical, linguistic, or ethnic reality. No specialist is able to pinpoint the birthplace of the Hamites (scientifically speaking), the language they spoke, the migratory route they followed, the countries they settled, or the form of civilization they may have left. On the contrary, all

the experts agree that this term has no serious content, and yet not one of them fails to use it as a kind of master-key to explain the slightest evidence of civilization in Black Africa.

Rather than be arrested for disturbing the peace and/or assault I have quickly walked out of churches during sermons because the pastor began to preach this "Ham" nonsense, adding that slavery was a blessing for Africans because it Christianized us. I am certain that each time these statements are made, Christ himself turns over in his grave, sits up, and yells: **"Say what?!!** Any preacher caught presenting this slavery-time twaddle needs to suffer the wrath of the congregation! How dare they teach this insult to Black children, then turn around and have the kids to recite: "I am somebody." The amazing thing is that Black folks pay preachers for the privilege of these psychological and spiritual assaults.

African Americans are not alone in this situation. People of color from many different nations who reside in the U.S. suffer from cultural confusion, identity crisis, retarded advancement, and non-survival. The beliefs, values, and ways of doing things within their mother cultures are at odds with those in the dominant Anglo-American culture. Very often any expression of a non-Caucasian mother culture is discouraged, suppressed, and punished in various ways. However, there are essential cultural elements that greatly contribute to their sense of identity, reality, health, wellbeing, and wholeness. When a significant number of cultural elements are lost, denied or taken away, the human spirit becomes dangerously diminished. Unrelenting social and cultural assaults naturally lead to physical illness as the individual's spiritual strength weakens and wanes. Such persons may experience anger, identity problems, sadness, depression, and any number of other negative behavior symptoms (Francis Cress Welsing, 1991). Persons who are subjected to social stresses like extreme institutional racism, violence, and cultural oppression spread throughout a nation find survival very difficult.

African Americans have lost a lot of racial and cultural consciousness since the 1960s Civil Rights Movement. As a result, we are now witnessing Black psychological escape and denial and some other truly bizarre behaviors that signal serious identity problems. Nathan Hare (1991:i) refers to Black middle class managers and professionals as "Black Anglo-Saxons" who began in the 1970s to express scorn for people who maintain Black Nationalist and Black consciousness sentiments. He discusses how Black males increasingly began to embrace White females *sexually* in their relationships shortly after the Civil Rights struggle. I am reminded of Eldridge Cleaver's (1968:149) commentary entitled "The Black Eunuchs" in which he presents the sentiments of an elderly, self-hating Black character named Old Lazarus: "Every time I embrace a black woman I'm embracing slavery, and when I put my arms around a white woman, well, I'm hugging freedom."

Hare (1991:i) also notes that Black females increasingly began to embrace White females *politically* with blond hairdos in the 1970s, a trend that has become a common practice today. Along with the blonde, orange, lavender and red streaked hair, Hare further discusses how African American women began to choose blue and green contacts for their eyes. This bizarre appearance indicates serious identity problems among Black people who dearly want to be, look like, and identify with Whites rather than just be themselves.

African Americans in the entertainment industries lead the way in "symbolically incorporating the physical characteristics of their white 'ego ideals'" without pausing to think about the social meaning and consequences. We all owe the next generation better examples of behavior so that they will be able to avoid the negative influences which direct them to self-destructive behaviors. Hare (1991:i) goes on to note the steady progression of adult Black identity issues that set poor examples for African American youth: "Black Anglo-Saxons in the late 1980s's and the year 1990 conspicuously incorporated the worldview and sociopolitical thinking of white people." When that happened, Whites were able to say "*Gotcha*" because it meant that such Blacks abandoned any concern about the survival of their children and had no other consideration than furthering their own selfish material ends.

Many African Americans have somehow come to believe that the most important thing for survival is the adoption of modern Western culture. They have been indoctrinated into believing that the African past does not matter. The reason this idea is taught so strongly is the importance of reducing African Americans' curiosity to conduct investigations into their true history and having them to eventually forget about the gross atrocities committed by the institutional slave trade. African Americans are always told to forget the atrocities of America's history of slavery which, by the way, continues to thrive in a new form. On the other hand, Jewish Americans are supported in their ongoing media campaigns so that the world will "never forget." Even when African American history is taught in the American educational system, the curriculum begins 400 years ago with slavery rather than thousands of years ago during Africa's classical period and its Golden Ages. The purpose behind this strategy is to place a permanent stigma upon Africans and to permanently embed the idea that they are people whose most noteworthy place in history is as slaves to a far superior master race.

African American cultural identity and fitness to survive involves the strength with which individuals have a sense of belonging to the totality of African history and experience. The strength of a Black person's sense of race consciousness and sense of cultural connection with the African Motherland determines that person's ability and fitness to survive and advance in socio-politically hostile America. The topic of culture includes discussions of race, total way of life, history, nationality, worldview, and religious beliefs. In other words, cultural identity is involved with:

➢ Geographic location of one's ancestral home;
➢ Genotype (genetic makeup) of one's ancestors;
➢ Phenotype (physical appearance) of one's ancestors;
➢ Ancient religious belief system, value system, worldview, and way of life of one's ancestors;
➢ *Total* history of one's people.

All of these factors combine and contribute to self-knowledge and self-empowerment that constitute a **whole person** with the internal fortitude to withstand any amount of socio-political oppression. In the words of Na'im Akbar (1985:27), "Without such knowledge, we are not only deprived of genuine power, but we are ill-equipped to develop power." If we help our children to develop strong, powerful images of themselves as African descendants, they will have the capacity to counteract the propaganda of self-destruction that bombards them from every social institution in this country. However, it is impossible to teach what one does not know. If Black adults fail to demonstrate a strong sense of race consciousness, history, community and collective responsibility, these factors will not be cultivated in our children. The end result will be yet another generation with no semblance of the racial and cultural identity needed to avoid **new forms of slavery** in hostile America.

The chapter that follows discusses the historical and cultural factors that have led to the crisis of identity that is found today among African Americans.

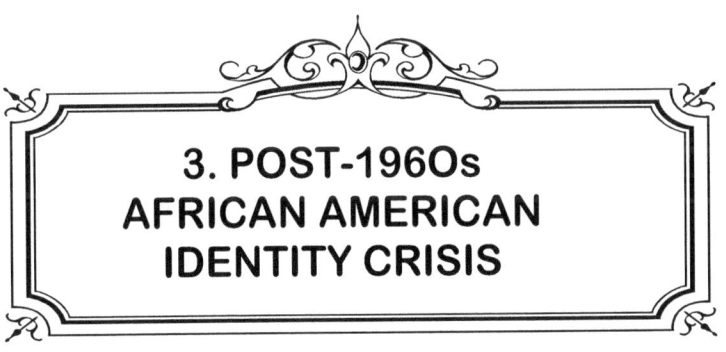

3. POST-1960s AFICAN AMERICAN IDENTITY CRISIS

*If you do not know who you are
and what you have done,
you cannot truly know anything else
because all knowledge begins with self-knowledge.
If you do not know where you are
or where you have been,
you cannot know where you are going.
And if you do not know where you are going,
any road will take you there.*
                    --West African proverb

Driving the Sane to Self-Alienating Insanity

One of the most critical mental health issues concerning African Americans is the problem of self-identity. Identity issues among African people are closely related to mental health, healing, and wellbeing because it involves self-hatred and affects the very core of a person's spiritual self. When people of African descent suffer spiritual imbalance it causes imbalance regarding everything else about them. A strong sense of identity plays a critical role in African Americans' ability to maintain their sanity within an insane, oppressive social system. In her book entitled *Neurosis and Human Growth: The Struggle Toward Self-Realization*, Karen Horney (1950) discusses the self-destructive nature of self-alienation:

Self-hate finally culminates in pure and *direct self-destructive impulses and actions* (her emphasis). These may be acute or chronic, openly violent or insidious and slow grinding, conscious or unconscious, carried out in action or performed in imagination only. They may concern minor or major issues. They aim ultimately at physical, psychic, and spiritual self-destruction.

Several recent studies have been conducted by psychologists. Mary E. Campbell (2007) explored the single-race identifications of African heritage individuals who have chosen a part-black multiracial label on a survey. She found that single-race identification choices on forced-choice questions vary considerably across family heritage groups. Those who choose a "black-American Indian" identity were extremely likely to select a black single-race identity, while other groups like "black-whites" have substantial variation in single-race identifications. Identification patterns vary significantly by age, family context and survey characteristics.

In a quasi-experimental focus group, Todd C. Shaw (2004) explored variations in African American expressions of patriotism in post-9/11 America. He found variations according to whether they are stated in a conversational context that is All-Black, Biracial, or Multiracial. All-Black groups voiced a wide range of sentiments about American patriotism and double consciousness. Biracial groups were often polarized in their responses.

In an older study, Suzette L. Speight, Elizabeth M. Vera, and Kennedy B. Derrickson, M.D.

(1996) examined the relationships among racial self-designation, racial identity attitudes, self-esteem, and demographic variables in a diverse sample of African Americans. She qualitatively explored reasons for particular racial self-designations. Results of her study indicated:

> significant differences in preferences for particular racial labels; 41% preferred Black and 30%o preferred African American. A content analysis of reasons for preferences indicated that participants preferring the term Black primarily appeared to have no particular ideological reason for choosing that term. However, those participants preferring the term African American indicated reasons related to its symbolic, political, and cultural meaning. Furthermore, pre-encounter and immersion racial identity attitudes varied significantly, according to racial self-designation. Gender, income level, and educational level were each significantly correlated with various racial identity attitudes.

Christel N. Temple (2006) takes a problem-solving approach by setting forth strategies for cultural renewal. Her study presents an American-based version of African globalism.

> The United States is a prime setting for African cultural renewal because it offers a dynamic set of human and technological variables that can link our present to the foundations of our classical African past. The most recent human variables to include in modern strategies for success are the masses of recent immigrants from Africa. In a historical perspective of renewal, it would seem

that because Africans can now voluntarily migrate to the United States, they would consider this a unique opportunity for expanding collaborative African globalism. Unfortunately, there is discord between newly arrived African groups and the traditional African American groups. However, the technological variables of the modern era can help to bridge the cultural gap between African Americans, Africans, and the classical African past. There are also perspectives available in literature that function within a social science context and offer additional strategies for a post-Western renewal.

Another study conducted by the PEW Research Center in 2007, in association with National Public Radio, found a growing values gap between poor and middle class African Americans. Their findings that reveal a decline in African Americans' optimism about Black progress in America are extremely interesting. Some findings are presented below. Additional findings from this study are placed in the Index.

African Americans see a widening gulf between the values of middle class and poor blacks, and nearly four-in-ten say that because of the diversity within their community, blacks can no longer be thought of as a single race.

The new nationwide Pew Research Center survey also finds blacks less upbeat about the state of black progress now than at any time since 1983. Looking backward, just one-in-five blacks say things are better for blacks now than they were five years ago. Looking ahead, fewer than half of

> all blacks (44%) say they think life for blacks will get better in the future, down from the 57% who said so in a 1986 survey.

Compare the African American outlook for the future with findings on Anglo-Americans' outlook.

> Whites have a different perspective. While they, too, have grown less sanguine about black progress, they are nearly twice as likely as blacks to see black gains in the past five years. Also, a majority of whites (56%) say life for blacks in this country will get better in the future.

These are only a few of the studies that focus on various perspectives on the issue of African American identity. The studies reveal the scope of identity confusion, lack of reflection, and "double-consciousness" factors that prevent a unified, purposeful self-identity that promotes inter-group cohesion.

African American culture is a continuation of African culture in the Diaspora. We have called ourselves Africans more than any other race/culture related term during our entire history in America. However, the strength of cultural knowledge and security among African Americans has been severely weakened since the 1960s. The issue is stated with expert clarity by clinical psychologist Dr. Bobby Wright (1989), who understood "the mind of an enslaved people. . . caught in a world stolen and remade for Europeans. The high African standards that gave the world civilization were now confusing or non-existent." As I mentioned in an earlier work (1996:3, *Realigning African Heads: Yoruba Curatives for Maafa-related Ailments*) the values, beliefs, and behaviors connected with American and European concepts of capitalism, progress, and the individual are alien, even antithetical to African cultural values that embrace the concepts of communalism, advancement, and the group (Borishade, 1996).

Western capitalism traditionally prioritizes material gain for a select few at any price, while African culture emphasizes the voluntary sharing of wealth among many in the spirit of communalism and human relations. African tradition was maintained within African American communities and on Historically Black college and university campuses as the practice of "Climb and Lift." In other words, as individuals progressed they were expected to lift others to a higher level. We need to be aware that it is the unbalanced, sick nature of Western society and culture that produces the "Crabs in a Barrel" mentality. When crabs live in their natural ocean habitat they do not act that way.

Africans' total history reveals progress and advancement of the whole society was based upon principles and practices of group sharing. Survival within a brutal social, cultural, and political framework that is diametrically opposed to African cultural and philosophical principles requires herculean efforts to maintain balance and sanity. African Americans have traditionally maintained cultural knowledge and self-help infrastructures within American society. However, these infrastructures have all experienced a radical decline since the 1960s.

Identity crisis and bizarre behavior are two consequences of the psychological injuries sustained by African people whose sense of self is assaulted in every way imaginable in hostile American society. Overwhelming emotions of race-related fear, anxiety, self-hatred, self-alienation, and even self-dehumanization among African people worldwide are symptomatic of the blunt trauma of being clubbed on the head with more than 400 years of death, oppression, grief, suffering, and indoctrination.

Western civilization is in a downward death-spiral and is battling to save itself. American society is sinking fast and dragging Black folks down in its wake. We allow ourselves to be confused and misdirected by the chaotic babbling and irrational behavior of a nation out of control and out of touch with reality. Many of the churches appear to be incapable of healing our people. Ironically, as small churches spring up like mushrooms and large ones build even larger edifices, the masses of African American people are increasingly worse off. This equation is unacceptable, and the reality of Black Church failure and lack of leadership can no longer be ignored. There is an urgent need to investigate the present relationship between many of the Black Churches and the Black community because as institutions they have fallen short of their traditional role as protector and sustainer of the people and wellspring of the culture. We desperately need for the traditional Black Church to return to its original historical role of leadership.

Africans on the Continent and throughout the Western Diaspora are suffering from a negative self-identity and self-hatred caused by negative portrayals and negative images perpetuated by White imperialism. It is imperative that some of this information should be presented at this time to provide Black readers with at least a thumbnail sketch of African American history.

A brief list of quantitative studies that show the relationship between African identity, self-esteem, social issues, and mental health are presented in the **Appendix**.

Historical and Cultural Assessment

African American cultural values took a serious nosedive since the 1960s, and that has resulted in devastating levels of identity crisis among many. We can put a pin in that period of our history as a starting point of social decline. Alarming increases in bizarre behaviors, teen pregnancy, crime, homicide, child mortality, and life-threatening diseases have followed as inevitable developments. A sharp increase in mortality rates are the end result, made all the more distressing because it is the young who are dying in record numbers.

We can better understand how African Americans began to lose life-sustaining cultural values by investigating the historical events that occurred before and after the Civil Rights Movement. The Black civil unrest of the 1960s was a bitter struggle by African Americans for a better life. The urban centers into which they were forced were overcrowded and Black populations began to slowly spill over the forced boundaries into juxtaposing hostile White communities. Blacks were fed up with the miseries and limitations of racial segregation and discrimination. They wanted a better life for themselves and a brighter future for their children, so they put their lives on the line for the right to vote without being threatened with violence and the right to gain equal access to goods, services, employment, housing, and education. That is what the 1960s Movement was about. It was not about merely wanting to sit beside Whites in restaurants, schools, and the like.

What is referred to as the Civil Rights Movement was actually a two-pronged movement that involved a push for **human rights** as well as **civil rights**. These were actually two separate but interrelated alternatives within the Civil Rights Movement that occurred at the same time with the same motivating factors. Both Integrationist and Nationalist sentiments have existed side-by-side in American society since the plantation days of American slavery. The Integrationist alternative was on one side of the struggle, focusing on the **non-violent** approach for **civil rights**, which addresses the rights of African Americans as citizens. The Black Nationalist alternative was on the other side insisting that the issue was one of **human rights**, arguing that African Americans' fundamental rights to life, liberty, and the pursuit of wealth and wellbeing were being violated.

Although both alternatives were a part of the same struggle for the same reason, each had radically different sets of advocacy themes, interpretations, goals, and objectives. Each faction has always held radically different views of themselves and their mission in America. The Integrationist tendency is to restrict the Black struggle to whatever is acceptable to the White ruling class. Therefore, much of their rhetoric is aimed at appealing to Whites. Nationalists are more outspoken and in general dare to address Black issues in a bold, straightforward manner. They speak and write directly to Black audiences with little or no concern as to Whites' thoughts on the matter. The existences of these two alternatives continue in contemporary American society today.

    Integrationist leadership may have begun with James Forten in the late 1700s, along with Sojourner Truth and Frederick Douglass in the 1800s. In the 1900s the great names of Alain Locke, W.E.B. DuBois, Adam Clayton Powell, Sr., Howard Thurman, Martin Luther King, Jr. and others are etched in African American history. Black Integrationists have always expected the American government to create positive changes and provide solutions. Integration into White society has always been viewed as the best route to gain respect, equal rights, and fair treatment in American society. Integrationists further believe that the moral fiber of African Americans will change the hearts and minds of racist Whites who will, in turn, insist on ending racial discrimination.

    In the 1960s Integrationists pushed for civil rights -- their rights as American citizens – and directed their rhetoric toward the U.S. Congress. **Nonviolent passive resistance** was the **Integrationist** approach to civil unrest and confrontation, an organized strategy that began in the 1960s, led by The Rev. Dr. Martin Luther King, Jr. and the Southern Christian Leadership Coalition (SCLC). The names of Fanny Lou Hamer, Stokely Carmichael (aka Kwame Toure), Rosa Parks, and Medgar Evers live on as testimonials of the people who committed their lives to the struggle. Stokely Carmichael began as an Integrationist, but made a radical move to Black Nationalism in the push for "Black Power." The high point of Integrationist advocacy and demonstrations was the March on Washington on August 28, 1963.

Black Nationalist activities were also heavily documented during the late 18th and early 19th centuries. Some of the early historical figures were Paul Cuffee, Martin Delany, David Walker, Denmark Vesey, Nat Turner, and Henry Highland Garnet. Following their example up until the 1960s are Henry Sylvester Williams, Marcus Garvey, Kwame Toure (aka Stokely Carmichael), Huey Newton, Bobby Seal, Elijah Muhammad, Malcolm X (aka El Hajj Malik El Shabazz), Muhammad Ali, and Louis Farrakhan. The Black Panther Party was launched by Huey Newton and Bobby Seal. The Black Panthers were considered the most dangerous because they insisted on the legal right for Black people to carry arms for protection, and carried out this practice on many occasions without being arrested. When police approached them Panther members would begin reciting "chapter and verse" of the legal statutes regarding their right to carry arms in a certain manner, and the intimidated police would have to back off. The Nation of Islam, led by Elijah Muhammad, offered African Americans a religious alternative. This became a movement in itself as tens of thousands of Black folks made a radical move away from what they believed were the crippling, mind numbing effects of Christianity as an arm of imperialism. This was the beginning of African Americans' criticism of the Black Church and the first behavioral expression, *en masse*, of their disappointment.

Categorically, Black Nationalists are separatists who believe that it is impossible to get along with Whites and that White racist attitudes and violent behavior will never change. To Nationalists, the only way to have peace, to advance, and to thrive is to live in separate communities and towns where Black people own and control their own homes, businesses, and institutions. Nationalists have always tended to be **militant**, which is very different from being violent. **Militancy** means they will not initiate a fight or a violent act. However, when confronted with violence they consider it their right and duty to meet offensive violence with defensive violence.

During the 1960s Nationalists advocated human rights and wanted to carry their plea to the United Nations, where issues of human rights are routinely discussed by a worldwide body of decision-makers. Quite naturally, this would bring embarrassment to the United States because it has been the most vocal advocate for international human rights. Malcolm X led the move to present the African American cause to the United Nations. However, he was assassinated some days prior to completing that mission. There have been two great Nationalist movements in the United States. The first was an international movement led by Marcus M. Garvey in the 1920s with his United Negro Improvement Association (UNIA). Garvey's teachings continue to influence Black people around the world. The second Nationalist movement was headed by Elijah Muhammad in the Nation of Islam that also emerged in the early 1900s and continues to successfully rehabilitate African Americans with prison records.

Maulana Karenga (1987:126) notes that the Integrationist faction initially overshadowed the Black Nationalist faction during the Civil Rights Movement. The **non-violent** integrationist push for civil rights peaked with the March on Washington, but quickly declined shortly afterward because it was controlled by forces outside the Movement. Dr. John Henrik Clarke (1995:40) reveals that the John F. Kennedy administration paid large sums of money to the major civil rights organizations to join together and cooperate.

> The attempt to come together ended in stagnation and a decline in their effectiveness. Martin Luther King, Jr. made his most famous and least effective speech at the March on Washington demonstration. In my opinion, it was a tragically missed golden opportunity to provide African Americans with a practical plan for the future. While he had the attention of the world, he was expected to announce a dynamic plan for change, not a dream. The plan might or might not be realizable, but that could be worked out later. Although it was not noticeable to many, the effectiveness of Martin Luther King, Jr. began to decline after the March on Washington and the "I Have a Dream" speech.

One reason for the decline was that non-violent Integrationists learned that their approach could not possibly work with a government and a society of people who are wholeheartedly committed to the most extreme forms of violence against any individual or organization that openly opposes its oppression. Integrationist failures laid the historical groundwork for the resurgence of Black Nationalism. Dr. Clarke (1995) comments on how

> The people were turning more and more to another voice that was stronger, clearer, and more dynamic. It was the voice of Malcolm X, who was calling on African Americans to believe in themselves again, to understand their enemy and to lose their fear of the enemy. He was also calling on them to reclaim their manhood and their womanhood and once more to have the confidence and the skill to rule nations. . . . In my opinion, the Movement was betrayed by confused ideologist, middle-class fakers, and just plain sellouts.

It soon became clear to White America that they would not be able to rely on pacifist Integrationist demonstrations with Whites committing all the violence with no fear of harm from Blacks' self-defensive measures. On the contrary, White-on-Black violence became risky business under the influence of the Black Muslim military wing called the Fruit of Islam (FOI) and Black Panther Party members who patrolled the streets of Black communities armed with rifles. Those two organizations filled an important void in unprotected Black communities where people could not rely upon police protection. Many Black policemen were equally, if not more brutal than Whites against their own people.

Historically, African Americans have been considered in international circles as the conscience of America. The Black struggle throughout the history of the United States has always revealed the deep and significant chasm that exists between America's lofty preachments and its racist, discriminatory practices. Blacks' role of acting as America's conscience during the 1960s Civil Rights Movement galvanized and inspired uprisings among non-African groups along the length and breadth of the nation. An upsurge of broad-based movements and direct-action campaigns shook the country to its foundation and developed a damaging negative image of the United States among nations of the world.

America's image was further tarnished during a tirade by Nikita Khrushchev when he disrupted the United Nations assembly by shouting, banging his fists on the desk, and pounding the desk with his shoe October 12, 1960. Khrushchev was reacting to an American speaker's criticism of Russian political oppression. The Russian leader's violent demonstration was also accompanied by accusations that the United Nations was controlled by the U.S. State Department; that America belonged to a group of imperialist "colonists"; and that America should take its own advice and cease its domestic and foreign oppression before criticizing USSR political policies. Both photographs were taken during that momentous meeting in 1960. One photo shows Khrushchev's shoe in front of him on the desk. Researchers have not succeeded in locating pictures of the actual shoe-thumping itself, after years of searching. However, the incident is indelibly stamped upon the minds of everyone who witnessed the televised news clip in 1960.

From Black to Multi-Racial Protests

African American resistance began to spread to other groups in an unprecedented manner. Vast numbers of American citizens' trust in the government and in America's dominant ideology and culture had eroded to a point of "no-confidence" in the 1960s. The thousands of citizens in Black communities across the country presented intelligent, sustained, disciplined protests and uprisings that caught and spread like wildfire among other groups with issues that were different but related to African Americans' struggle for basic civil and human rights.

Black protestors galvanized multi-racial rebellion among divergent interest groups, such as GIs, welfare mothers, students, and prisoners. African American activism inspired a predominantly White New Left Movement that fought to end U.S. intervention abroad. New Left opposition to the Vietnam War erupted in militant protest demonstrations. The New Left began to advocate for an end to the war and a more fair and humane way of life at home in America. The Black Movement that burst upon the American political scene in the 1960s led to a historically unparalleled, deep-rooted multiracial resistance among Chicanos, Puerto Ricans, Asian Americans, and Native Americans. While African Americans were articulating strategies and objectives of "**Black Power**," Native Americans began to follow suit with reference to "**Red Power**." African Americans referred to Black collaborators and accommodationists as "**Oreos**" (Black outside, White inside), and Native Americans came up with the term "**Apples**" (red outside, white inside) for Native people who held no sense of loyalty for the Native American cause.

Still another wave of resistance came in the form of the women's liberation struggle. Women's activism inspired yet another movement by lesbian women, homosexual men, and disabled people who all began to insist on their particular rights. African Americans were members of several divergent groups, and as such they helped to influence the vision and activities of those groups from within. A debt of gratitude is owed to African Americans who placed their lives on the line in the cause of justice in America that benefitted so many besides themselves, at home and abroad.

Government Backlash Strategies

Critical analysis identifies some unforeseen things that began to occur as a reactive U.S. government moved to halt the Civil Rights Movement. One U.S. government strategy was to move White teachers into predominantly Black neighborhood schools. At the same time, the Black middle class began to move into the suburbs, happy to get away from the grossly overcrowded Black urban centers. As a result, the Black community lost the role models, mentors, and family support systems upon which they relied to maintain their history, cultural values, economic strength, and social stability held for so long among themselves.

Gone were the committed Black *master teachers* who had been a constant presence in the past, insisting upon excellence of character and inspiring a love for learning. The teaching of African American contributions to history, literature, science, music, medicine, etc. became *passé*. It didn't matter that information about racism was not presented in the textbooks. Prior to the 1960s Black teachers were always there to teach between the lines, in the margins, off the pages, and out of the box while instructing students on how to survive in the *real* America. After the 1960s they were no longer present to provide living proof and testimonial of past accomplishments. They were no longer there to instill in Black children the shining certainty of contributions yet to be made by them. The weekly presentation of alternative information ceased, and new generations of Black children have suffered the loss. There was nothing to prevent seeds of Black inferiority from germinating in young Black minds surrounded by a hostile social environment where every institution played a part in communicating White supremacy.

Many Black folks believe in White Supremacy more than Whites themselves. Imagine the wife of an A.M.E. (African Methodist Episcopal) bishop suggesting at an annual conference that the church should minimize singing the Black gospel songs and emphasize the White hymns instead. If that is not bad enough, there is the case of a Black charter school in Florida run by a Black church where a Black principal warned a teacher, "Don't teach nothin' about Black folks, and don't even mention Africa," among a student body that was 99% African American. Such incidents occur with people of

African descent who are alienated from themselves and eaten to the core with self-hatred.

A second government strategy to undermine the **Black Power** aspect of the Civil Rights Movement was the dismantling of the Black communities. **Urban Renewal** bought the land upon which Black homes and businesses rested and completely restructured the Black communities. Today, **gentrification** is a different name for the same strategy being used for a similar purpose. This eliminated the Black economic base where the dollar turned over almost thirteen times and took at least a year to leave the community.

Up until the 1970s no one had to go outside the community for anything, unless they just wanted to. Everything was within walking distance, so the only time you needed a car or a bus was to get to work or to a hospital. During the week children who needed school supplies could stop at a neighborhood store and get what they needed. If kids didn't have money the cost was added to a tab and presented to parents the next time they met up with the store owners. Local department stores were owned by Blacks, so there was no need to go downtown for everyday clothing and holiday outfits. There were Black pharmacies, ice cream parlors, shoe repair shops, cleaners, and laundries. Elders in many communities who had migrated from the South knew how to make bars of laundry soap and powdered detergent. On wash days, at a time when the washboard was still used, people purchased laundry soap and powdered detergent from their neighbors almost as often as they did from the store.

There were local barbers and beauticians. Teachers tutored students free of charge after school and doctors took care of patients in their home clinics every evening after leaving work at the hospitals.

Many Black men were self-employed doing electrical, plumbing, and other types of light contracting work, such as light hauling and landscaping. People with mental or physical handicaps who lived alone and had no family members around were supported by the entire community in whatever entrepreneurial efforts they came up with, like window washing, house cleaning, sewing, and yard work. If they became sick community people made sure they were cared for. If a crime was committed the community took care of it before the police. When people stole from neighbors, the thieves' own relatives would turn them in to the victims and return the stolen items, wherever possible. Those were the days when the word community meant something.

A third strategy used by the U.S. government aimed to destroy the renewed sense of Black pride and Black culture. When segregationist laws were overturned during the 1960s, subtle media messages bombarded Black Americans about the need to assimilate culturally and become more like White Americans. African Americans bought into the anthropology concept of *assimilation.* The idea spread until Black people themselves began to discuss the necessity of adopting Anglo-American culture. On the surface this appeared to be a harmless, sensible thing. However, close inspection and hindsight reveal that Anglo cultural features are capable of disrupting and destroying the African psyche.

When Anglo cultural features are adopted by a person of African descent it is analogous to a very sophisticated computer worm being introduced into a computer system. Viewed from the Black perspective of world history, Western cultural assimilation serves the same purpose as the computer virus. It destroys the system from within. Consider four features of Anglo culture that have infectious "wormlike" characteristics. The first is "**racism**," the belief in White supremacy. The second feature is "**sexism**," the belief in male superiority. Third, "**imperialism**" is the Caucasian belief in their *God-given right* to rule non-Caucasians. The fourth feature is "**hegemony**," which is the Caucasian belief that they have the further *God-given right* to impose or force European religion, culture, and values on non-Europeans. We might refer to these European/American cultural features with the acronym "RSIH" (racism, sexism, imperialism, hegemony).

By using blatant negative portrayals or subtle implication, schools, churches, mass media, and especially pop culture have assaulted the psyches of African Americans with these four features of Anglo belief and culture. Black people's mental assimilation of these four features, especially through various entertainment media, is tantamount to a computer being infected with a worm that begins to eat through the entire system until it completely loses all of its original integrity and crashes. Once the person's mental/psychological "hard drive" is infected with worm-driven features of RSIH that become *bona fide* beliefs, those elements systematically begin to destroy all normal, balanced cognitive and behavioral functions of the system. Survival is impossible when the system is turned against itself to ensure self-annihilation. One sure beginning sign of infection is bizarre behavior witnessed in the way men wear their pants below their buttocks and women who flash yellow, pink, and green hair with blue and green contact lenses.

Another metaphor for the assimilation of the "four Anglo-European infectious diseases" is the HIV virus. Once it enters an individual's system it begins to attack and destroy the protective disease-fighting elements of the system and begins to replicate itself at the same time, until the organism dies. This metaphor can be expanded to fit the manner in which persons whose psyches are "infected" with the "RSIH virus" begin to infect others. The sick person begins spreading the infection by persuading others to become like-minded and influencing them to engage in bizarre and risky behavior. The entertainment industry is an excellent example of how the "sickness" is spread abroad, especially among the young who have little or no defenses against it.

Since the 1960s, Black Americans have been deprived of the teachings of cultural values, beliefs, understandings, and traditions that supported and ensured thousands of years of African civilization, progress, and contributions. Among inner city masses pride in Africanity has been replaced by a deeply rooted belief in Black inferiority and self-hatred. There are African Americans who are so filled with self-loathing that they do not want to live in a community with their own people. It is disturbing each time they see another person of African descent because it reminds them of who they are. Living in Washington State is tantamount to living in a weird "nether world," because with a 5% Black population, African Americans refuse to give each other eye contact and hardly want to pass each other on the sidewalk. It is the first thing noticed by outsiders moving into the area. This is a seriously sick, upside-down mentality, because seeing a person who looks like oneself is normally a natural, wholesome, self-affirming experience for every human being.

The fundamental definition of mental illness is that an individual is out of touch with reality, and this describes the identity crisis behavior of many African Americans. Individuals who are clearly of African descent by phenotype/physical appearance, but claim every other racial type on the planet suffer from self-hatred and are not completely in touch with reality. If a person is against himself/herself, there is no way for that individual to survive and succeed in life. The individual would immediately disappear in the crowd if taken to any part of the Congo, Mali, Angola, Nigeria, Kenya, etc. However, such persons reveal the level of their psychosis by claiming Irish, French, British, or Native American ancestry and denying African heritage. One individual that I often think of is a man who strongly resembles Marcus Garvey but never ceased to refer to his Irish background. After I asked him if he ever "hung out" at any of the Irish pubs with his countrymen, he never spoke to me again because I momentarily jerked him out of his fantasy world.

This is indicative of psychological sickness brought on by acculturation into the "four Anglo-European infectious diseases."

Some persons of African descent state that they are Americans, not Africans. Their denial strategy uncritically focuses on *citizenship* while ignoring *genetic heritage*. It is rare to find other groups whose ancestral roots are not Anglo-European deny and reject their ancestral origins (One exception is Latin Americans). It is not typical even among the groups whose grandparents immigrated to America from Europe. This African American behavior clearly indicates the person is "infected" by the "four Anglo-European diseases" which manifests in the form of identity confusion and denial.

Another example of Caucasian RSIH infection is found among parents who believe White teachers are superior to Black ones. The sickness convinces such parents that it is irrelevant that over and above the regular instructions, the Black teacher can pass on to Black students the information they need to survive in America's racially hostile society. Symptoms of the illness prevent the infected individual from considering that the Black teacher automatically had to learn more, have more experience, and overcome more obstacles than the White teacher, just to compete for and succeed in the same job.

African American policemen are a case in point. During the 1960s civil rights disturbances Black policemen joined with White ones to perform violence against peaceful civil rights marchers and protestors. Some are known to hold the philosophical position that once they don their uniforms they cease being Black and become blue. Such Black policemen are so sick, so filled with self-loathing that they are even more brutal when dealing with their own people than racist Whites. A poignant article written by Richard Rothstein (January 28, 2007), a citizen of New York City, asks: "Are Black officers a defense against racism in our criminal justice system or are they enablers of racism?" Rothstein draws an analogy between "Black cops and gay Republicans" in his troubling commentary of how the racist social system of America lures and co-opts the minds of the very minorities that it targets for discrimination and oppression.

> Gay Republicans take the position that they can change the system by working from within. The majority of gay men and women, myself included, see Gay Republicans as Uncle Toms who enable homophobia, wallow in self-hatred and sell their souls to gain acceptance by the so-called majority, a majority that openly crusades to deny us, as Gay Americans, our civil rights and our equal right to life, liberty and the pursuit of happiness.
>
> I've never before considered the New York City Police Department in this way. Have I been wrong? Are the Abner Louima, Amadou Diallo and Patrick Dorismond incidents of the Giuliani days the rule rather than the exception? Are there no white or black cops, but only racist blue cops in this city?

It is bad enough when brutal, nightmarish incidents happen to far too many law-abiding African

Americans at the mercy of White police officers. It is much worse having Black officers adopt the same racist attitudes and behaviors as the White ones, and having them acculturate into the closed "blue wall of silence" mentality that pervades White police culture. It is difficult for law-abiding African American citizens to comprehend Black police participation in the "*us against them*" point of view, knowing that to Whites the Black policeman is still considered as one of the "*Black them*," and that s/he has a mother, a father, a sibling or some other relative in the community. It usually takes the random, senseless brutalization or murder of a close relative to change the attitude of a Black policeman who is infected by RSIH, such that s/he has become mentally, spiritually, and culturally co-opted to think and act in this self-destructive manner.

Pop culture makes many of us look foolish. In nature, deeply pigmented humans have dark hair and dark eyes. What possesses some of us to buy green contact lenses and don blonde hair is beyond me. Someone will invariably bring up the example of Australians who have dark skin and blonde hair. This argument is invalid because that phenotypical trait occurs only among children in a few isolated tribes that live far up in the mountains, whose hair turns dark once they reach the age of puberty. Admittedly, I am from what some call the "old school" of folks who find this behavior strange. Adornment is a feature of African culture, but we have a habit of taking things to the seventh dimension. It is no joke that I have met people on the street who looked possessed, to the point that I wanted to adopt a defensive posture with my fingers formed in the form of the Christian cross.

Today we have grown men who do not understand the concept of UNDER-wear, and they are setting the wrong behavioral standard for youth. That behavior is uncouth, uncivilized, unhygienic, and indicative of anti-social sentiments. Let's take an archaeological perspective of this phenomenon. The irony is that it took human beings almost five million years to develop a hip bone and hip joints that allow erect posture and the ability to walk upright with ease. African people take pride in having the most well-developed, muscular buttocks among the human species. It is the muscles in the buttocks that support erect posture, and Africans have been standing erect and walking around on two legs longer than any of the other human beings. Now Black men are wearing their pants in such a way that makes their buttocks look completely flat, and forces them to walk as if they are evolutionary throwbacks.

Some of these statements will raise the ire of a lot of people, but so be it. There is no point in becoming angry with me for telling the truth about behavior that everyone knows is clearly bizarre, if not borderline insane. People who act this way should get angry when no one attempts to pull them back into an acceptable "zone of sanity." I speak as Grandmother or "Big-Momma," if you will, and refuse to relinquish that role. It is my responsibility to tell my children the truth for their own good, and to say it in a manner that they understand and respond to at some level. If my children are sick, I am expected to deliver the "medicine" that makes them well. Whether or not they accept the "medicine" is up to them, but they will never be able to say that no one ever offered them truth and healing.

It seems a foregone conclusion that if a loss of cultural values and racial identity can cause such devastating social, moral, mental, and spiritual decline in forty short years, then restoring those cultural and psychological elements should provide a powerful intervention strategy for much of what is referred to as *identity crisis*. Contemporary history is not the first time African people have been confronted with the life-threatening elements of identity crisis. We have been fighting against it since the days of slavery.

Black folks everywhere need to read the historical accounts of three Afro-Brazilian women in the early 1800s when they were freed from slavery. These three women acknowledged the fact that they and the other freed Africans had suffered cultural losses that were desperately needed for survival. In order to find a remedy they returned to West Africa to immerse themselves within the sources of African cultural heritage that had been lost. After studying the religion and culture in Sierra Leone and Nigeria long enough to become masters in the knowledge, the women returned to Brazil. The power of their knowledge and teachings sparked the *Lagosian Cultural Renaissance*, a vast international movement of traditional Yoruba religion, culture, and traditions that swept across Africa, Latin America, and the Caribbean.

As a result of these women's activities, millions of Afro-Latin Americans and millions more with no African heritage consciously adopted African religion, language, and traditions as their way of life for all time. Afro-Latin Americans who understood the importance of restoring and preserving their racial and cultural identity fully embraced the value of African cultural and racial purity. The *Lagosian Cultural Renaissance* of the 1800s is the forerunner and the cultural foundation of the *Harlem Renaissance* that took place in New York City 100 years later.

The *Harlem Renaissance* is another notable historical movement that occurred when African Americans grew tired of being forced by White publishers to produce art and literature that artificially conformed to Anglo-American realities and cultural standards. Artisans, writers, and poets began to draw from African traditions for artistic inspiration and expression in the 1920s and 1930s. That cultural movement gave rise to a virtual explosion of artistic creativity in literature, performing arts, visual arts, philosophy, and more. It is an entirely possible and feasible notion that a third look toward Africa for guidance in the areas of philosophy, cultural values, social stability, and human development might provide the flash that creates yet another *African Cultural Renaissance* to burst upon the canopy of world history. If it happened twice, it can happen again!

If it happens again, such an occurrence can easily signal the return of Africa as a world power, as it once was. This is a distinct possibility because of Africa's natural wealth and resources. Africa remains the richest continent on the face of the earth. This is the reason why everyone wants Africa. In the event that Africa is taken over by colonial powers again, Africans worldwide will be re-enslaved with no possibility of redemption.

It is not good enough to merely propose the possibility of a third *African Cultural Renaissance* to rekindle the fires of African American character development, excellence, and achievement. Such a proposition must include information, strategies, and application of those African cultural features--those creative, healing embers that still smolder in the psyche of African folks everywhere. The problem is our self-inflicted shame in our own Africanity that cannot be excused in this day of enlightenment that provides easy access to information on the internet.

The above information presents relatively recent historical accounts. What is needed is documented knowledge of Africans' **total history** that forms the basis of **ancestral knowledge** and **cultural security**. These are the two most powerful weapons for psychological, cultural, and political resistance in any society. Ancestral knowledge promotes a strong sense of **group identity** and provides guidelines for collective behavior. Cultural security contains a solid base of collective beliefs, assumptions, understandings, and ideologies that can motivate powerful collective activity. Keto advises us about the importance of African *total history* in his book entitled *The Africa Centered Perspective of History: An Introduction* (1991:5):

> History as a conceptualized field of the study of the past is different from "total history." History in the restrictive sense of a "reconstructed past" automatically implies a selective and interpreted history which is the handiwork of scholars, dead and alive. Only "total history" encompasses "the sum total of what happened in the past—what

was done by billions of people over millions of years in trillions of occurrences.

In addition to the government measures discussed above that resulted in Black identity crisis, a massive counter-intelligence program was devised and put into action to absolutely neutralize African American organized resistance to racist oppression. The activities of the FBI to put down the 1960s broad-based progressive movement are presented in the following chapter.

4. COINTELPRO vs. 1960s PROGRESSIVE MOVEMENTS

> *There is no easy walk to freedom anywhere and many of us will have to pass through the valley of the shadow of death and again before we reach the mountain tops of our desires.*
> --Nelson Mandela

Neutralizing the Progressive Movement

A vast U.S. government program called "COINTELPRO," an acronym for the Counter-intelligence Program, was organized in the late 1950s. The program's targets were American citizen groups who began to protest against unfair government policies at home and abroad. The mission of the COINTELPRO Program was to repress domestic grassroots political opposition through covert action under the guise of legitimate law enforcement. The FBI investigated about 20,000 people between 1956 and 1971 solely on the basis of their political views. Most were never suspected of committing any crime (Wolf et. al., 2001).

The anti-communist paranoia of the 1950s "Age of McCarthyism" produced the counterculture of the 1960s, according to Wolf (2001). In his own words stated July 26, 1950, J. Edgar Hoover was the Director of the FBI during that era. He contended that Communists cleverly camouflaged movements such as peace groups and civil rights groups to achieve their sinister purposes. Therefore, Hoover considered these movements as motivated by Communist enemies of the American way of life. It is very telling that no links to Soviet Russia were uncovered in any of the social movements disrupted by the FBI during the entire COINTELPRO period.

Brian Glick's (1989) book, entitled *War at Home: Covert Action Against U.S. Activists and What We Can Do About It,* argues that the American government has been waging a domestic war against its citizens since the 1960s. He reveals the nature and scope of ongoing government attacks on social justice movements that flared up in the U.S. since the 1960s. In the Introduction he states: "Government harassment of U.S. activists clearly exists today, violating our fundamental democratic rights and creating a climate of fear and distrust which undermines our efforts to challenge official policy." It was COINTELPRO operatives who burglarized the Watergate offices of the Democratic National Committee under the Nixon administration. It was during the Watergate period when COINTELPRO was first exposed. Despite the seriousness of the charges, the incident was virtually ignored by the national press and the journals, demonstrating media subservience to power and government ideology.

Social change and unrest shook the very foundations of America throughout the 1960s, brought on by protesters against the combat in Vietnam, protesters and priests burning draft cards and American flags, and massive Black rebellions that swept across almost every major U.S. city in the Northeast, Midwest, and California. Protesters were denounced by Presidents Nixon and Johnson, who feared violent revolution. The opposite opinion was voiced by President Kennedy, who stated "Those who make peaceful revolution impossible will make violent revolution inevitable" (Wolf 2001:3).

Glick (1989) reports that the FBI and local police began to move outside the law when congressional investigations, political trials, and other traditional legal modes of repression failed to counter the growing protest movements. They used methods that amounted to a home front version of CIA covert actions used throughout the world. Wolf et.al. (2001) make a poignant commentary concerning FBI extra-legal activities in the face of America's claim of democracy.

> ...Yes, there are elements of democracy; there are things that you're grateful for, that you're not in front of the death squads in El Salvador. On the other hand, it's not quite a democracy. And one of the things that makes it not quite a democracy is the existence of outfits like the FBI and the CIA. Democracy is based on openness, and the existence of a secret policy, secret lists of dissident citizens, violates the spirit of democracy.

FBI headquarters set policy, assessed progress, charted all new directions, demanded necessary increased production, and carefully monitored and controlled day-to-day operations, according to FBI researcher Brian Glick. Local FBI field offices communicated at great length with national COINTELPRO supervisors concerning every operation, freely and without fear of public exposure.

The ensuing bureaucratic paper trail was prolific. The moment that paper trail began to surface, the FBI discontinued all of its formal domestic counterintelligence programs. However, the Bureau never ceased its covert political activity against U.S. citizens who protested against U.S. government policies at home and abroad. FBI files have never been seized by the U.S. Congress or the courts, nor have they been sent to the National Archives. Many counterintelligence operations were never committed to writing, there have been no open investigations, and former operatives are legally prohibited from discussing FBI and COINTELPRO activities (Wolf et.al.:3, 8).

Gary Lee's (1995) article "How COINTELPRO Helped Destroy the Movements of the 1960s informs as to how COINTELPRO successfully stifled the 1960s movements. The program pitted Whites against Blacks, Blacks against Latinos, students against workers, men against women, workers against people on welfare, Christians against Jews, Jews against Muslims. COINTELPRO placed FBI infiltrators within organizations to create internal problems. Leaders of organizations were attacked, money was repeatedly stolen and equipment was sabotaged by infiltrators to intensify pressure and create mistrust and suspicion.

COINTELPRO finally enabled the FBI and local police departments to outright eliminate leaders of mass movements in a manner that did not undermine the image of the United States as a democracy that supported free speech and the rule of law. The organization attacked and "neutralized" leaders before their skills could be transferred to others and before they were able to establish stable structures to carry on their work. "Neutralization" was defined as "shooting to kill." History has yet to relate the true story behind the assassinations of Martin Luther King, Jr., Malcolm X, Medgar Evers and others. With the assistance of mainstream media, prominent leaders were portrayed to the public as crooks, thugs, philanderers, or Communists. Others, like the Black Panther Party leaders, were murdered in shootouts under phony pretexts in which the only shots were fired by the police.

It is necessary to take a brief step all the way back to the beginning of this country to understand that the above developments did not just spring up during the 1960s. The illegal use of law enforcement and the injustices of the justice system are found in the blood, bones, and chromosomes of America as a nation.

American Apartheid

By my estimation, there have been a total of about 347 years of apartheid in America and a mere 40 years of legal integration. Despite America's claims for being the poster-child for democracy in the world, its historical record demonstrates a very different situation.

Before going further, we need to present some of the historical events that followed the end of the Civil War in 1865. Although it was also the end of slavery, **Black codes** and **Jim Crow regulations** continued to restrict the rights of Africans. Despite that, the Republican Party was the "party of Lincoln" to which almost 100% of the Black population belonged at that time.

The thirty-ninth meeting of Congress convened December 4, 1865, dominated by northern radical Republicans. Charles Sumner and Thaddeus Stevens were the most vocal of all the northern radical Republicans. At that time, Congress passed the first **Civil *Rights Act*** on April 1866, which extended citizenship to Africans in America and stipulated that discrimination would be tried in the federal courts. This *Act* was the precursor of the ***Fourteenth Amendment***, ratified on June 13, 1866 that granted **full citizenship** to Africans. The *Fourteenth Amendment* struck two blows to the South's most sacred canons: states' rights, and African inferiority. Congress next passed a bill on January 8, 1867 that conferred suffrage on Africans in the District of Columbia. Three weeks later, they passed still another measure that forbade territorial legislatures from denying the ballot to Africans (Quarles, 1987:131-132).

Those legislative events were followed by the March 2, 1867 **Reconstruction Act**, which was the Republican Congress' way of using the *Fourteenth Amendment* to protect and enfranchise Blacks who would in turn help to build loyal governments in the South after the Civil War. On one hand, the Act reinforced Africans' right to vote and fully participate in the reconstructed southern states' governments. On the other, it required that delegates from the southern states had to be chosen by an electorate which included Africans. The *Fifteenth Amendment*, ratified March 30, 1870, delivered another severe blow to the southern states by denying state or federal governments the right to restrict the Black vote (Quarles, 1987:133-136).

Now we can return to the subject of **American Apartheid,** beginning in 1619 with the start of slavery. From 1619 to 1866 with the writing of the first Civil Rights Act, we have **247 years of Apartheid.**

Reconstruction was short-lived, ending in 1876 with what is referred to as the "Hayes betrayal." Rutherford B. Hayes won the 1876 rigged presidential election aided by a corrupt Electoral College. That event has been called the "legal and illegal corruption of imperialist democracy" (Copeland, 2000). Hayes restored the power of the Southern ruling class and withdrew all federal troops from the South. The Supreme Court then re-interpreted the Fourteenth and Fifteenth Amendments in such a way as to weaken protection of Africans. This adds up to **9 years of integration**.

Black disfranchisement began abruptly in 1876, and continued until 1964. Those were the years of Jim Crow laws, violence, lynching, segregation, and disfranchisement. On one hand, Black people were killed for attempting to vote. On the other hand, the practice of rounding Blacks up in pickup trucks to vote for racist Whites at the point of a gun or rifle was common. It was a time of armed suppression of Black liberation. Such stringent measures were aimed at Blacks that poor Whites were caught up in the legal oppression. Copeland

(2000) argues that the end of Reconstruction was definitely the end of Black democracy.

> The majority of the Republican leadership had been secretly helping the former slaveholders to regain their former political power in the South—first of all by allowing them to beat down the Black people.
>
> The election deal that promised the Southern ruling class a free hand in the South was thus only the parliamentary side of the bloody counter-revolution that the Democratic Southern ruling class had already carried out. Its consummation set the seal of legality, Republican consent, and finality to the armed suppression of Black freedom. ...

Change came about almost 100 years later due to the civil rights unrest when African Americans took to the streets in protest and marched on Washington demanding change. This period comes to **88 years of apartheid**.

The fourth *Civil Rights Act* of 1964 (Why were so many of them necessary?) ushered in a period of legal integration. The forward strides made by African Americans and other progressive groups began to erode in 1995 during the Clinton administration with the Republican Congress' "Contract with America." Some refer to it as a "Contract *on* America" because the emerging neo-conservatives began to roll back many of the changes that liberals had fought for over the years.

Copeland (2000) reveals how what he calls the "Tweedledum-Tweedledee" character of modern capitalist politics" that we are witnessing in 2007 is really just an extension of the "Hayes betrayal" of 1876.

Both Republican and Democratic parties were, from then on, the exclusive parties of U.S. big business with no other significance (besides the enrichment of professional bourgeois politicians) than to continue the rule of big business with one or another reformist or reactionary method.

This revelation puts the craziness of present politics and what some are referring to as "disaster capitalism" into a proper perspective.
Here we have **31 years of legal integration** between 1964 and 1995.

Race relations, civil rights, and human rights issues and legislation have been on a greased downhill run toward apartheid and the suspension of constitutional rights and liberties since 1995. The bombing of the Twin Towers in 2001 has served the interests of the multinational corporations that are now running the U.S. government. Our minds are being programmed into a matrix-like false reality, and many of us are voluntarily giving up our rights and voting against our own self-interests for the benefit of big business. Between 1995 and 2008 represents **13 more years of apartheid**. When we do the math it adds up to **348 years of apartheid** and **40 years of legal integration.**

FBI and COINTELPRO Targets

According to Glick (1989) FBI documents disclosed six major official counter-intelligence programs in addition to COINTELPRO. Covert operations were aimed against African American,

Native American, Asian American, Arab American, and Iranian, activists. Neutralization programs were aimed at every progressive movement and group in the country, across racial and ethnic lines.

Communist Party-USA

This was the first and largest program, which led to the Party's decline in the 1950s. In a turnaround, the Party was used in the mid-1960s against civil rights, civil liberties, and peace activists. Organizations targeted in this manner included the NAACP, SCLC, the Mississippi Freedom Democratic Party, the National Lawyers Guild, the National Committee to Abolish the House Un-American Activities Committee, Women's Strike for Peace, the American Friends Service Committee, and the National Committee for a SANE Nuclear Policy.

Black Activist Groups

Counterintelligence programs were aimed against every African American protest group: Black Nationalist and Black Integrationist organizations; National Welfare Rights Organization; League of Black Revolutionary Workers; Republic of New Afrika (RNA); the Nation of Islam; Congress of African People; Black student unions; Black churches; and community organizations.

White Hate Groups

White hate groups were actually a component of the FBI's operations against progressive activists who were COINTELPRO's main targets. The FBI actually gave covert aid to the Ku Klux Klan, Minutemen, Nazis, and other racist vigilantes. These groups received substantial funds, information, and protection from the FBI and suffered only token FBI harassment so long as they restricted their violence against COINTELPRO targets.

New Left Activists

"New Left" activists included a cross-section of the predominantly White American population, including such groups as: Students for Democratic Society (SDS); Peace and Freedom Party; Institute for Policy Studies; anti-war, anti-racism, student, GI, veteran, feminist, lesbian, gay, environmental, Marxist and other anarchist groups; food cooperatives, health clinics, child care centers, schools, bookstores, newspapers, community centers, street theaters, rock groups, and communes.

Independence for Puerto Rico Activists

The FBI and COINTELPRO organized to disrupt, discredit, and factionalize the island's main centers of anti-colonial resistance, especially the Puerto Rican Socialist Party (PSP) and the Socialist League (LSP). The Young Lords Party that was fighting for human rights for Puerto Ricans living in the United States was also targeted.

Border Coverage Program

This program targeted radical Mexican protest organizations like the Brown Berets, the Crusade for Justice, La Alianza, and the Chicano Moratorium to End the War in Vietnam.

Socialist Workers Party

FBI operations targeted this group and its youth organization, the Young Socialist Alliance.

Whoever supported or worked with them were also targeted, such as Malcolm X and the National Mobilization Committee to End the War in Vietnam.

Various techniques were used against all these organizations and groups by COINTELPRO, with great success. FBI commitment to undermine and destroy popular movements was extensive and relentless, similar to the activities of any police state and unlike anything seen among Western industrial democracies. Wolf et.al. (2001:4) discusses the scope of FBI and COINTELPRO commitment "to expose, disrupt, misdirect, discredit, or otherwise neutralize" the enemies of the State. During the Nixon administration, a Bureau document entitled "FBI Paramilitary Operations in Indian Country" outlined a how-to plan that defined "neutralization" as "shooting to kill."

Victimization and Infiltration

The full force of FBI disruption programs were brought against Black Nationalists. FBI agents were instructed to undertake actions to discredit Nationalist groups within what was considered the "responsible Negro community as well as Black radicals." The "responsible White community" and the White liberals who hold sympathy for Black Nationalists just because they are Negroes likewise had to be convinced that Nationalists were enemies of America. Hoover issued a memo on March 4, 1968 that laid out the goals of the COINTELPRO. In accordance with these goals, Martin Luther King, Jr. Malcolm X, Stokely Carmichael, Eldridge Cleaver, and Elijah Muhammad were targeted (Wolf et.al.

2001:4-5). Clearly stated, the FBI and COINTELPRO intended:
> To prevent the coalition of militant black nationalist groups; to prevent the rise of a messiah who could unify and electrify the militant black nationalist movement; to prevent violence on the part of black nationalist groups; to prevent militant black nationalist groups and leaders from gaining respectability; and to prevent the long-range growth of militant black nationalist organizations, especially among youth.

The FBI used paid informants called *agents provocateurs* as one of its techniques to disrupt organizations. These infiltrators would raise controversial issues at meetings to take advantage of ideological divisions, to promote enmity with other groups, or to incite the group to commit violent acts. They went so far as to provide groups with weapons. FBI provocateurs have been used repeatedly over the years to initiate violent acts, forceful disruptions of meetings, and demonstrations, attacks on police, bombings, and so on. They followed an old strategy of Tsarist police director T.C. Zubatov: "We shall provoke you to acts of terror and then crush you" (Wolf et.al. 2001:7).

Wolf et.al. (2001) present a written statement by COINTELPRO specialist William C. Sullivan shortly after Martin L. King's "I Have a Dream" speech:

> We must mark [King] now, if we have not before, as the most dangerous Negro in the future of this Nation from the standpoint of communism, the Negro, and national security ... it may be unrealistic to limit [our actions against King] to

legalistic proofs that would stand up in court or before Congressional Committees.

At the time, Dr. King was leading the Southern Christian Leadership Conference (SCLC) in a massive campaign to secure Black voting rights across the rural South. The FBI believed that success of this campaign threatened the ultimate dismantlement of some of the most blatant aspects of the U.S. system of segregation in the South. FBI supervisor J.G. Kelly forwarded a newspaper clipping in mid-September of 1957 stating that the SCLC was "a likely target for communist infiltration." However, the SCLC became infiltrated by FBI agents, not by Communists. By October 15, 1960, the Bureau infiltrated SCLC organizational meetings and conferences as the issue of Black voting rights in the South gained attention and support across the nation. In order to lend credibility to FBI counterintelligence activities, J. Edgar Hoover sent a letter to Attorney General Robert F. Kennedy falsely claiming that King enjoyed a "close relationship" with Stanley D. Levison, "a member of the Communist Party, USA. Hoover also claimed that one of Dr. King's speeches had been written by Isadore Wofsy, a high ranking leader in the Communist Party (Wolf et.al. 2001:11).

Ku Klux Klan

FBI agents and informers made up at least one quarter of all active Klan members during the 1060s. Internal FBI documents revealed that they were neither neutral observers nor objective investigators. Rather, they were active participants in beatings, bombings, and murders that claimed the lives of about 50 civil rights activists by 1964. They served in top leadership posts in at least half of all Klan units, and promoted the Klan's fascist agenda. FBI infiltrators' loyalty and commitment were confirmed by their participation in terrorist acts.

Historical records show that the FBI "Klan – White Hate Groups" arm of COINTELPRO was actually launched to infiltrate and support the Ku Klux Klan. Documented FBI activities of the 1960s forward clearly contradict the FBI's role as heroes in the film "Mississippi Burning, written by Alan Parker." This was a slick Hollywood popularization of the period to cover up the fact that the FBI was instrumental in building the Ku Klux Klan in the South. Wolf et.al. (2001:19) reveals that the FBI's role during the 1960s was not to protect civil rights workers, but to assist the Ku Klux Klan in their campaign of murder and terror.

According to Wolf et.al. (2001), the Klan continues to exist as a supplement to the armed power of the State, available to be used when the State finds it necessary. He further discusses how the FBI consistently refused to protect civil rights workers under attack across the South, and the Bureau consistently refused to warn those whom they knew were under imminent threat of violence. Police agreed to show up fifteen or twenty minutes after the time that Klansmen carried out an attack on civil rights workers. Klansmen received lenient treatment if they managed to get arrested by some fluke. No serious efforts were made to explore the role of White Citizens Councils that served as fronts for the Klan, and no one investigated the widespread complicity in racist violence on the part of local police.

White Citizens Councils

White Citizens Councils (WCC) were first established in Mississippi following the U.S. Supreme Court decision that racial segregation in public schools was unconstitutional in the case of *Brown v. Board of Education* on May 17, 1954. The immediate reaction was formation of Councils in opposition to integration. Robert "Tut" Patterson founded the organization in Indianola on July 11, 1954 to try and stop the implementation of the *Brown* decision. The organization was spearheaded by individuals of prominence and wealth who were part of mainstream American society: primarily plantation owners, doctors, lawyers, legislators, preachers, teachers, and merchants. As such, they wield tremendous power at voting booths and in the halls of government.

The WCC openly renounced violence; however, they simultaneously encouraged White violence against Blacks, especially in the case of the Ku Klux Klan. They were referred to as the "Uptown Klan" because they donned suits and ties instead of white sheets and hoods. The organization's strength was in its ability to bring economic reprisals against anyone who supported desegregation. Members would threaten and harass anyone who spoke in favor of civil rights. As a result of WCC efforts, it took about ten years before any desegregation took place in Mississippi in accordance with the *Brown* decision. According to the *Sisters of Selma* website, "uppity blacks found themselves jobless, black professionals had credit, insurance, or license problems, and all blacks who tried to register to vote were placed on a blacklist." After a long history of hate, intimidation and violence, the group fell apart. However, it was resurrected years later by some former members.

Council for Conservative Citizens

By using mailing lists from the WCC, former members were able to form a new organization called the Council for Conservative Citizens (CCC). Like the former organization, CCC members were well organized, and were able to present a united front in vehemently opposing integration, same-sex marriages, immigration, inter-racial marriages, and abortion. The CCC claims that it is not a racist organization; however, the Southern Poverty Law Center has labeled them as a "hate group."

The Klan, the WCC, and the CCC have all worked in concert with the FBI and COINTELPRO. Counterintelligence programs have been so successful that they have had serious long-term consequences for African Americans, not only neutralizing mechanisms to deliver services to Black people, but also creating a sense of depression and hopelessness. Some of the methods include: psychological warfare from the outside; harassment through the legal system; and extra-legal force and violence (Fraser (1961).

Psychological Warfare from the Outside

Agents and informers spied on political activists to discredit leaders and to disrupt activist organizations. The FBI and police used a variety of "dirty tricks" to undermine progressive movements, including planting false media stories, publishing bogus fliers, forging correspondences, making anonymous telephone calls, having parents, employers, landlords, school officials and others to cause trouble for activists.

Martin Luther King and the SCLC were repeatedly accused by the FBI of having ties to the Communist Party. Although none of the claims were substantiated the Bureau planted at least five disinformational "news stories" in the media claiming SCLC had communist connections. On the basis of the false media claims, Attorney General Kennedy authorized round-the-clock surveillance of King's home and all SCLC offices. Telephone taps were placed on King's residence and all SCLC offices (Wolf et.al. 2001:12).

The Bureau became desperate in its attempts to discredit King when it was announced that King would receive a Nobel Peace Prize as a reward for his work in behalf of African Americans. FBI audio technician John Matter doctored a set of audiotapes taken from King's tapped telephone conversations to demonstrate that the civil rights leader's "sexual perversion and depravity" with prostitutes. The FBI threatened to release the audiotapes to the media if King did not commit suicide before receiving the Nobel Peace Prize. FBI Associate Director Cartha D. DeLoach personally delivered a copy of the transcript to Benjamin Bradlee, Bureau Chief of the *Newsweek* Washington Bureau. Bradlee refused the material, and disclosed FBI plans to unfairly discredit King to Jay Iselin of *Newsday*. As a result of being found out, Senator Edward V. Long ordered Hoover to dismantle the electronic surveillance of King and the SCLC. Not to be deterred, FBI efforts to discredit the reputation and mission of Martin Luther King never slackened, right up to his death in Memphis,

Tennessee on April 4, 1968. Bureau efforts to "expose" King's communist connections even continued for at least a year after his death (Wolf et.al. 2001:13).

Protestors seeking independence for Puerto Rico were attacked in similar fashion. Juan Mari Bras, leader of the *Movimiento Pro-Independencia de Puerto Rico* (MPIPR), suffered a near-fatal heart attack on April of 1964 after receiving an anonymous counterintelligence letter. His illness and the effects of the letter on the MPIPR leaders brought the (Puerto Rican Independence Movement to a near halt. Bras was already suffering from tremendous strain and overwork, and his supporters claim that the letter played a part in triggering his heart attack. The contents of the anonymous letter created a climate of distrust and dissension, from which it took some time for the organization to recover.

Harassment through the Legal System

The FBI and police abused the legal system to harass activists and make them appear to be criminals. Policemen gave perjured testimonies and presented fabricated evidence for false arrests and wrongful imprisonment. They used conspicuous surveillance, unfairly enforced tax laws and other government regulations. They also intimidated activists and silenced their supporters by using grand jury subpoenas.

There are large numbers of Americans who have been jailed because they dedicated their lives to the transformation of the U.S. for the better. These are the idealists who were willing to die to end brutality, racism, economic discrimination, imperialism, and war. Wolf, et.al. (2001:33) defines them as "political prisoners":

> When the government can select a person for criminal persecution because of their political activity, when they can fabricate evidence against that person and suppress evidence proving that fabrication, and prosecute a person and put them in prison for any amount of time, let alone for life, then you have a political prisoner.

COINTELPRO-instigated violence forced Black Panther Party members underground. They were hunted down by local police as well as federal law enforcement officials. Black Panther Party leaders and members like Dhoruba Bin Wahad, Huey P. Newton, and Marshall E. Conway were routinely jailed on false FBI charges. Harold Russel, Woody Green, Twyman Meyers, and Zayd Shakur were killed during law enforcement confrontations. Others were captured and charged with crimes. All Black Panther members were tried at a time when the American public and juries knew nothing of COINTELPRO's existence (Wolf et.al. 2001:48).

According to Wolf et.al. (2001:38-48), Mumia Abu-Jamal was imprisoned for the falsely created charge that he was involved in a crime he did not commit. "Geronimo" Pratt was personally targeted in 1969 for "neutralization" by COINTELPRO after it was learned he would become the next head of the Los Angeles branch of the Black Panther Party. Pratt faced trumped-up charges of a Bank of America robbery that FBI already knew was committed by United Slave (US) members.

Exculpatory evidence was withheld and other U.S. Constitutional violations were committed during the trials of Dhoruba Bin Wahad and Geronimo Pratt. They, as well as Anthony Jalil Bottom, Herman Bell, Robert Seth Hayes, Sundiata Acoli, Abdul Majid, and Bashir Hameed remain in prison today because post-conviction motions in their behalf were unsuccessful. Albert Nuh Washington died in prison in 2000, followed by Teddy Jah Heath in 2001. They were denied compassionate release in their last days of life, although both had spent over 25 years in prison.

Extralegal Force and Violence
Outright violence was a hallmark of FBI techniques aimed at neutralizing and destroying dissident organizations formed by African Americans and other ethnic groups in the U.S. Apart from murder and assassination, the FBI and police threatened, instigated, as well as conducted break-ins, vandalism, assaults, and beatings with the objective of frightening dissidents and disrupting their movements. Many of the attacks on Black, Puerto Rican, and Native American activists were so extensive, vicious, and calculated that they can accurately be termed a form of official terrorism.

Right-wing paramilitary groups and *agents provocateurs* were organized and financed by the U.S. government to carry out extensive terror and disruption campaigns. The most effective means of disruption occurred through infiltration and provocation of existing groups, especially on college campuses. Wolf et.al (2001:7-27) claim that "much of the violence that occurred on college campuses can be attributed to government provocateurs." This brings to mind the students that were shot down by the Ohio National Guard on the Kent State University campus on May 4, 1970.

At least 10,000 American homes were subjected to illegal breaking and entering by the FBI, acting without judicial warrants. Burglaries called "black bag jobs" were performed in order to obtain written materials, mailing lists, internal documents, position papers of organizations and individuals. Black activists were repeatedly arrested on any excuse until they could no longer make bail. FBI also used violent and emotionally disturbed individuals to present false testimony against key Black activists for crimes as serious as murder, in full knowledge that they did not commit those crimes.

The American Indian Movement (AIM) was another group that was targeted for disruption and neutralization. AIM was a vehicle for indigenous pride and self-determination in the late 20th century. The organization had the full support of the traditional Oglala nation. However, from the 1960s to the 1970s, FBI pressure on people on the reservation, especially the elderly people, wore them down until they suffered a kind of fatigue. Traditional Oglalas finally asked the protesters to disengage after a bloody firefight on the Pine Ridge Reservation in South Dakota in the 1970s. More than sixty AIM members and supporters died violently and at least 342 others suffered violent physical assaults between 1973 and 1976, at Wounded Knee and in other nearby locations.

Examples of FBI and COINTELPRO efforts to put down the American Indian Movement were the assassinations of Richard Oaks, Larry Cacuse, and John Trudell. Oaks was leader of the 1970 occupation of Alcatraz Island, where Native Americans representing all the tribes gathered in protest. He was gunned down in California the following year. Cacuse, a Navajo AIM leader, was shot to death in Arizona in 1972. Their deaths were followed by that of John Trudell, another AIM leader. Trudell was warned by FBI personnel that if he delivered a scheduled speech in Washington there would be "consequences." Trudell made his speech, in which he detailed the nature and scope of federal repression in Indian country. That very night his wife, mother-in-law, and three children were "mysteriously" burned to death at their home in the Nevada Duck Valley Reservation (Wolf et.al. 2001:18).

Wolf et.al. (2001:15) further reports how, during the winter of 1972-1973, hundreds of Native Americans from reservations across the West had gathered to commemorate the 1890 massacre of Wounded Knee. A series of unsolved murders on the reservation and a struggle between the administration of the Oglala Sioux tribal president, Dick Wilson, and opposition organizations on the reservation had already created a tense situation. Wilson's guards who patrolled the reservation unleashed a reign of terror against all who opposed him.

Things came to a head on Feb. 28, 1973 when Wilson's men blockaded roads to the hamlet supported by FBI personnel and the U.S. Marshalls

Special Operations Group. General Alexander Haig, the then military liaison in the Nixon White House personally directed Colonel Volney Warner of the 82nd Airborne Division and Colonel Jack Potter of the 6th Army in the armed melee. These Pentagon "advisors" coordinated a massive flow of military personnel, weapons and equipment to Wilson and his men besieging Wounded Knee. A 71-day siege ensued with U.S. military officers, supply sergeants, maintenance technicians, chemical officers, and medical teams all working in civilian clothes to conceal their unconstitutional involvement in the "civil disorder" that had to be put down at all costs. AIM's direct confrontation ended, out of respect for the request of the traditional people, although the resistance remains and the struggle continues in other forms (Wolf et.al. 2001:6).

Mari Bras, leader of the Puerto Rican *Independentista* Movement, testified before the United Nations Commission on Decolonization that he received a detailed description of the death of his son who was killed in 1976 at the hands of an assassin. Bras assumed the FBI was behind it because the memo was almost joyful about the terrible effect his son's death would have upon him personally and upon his gubernatorial campaign in 1976. It was speculated that the FBI was also behind the firebombing of Bras's home in 1978 (Wolf et.al. 2001:14).

Two young activists in the Puerto Rican *Independentista* Movement were killed in a clear example of direct FBI involvement. Arnaldo Dario Rosado and Carlos Arrivi were lured into a trap by an FBI *provocateur* named Alejandro Gonzalez

Malave. The two activists were shot to death by police near the mountain village Cerro Maravilla. According to a witness, "it was a planned murder, and it was carried out like that." The two men were forced to their knees, handcuffed with their arms behind their backs, tortured, and murdered, despite the fact that the two men offered no resistance. Gonzalez Malave admitted that he was an infiltrator reporting to both the local police in Puerto Rico and the FBI. He also admitted to setting the two victims up for execution. After the murders, a police officer named Julio Cesar Andrades testified that the assassination was planned "from on high" in collaboration with the FBI (Wolf et.al. 2001:15).

Operations against the *Independentistas* continued well into the 1980s, according to Alfredo Lopez (1988). He reports around 170 documented accounts of attacks, beatings, shootings, and bombings of independence organizations and activists at rallies and pickets. *Independentistas* were attacked just walking the streets. Two restaurant workers were killed in the 1975 bombing of a rally at Mayaguez. Although many right-wing organizations claimed credit for the more than 170 attacks, not one person has been arrested or brought to trial.

There has been little or no mention of the FBI and COINTELPRO programs of violence and disruption carried out for the U.S. government. Things were summed up by FBI Director Clarence M. Kelley: "Faced with sufficient threat, covert disruption is justified" (Wolf et.al. 2001:52).

This chapter has presented only a birds-eye view of the ruthless, brutal nature of Anglo American behavior during the 20th century. It provides a glimpse of the "no holds barred" commitment to repressive violence aimed to put down the popular progressive movement of the 1950s and 1960s, and to neutralize all parties engaged in the movements that swept through the country. Without knowledge of the 400 or so years of European and American imperialism that precedes the 1960s era, it is difficult to understand how this can occur in the United States of America – the country that presents itself to the world as the ultimate beacon of hope, freedom, and democracy.

The following information demonstrates that racism did not suddenly appear in America. Rather, it is a social construction created by Caucasians in recent history for the purpose of political domination. The chapter outlines methods used by Europeans and Americans to develop false, twisted concepts of race and racial hierarchies 400 years ago as tools for White minority domination over people of color worldwide.

5. TWO MODELS OF HISTORY AND CULTURE

One of the ways of helping to destroy a people is to tell them they don't have a history, that they have no roots.
--Archbishop Desmond Tutu of South Africa

There are two competing models of history and culture. The first is the *Ancient Model* that uses physical evidence from archaeology and ancient written documents about the African origin of religion, knowledge, and civilization in the world. This model continues to stand the test of time and scholarly scrutiny after thousands of years. Scholars and researchers have no problems finding a wealth of documents that support the factuality of claims within this model.

The other is the *Aryan Model* which was recently developed by Europeans in the past 300 years. This model presents a re-fabricated historical account that claims the well-known ancient Greek scholars were misled or wrong in giving Africans credit for everything they knew, and that it was Caucasians who created the highest forms of knowledge and civilization known to the world. Scholars and researchers who use the recent Aryan model make several claims of this type, but have problems finding valid historical documents to support its false claims. One of their greatest difficulties lies in the fact that the ancient Greeks documented their personal experiences; what they saw, what they knew, and that they experienced firsthand about the relationship between Africa and Greece during their lifetimes. Another serious difficulty is in the field of archaeology, where there is no physical evidence to support Aryan Model claims.

The Ancient Model of History and Culture

For the purposes of this book, the *Ancient Model* should be considered as the **African Model** *of history and culture*. Many ancient and modern scholars acknowledge that a preponderance of physical evidence supports the claim that all Western culture and civilization have African origins. There were also Phoenician contributions to Greek culture, but they had also borrowed heavily from the Egyptians, Ethiopians, and Sudanese who were initiators and forerunners in culture and civilization.

Every student who has studied the Greek foundations of Western culture knows that all the textbooks begin with Egyptian civilization before any attempt to discuss Greece. In the process, Egyptians are portrayed as being White, Semitic, or "Oriental" (whatever that is), depending on who is making the argument. It cannot be denied, however, that at the time when ancient Greece was just developing its *first ever* high point in civilization, Africa was already in its long *Second Golden Age* of civilization with highly developed governmental structures, science, mathematics, religious and philosophical systems, division of labor, colossal architecture, medicine, surgery, visual and performing arts.

There are several scholars whose works have to be cited in any discussion of the *Ancient Model*. Senegalese scholar Cheikh Anta Diop's (1974) most popular work is *The African Origin of Civilization: Myth or Reality* that sets forth his theory that Africa is the "Southern Cradle" in which all humanity and civilization first developed. Diop (1974:xv) quotes Dr. S.B. Leakey on this issue:

> The triumph of the monogenetic thesis of humanity, even at the stage of "Homo sapiens-sapiens," compels one to admit that all races descended from the Black race, according to a filiation process that science will one day explain.

Dr. John Henrik Clarke (1995:14) in his book *Who Betrayed the African Revolution? And Other Speeches* asserts the documented fact that Africans are the ancestors/predecessors of Europeans, since it is we who created them. He quotes the words of R.R. Palmer and Joel Cotton:

> ... Europeans were by no means the pioneers in human civilization. Half of man's recorded history had passed before anyone in Europe could read or write. The priests of Egypt began to keep written records between 4,000 and 3,000 B.C.E. While the Pharoahs were building the first pyramids, Europeans were creating nothing more distinguished than garbage heaps ...

Dr. Yosef ben-Jochannan's (1971) massive work entitled *Africa, Mother of Western Civilization* and another massive publication by Gerald Massey

(1991) *A Book of Beginnings* set benchmarks and provided a foundation for similar works by Africa-centered scholars. Dr. John Henrik Clarke (1995:93) remarks that Massey, an agnostic, was neither an Africanist nor an African lover. Nevertheless, this consummate scholar kept tracing European religion back to Africa until he finally proclaimed: "I will prove that all European religions were taken from outside of Europe." Massey's general theme was expanded in Martin Bernal's (1987, 1991) two-volume work entitled *Black Athena: The Afroasiatic Roots of Classical Civilization.*

Clarke (1995:93) also refers to important works by White scholars, such as Count Volney's *The Ruins of Empire,* and Frenchman De Lepsis who did an assessment of the monumental ruins of Egypt. Fifth century Greek historian Herodotus recorded his eye-witness accounts of Egypt and Ethiopia and described the complexion and physical appearance of both as being the same. Roman historians on Africa include Pliny the Elder and Pliny the Younger similarly left records that demonstrate the high civilization found in Africa. These are by and large the most prominent contemporary and ancient scholars who have written extensively on the subject of Africa's contributions to Western civilization, which is the starting point for all Western culture.

All of the scholars center their discussions in ancient Egypt, Ethiopia and Sudan, with Egypt having the greatest significance in the development of Classical Greek culture. They use archaeological and historical evidence, as well as eye-witness accounts in the case of ancient records; however,

Gerald Massey includes linguistic evidence. All of the above scholars make it clear that ancient Egypt was a Black African civilization, but Bernal argues that Semitic influences were also a factor in what he refers to as the "Afro-Asiatic" roots of Classical Greek culture. One must be careful in reading Bernal. Since ancient Hebrews identified and associated themselves with the Asian Hyksos who invaded and occupied Egypt for about 200 years, Bernal's term "Afro-Asiatic" suggests that Hebrews had a major role in laying the foundation for Egyptian culture. The term "Afro-Asiatic is also misleading because it further implies that the Africans in Egypt were significantly Semitic by both blood and culture. This is problematic because Semitic people were still predominantly nomadic when Africans had already developed a sedentary lifestyle and had established their pharonic, pyramid-building phase of civilization.

The authors mentioned above present various types of compelling documented evidence that black-skinned Africans, especially Egyptians, Ethiopians, and Sudanese created the first religion and the first cradle of civilization. Diop, ben-Yochannan, and Massey discuss the tribal and cultural connections among ancient Egyptian, Ethiopian and Sudanese peoples. Massey uses extensive linguistic evidence, and demonstrates the African origins of Judaism, Christianity, and Islam. To a lesser extent, ben-Jochannan also documents the African influence on Judaism and Christianity.

Diop (1974) sets forth the bold assertion that: "Instead of presenting itself to history as an insolvent debtor, [the] Black world is the very initiator of the western civilization flaunted before our eyes today." Diop recounts African religious, scientific and philosophic contributions to ancient Greeks, such as: Pythagorean mathematics, Greek architecture, the theory of the four elements of Thales of Miletus, Epicurean materialism, Platonic idealism, Judaism, Christianity, Islam, and modern science. Physical evidence demonstrates that all are rooted in Black Egyptian cosmogony and science. The mathematical principle of *pi* was articulated in Western culture after more modern scientists studied the dimensions of Egyptian pyramids. In religion, Osiris the Redeemer-god sacrifices himself, dies, and is resurrected to save mankind. Other cultures adopted this religious story, such that there are at least sixteen such resurrected saviors who are central figures in religions much older than Christianity.

Bernal (1987, 1991) focuses extensively on primary source documents written by ancient Greek historians and philosophers like Herodotus, Isokrates, Plato, Aristotle, and Thucydides to support his argument that Egyptian knowledge, thought, and science were transmitted into Greece and contributed to the classical period of Greek culture. He further argues that the Eurocentric Aryan Model was formed by Christianity and Caucasian Nationalism in the 19th and 20th centuries.

Several 18th and 19th century scholars conducted research into the origin of scientific knowledge in the ancient world, and all agreed that Western civilization was founded by Egyptian Africans. Charles Francois Dupuis argued that the field of astronomy began with Egyptians. The research and writings of Count Constantine Chasseboeuf de Volney and Abbe Gregoire explicitly ascribed the "greatest degree of human knowledge" to ancient Africans. French Count C.F.de Volney wrote in 1793:

> There are a people now forgotten (who) discovered while others were yet barbarians, the elements of the arts and sciences. A race of men now rejected for their black skin and wooly hair, founded on the study of the laws of nature those civil and religious systems which still govern the universe.

After studying ancient Egyptian sculptures in 1849, John Stuart Mill concluded that the Egyptians were African because that is how they portrayed themselves. Investigation of Greek writings led him to add: "It was from negroes, therefore, that the Greeks learnt their first lessons in civilization." Admiration for Egyptian knowledge and civilization reached new heights in the 18th century Enlightenment era due to the rise of Freemasonry. Freemasons considered themselves to be the idealized Egyptian priests of the modern age (Bernal, 2003). However, they are limited to a mere 33° of African knowledge, rather than the full 360° that is accessible only to the African people from whom it was borrowed.

African American scholars and intellectuals like R.A. Young, David Walker, Frederick Douglass, W.E.B. DuBois, St. Clair Drake, Chancellor Williams, and John Jackson all joined in the effort to educate others about the Ancient Model that demonstrates the Africanity of ancient Egyptians and their tremendous contribution to Greek civilization, which is the starting point for all Western civilization. Bayo Oyebade (1990) reminds readers that the study of Africa from an African perspective is indeed not new because it even dates back to the closing years of the colonial period in Africa. This approach increased in the scholarly works of African Americans in the 1960s, especially during the height of the "Black is Beautiful" phase of the Civil Rights Movement. The 1980s development of the Africa-centered academic discipline that uses an "Afrocentric" perspective as a theoretical and philosophic approach became part and parcel of academia, led by scholars such as Molefi Kete Ashante, Tshetloane Keto, and Maulana Karenga. They are joined by many other scholars who have been trained in the discipline and continue to carry this academic movement forward.

Aside from African contributions to world civilization and science, it needs to be mentioned that the greatest contribution by Africans to the world is the gift of humanity. The best internationally known scientific minds in archaeology and genetics have demonstrated that Africans are the parents of all human beings. Their studies show that African women are the only people with the MtDNA that contains the genetic makeup of every race of people in the world. A worldwide genetic study also found that as Africans began to mix with others who, over tens of thousands of years, had developed into lighter skinned races due to environmental adaptation, the MtDna of their female offspring began to lose its rich variation. It is speculated that in case of a gene-mutating nuclear accident, African women may be the ones that are most fit to preserve humanity as we know it because they carry the most highly varied dominant genes of all the so-called races on earth.

The Aryan Model of History and Culture

The most obvious features of the *Aryan Model* are its racism and anti-Semitism. This re-fabricated version of the *Ancient Model* was a racialist model of history developed by a narrow group of British and European intellectuals: clergymen, physicians, professors and philosophers. Many of them had never seen Africans and depended on second-hand accounts. In the United States the model was further developed by intellectuals and slave-masters like Thomas Jefferson who, ironically, claimed to believe the notion that "all men are created equal." (Jefferson, sometimes considered to be America's most eloquent champion of equality, lived a life of contradiction. He fathered around six children by Sally Hemings, his slave concubine, and never made provisions to set any of them free even after his death.)

The European designers of this model of history were interested in developing a unified history and heroic image of Europe. We must remember that the Christian Church plunged Europe into the Dark Ages, which lasted from the sixth century A.D. until the 14th century A.D.; some 800 years of suspended intellectual progress, cultural stagnation, and utter ignorance. By the 18th century, Europe's historical accounts were made up of only a sparse collection of epics and folktales. The search began for the origins of what they considered the vigorous European genius. What they needed was a sufficiently heroic account of events that would demonstrate Caucasian superiority.

Europeans began to scour the Greek Classics in search of Europe's childhood. The Greek classical period was as far as Europeans could go in tracing any semblance of a glorious, heroic history. They discovered what they needed in the writings of Homer and other Greeks of the Classical period. It was the *ancient* Greeks they wanted as ancestors, not the Greeks of their time who were looked down upon as degenerates (Kaiwar 1989:33-35).

The Aryan Model presents Africa and people of African descent as being culturally and historically non-existent, when the evidence clearly shows that the world should be grateful to Africans for the gifts of life, civilization, culture, and science. The Western world apparently cannot tolerate the thought of being beholden to Black folks, so they made sure that the *Ancient Model* was overturned. The end result was a form of history that no longer chronicled ancient wars and the achievements of monarchs, dynasties, and heroes. History became the biography of a people.

Bernal (1989) provides the motivations behind the re-fabricated design of the *Aryan Model*:

> For the past 200 years, ancient Greece has been viewed as setting artistic and intellectual standards for later Europeans to follow. At the same time, it is implied that as no other continent possessed a Greece, its existence places European culture on a higher plane than those of

other continents. This theory was used to justify European and North American supremacy over the non-white peoples of other continents.

Vasant Kaiwar's (1989:32) heavily documented essay "Racism and the Writing of History, Part I" explores the construction of the *Aryan Model* of history and the manner in which historical achievements of African and Near Eastern civilizations were suppressed by racist, anti-Semitic Europeans and Americans.

> The elimination of these two from the ranks of great civilizations, and from having made any contribution to Greek language and religion, coincided temporally with Black slavery, imperialism, and subsequently with anti-Semitism in Europe. It also represented a momentous shift in historical interpretation in that the Ancient Greeks themselves and Europeans through the Enlightenment had believed that, to one degree or another, Egyptians and Phoenicians had played a formative role in the development of Greek civilization....[It] shows how the enslavement of Blacks deeply affected European perceptions of Africans and their subsequent efforts to downgrade them. Mendacious arguments were used to suggest that Egyptian civilization could not have been African, and that it was necessary for Asians to bring civilization and high culture to Egypt.

Diop (1974:100) also sets the historical record straight regarding the Asian or the Semitic world being the first cradle of civilization.

> To assign Egyptian civilization an Asiatic or any foreign origin whatsoever, we must be able to

demonstrate the prior existence of a cradle of civilization outside of Egypt. However, we cannot overemphasize the fact that this basic, indispensable condition has never been met.

Diop (1974:xv) takes this argument further by asserting that:

> Anthropologically and culturally speaking, the Semitic world was born during protohistoric times from the mixture of white-skinned and black-skinned people in western Asia. This is why an understanding of the Mesopotamian Semitic world, Judaic or Arabic, requires constant reference to the underlying Black reality. If certain Biblical passages, especially in the Old Testament, seem absurd, this is because specialists, puffed up with prejudices, are unable to accept documentary evidence.

Dr. John Henrik Clarke (1995) adds to this discussion by providing some historical facts about Hebrew culture in particular:

> When I use the word "Hebrew" I might be confusing you and myself because I know better. I know that when these Western Asians entered they were not Hebrew, but they were Hebrew when they left. When they entered Africa they had no clear religion, no clear language, and no clear culture; they had all three when they left. So who are we talking about? We are talking about a people who effected a wedding between their culture in Western Asia and the culture they encountered in Africa, and who belonged to the Hebrew faith.

As 19th century Europeans and Americans took it upon themselves to become the arbiters of the world's destiny, the result of their racism and imperialism is a historiography that presents the categorical inferiority of non-Caucasian nations. The Eurocentric "scholarship" has produced nothing more than a specious historiography and a set of pseudo-sciences upon which it relies. One example of this is found in the words of J.F. Lauer in the 18th century. He claimed that Egyptian priests had built up a store of practical and technical knowledge, but they were completely ignorant of the real value and applicability of their knowledge. To Lauer, the only historic role of the Egyptians was to pave the way for the energetic, innovative Greeks. In other words, 3,000 years of Egyptian history, advancements, and splendid achievements were reduced to a mere backdrop for the arrival of the Greek genius (Kaiwar (1989:38).

In like manner, Egyptologists like Maspero and Wallis Budge (1904) wrote disparaging remarks about Egyptian religion. Egyptians developed an entire complex religious system and symbolic mythology based upon the notion of the One God who created "divine unity" throughout the universe. Maspero and Budge were committed to the notion that the Aryo-Semitic monopoly of civilization rested on the "invention" of the great principle of monotheism. They were committed to defending monotheism against so-called barbarian races whose religious traditions was seen as nothing more than pantheism. According to Maspero, "the Egyptian possessed the spirit of a subtle metaphysician, a talent liberated when Christianity provided a suitable subject." Budge argued from a standpoint of linguistics, stating that no African language, including Egyptian, had the vocabulary to express metaphysical and philosophical discourse:

> . . . [Even] an Egyptian priest of the highest intellectual attainments would have been unable to render a treatise of Aristotle into language which his brother priests, without teaching, could understand. The mere construction of the language would make such a thing impossible, to say nothing of the ideas of the great Greek philosopher, which belong to a domain of thought and culture wholly foreign to the Egyptian.

Since the *Aryan Model* is constructed from falsehoods, it has always presented problems for the designers, even from the outset. Kaiwar (1989) explains that on one hand German romantics who pioneered this false historiography were ecstatic about discovering that the Indian Sanskrit language was ancestor to all Indo-European languages. On the other hand, the news was upsetting because the dark-skinned inhabitants of the Indian subcontinent were considered degenerate. The Germans were forced to turn history on its head by claiming that a "racially pure" Nordic-like race of pioneers left their ancestral home in the Caucasus Mountains and migrated south to the Indian subcontinent where the land was occupied by inferior dark-skinned natives. The so-called Aryans were given credit for planting the seeds of its civilization among dark-skinned peoples living in southern climates whom Caucasians considered as being barbarians. An attending notion attached to this historical interpretation was a warning against racial mixing with dark-skinned people. This notion quickly became the orthodox colonial historiography of India, and "high-caste Hindu Nationalists made it part of their project for a "revival" of a Hindu-Sanskritic India.

Kaiwar (1989:35) further notes that this specious historiography contained the romantic-racialist notion of a German nation that held only pure racial types: blonde hair, light colored eyes, and severely exclusive to all other racial types. German National Socialism became directly associated with this notion. Therefore, Greeks had to be fabricated into a Nordic people who had no semblance of African or Semitic blood. Ancient Greeks were given godlike status so that modern Europeans could share the godlike mantle as natural rulers of the world.

> ... [In] the Greeks *alone* we find the ideal of that which we would like to be and produce... from the Greeks we take something more than earthly – almost Godlike.

Despite all the false claims, the Aryan Model can only be characterized as an ideological argument. Since there is no compelling evidence to support the model, it should not be considered as a *bona fide* academic claim. It must be admitted, nonetheless, that the European and American exercise in creating a false history of themselves has been planned and executed very successfully up until now. However, people of color all over the world are breaking the bonds of mental enslavement and psychological illness by researching and documenting their own histories from their own cultural perspectives. It is time for Africans worldwide to follow suit.

African Delusions from Anglo Illusions

The concept of White supremacy claims that the "races" with the lightest skin tones are superior to those with darker skin coloring, which allowed them to place themselves at the very top rung of all expressions of humanity worldwide. Of course, common sense informs that if this were factual, then Caucasian genetic features would be scientifically labeled as "dominant" rather than "recessive." As a result of the constant and brutal bombardment of White supremacy messages and oppression, we *have* come a long way – *backwards* -- Baby! For hundreds of years we have fought for civil rights and human rights. We lost both battles when we bought into the politicians' insistence that assimilation is a necessary component of integration. Assimilation is an anthropology term that describes the rejection or abandonment of beliefs and values in one's mother culture in favor of the beliefs and values in a completely different culture. This is the very core of the tragedy, suffering, and social decline that African Americans are experiencing today.

Many African Americans suffer from self-hatred, identity crisis, self-alienation, lack of discipline, and uncontrolled rage. It does not require a psychologist or psychiatrist to recognize that these are mental health problems. Likewise, a criminologist is not needed to understand that the antisocial behavior, lack of discipline, violence, and rebellion acted out by our children is indicative of some serious moral and spiritual states. Nor is it necessary to be a sociologist to understand that these emotional and spiritual states are directly due to race-related, White supremacy strategies on individual and institutional levels that are designed to produce these self-destructive results.

The assimilation strategy has transformed a nation of strong, achieving Black people who were proud of their African heritage into self-hating, self-enslaving Black *Afro-Saxons*. The spiritual and psychological illnesses as well as the alarming rate of social decline experienced by African Americans today can be understood by an explanation of what assimilation into the values of Caucasian culture means. Simply put, we are dealing with the rejection of our own healthy *African Model* of cultural beliefs, knowledge, and values that have supported more than 40,000 years of survival, high civilization, and achievement. In its place we adopted the enslaving beliefs of the *Anglo-Saxons' Aryan Model*.

Earlier, I outlined the four features of the *Aryan Model of History and Culture*: racism, sexism, imperialism, and hegemony (RSIH). *Racism* is a belief in white supremacy. Many Africans are black-faced White supremacists because in their hearts they truly believe that Caucasians are superior to them and other non-Caucasians.

Sexism is a belief that males are superior to females. An enormous number of African American women have accepted the imposition of this inferior status. A large number of Black men also have bought into Caucasian sexism. Some can be recognized by a motivation to gain status, recognition, and liberation from oppression for themselves, but they want it to be withheld from Black women.

Imperialism is the belief that Caucasians have the right to control and rule non-Caucasians politically and economically. Most of us know at least one individual who states a preference for Caucasian supervisors and politicians, even when they know the White person is disrespectful toward them.

Hegemony is a belief that Caucasians have the God-given right to impose their religion, culture, values, and standards of beauty upon non-Caucasians and non-Christians. Numbers of Black pastors in Black churches preach to their congregations that the enslavement of Africans was a blessing because it introduced Christianity to us.

Michael Jackson's suffering is a painful example of what can result from the silly notion that Caucasian racial characteristics are the standard of human beauty for the rest of the world. It is a sign of confusion and self-hatred when Black folks refer to "good hair" and prefer characteristics that are farthest away from the African ideal. What is *in* the head is more important than what is *on* the head, so straightened hair does not disturb me. Straightening combs were found in the tombs of African queens in Egypt. Caucasians themselves do not believe they are the worldwide standard of beauty, evidenced by their preoccupation with tanning their bodies at the risk of contracting skin cancer, injecting collagen into their lips, and increasing the size of their buttocks with either foam rubber or surgically implanted body fat.

Some people who call themselves African American are still uncomfortable with their Africanity. Others reject the term African completely and ask to be identified only by their place of birth because they are apparently unable to distinguish between their race, the land mass of their ancestors, and their present nationality. Many prefer to be called "Black," which tells us nothing because people with dark skin tones are found all over Asia and Australia. Then, there are folks who claim to know something about African American culture *(the branch and leaves)* but know nothing and prefer not to know anything of depth and substance about original African culture *(the tree)*.

The really sad cases are people who are obviously an African phenotype, yet are so self-alienated that they sojourn into a fantasy world to trace their lineage among people who are racially and culturally alien to them, and who are socially hostile toward them, to boot. I have known several such persons whom even Stevie Wonder would recognize as being Africoid in appearance, but who reject having any semblance of African blood. The most pitiful case in my experience was a brother who resembled Marcus Garvey but identified himself as an Irishman.

Not enough Black scholars bother to research the contributions African people have made to worldwide civilization. I have yet to hear an educated African colleague object to the exclusion of African religion in the textbooks on world religions. Ignorance of African history and civilization is especially alarming among theologians in African

American seminaries and pastors of Black churches. It takes very little research to discover that African religion is the basis and origin of Christianity and that the Christian holidays and "holy days" have an African origin. There have been a number of gifted and well-known African prophets, going back 6,000 or more years. Yet, most Black preachers and theological scholars do not know about them, and those who know maintain silence on the subject. Belief in White supremacy produces an enslaved African mind that is incapable of believing that African people have done anything significant since the beginning of time. Slavery has become their comfort zone.

We are not surviving as a people because we continue to participate in anti-African beliefs and destructive behaviors set forth in the European *Aryan Model.* Survival is impossible because we cannot be against ourselves and sustain our lives at the same time. Nor can we survive if we are against our own people and for our enemies. During slavery it was the house slaves that fit Hare's (1991) description of Black Anglo-Saxons who always helped the White slave owner to keep the other slaves in line. Their betrayals and willingness to identify with their White slave-masters helped to secure their own enslavement along with the others, which clearly seems insane. Little has changed today on the various plantations where African Americans are employed.

A Case in Point
Justice Clarence Thomas is a man with power, but is despised among African Americans.

He is among the sad group of self-loathers who only presented the picture of his White wife's niece during his nomination period as justice of the Supreme Court when asked by the press to submit a family photograph. Since his appointment to the Supreme Court he has joyfully and gratefully held his White masters' hands to lead the way in rolling back much of the progressive civil rights and affirmative action legislation that allowed *him* to acquire higher education, by the way. Once he had his education through affirmative action programs, it was no longer good for the country. The National Bar Association, with the nation's largest organization of African American attorneys and judges, did not endorse Thomas's 1991 appointment to the Supreme Court. Thomas' eventual Supreme Court victory holds a bitter aftertaste, when we consider that the Maryland School System disinvited Thomas to speak at one of the schools, and The Rev. Al Sharpton has held at least one protest demonstration on the front lawn of Thomas's house. Thomas learned too late that the money earned from his betrayal will not buy respect.

If Black folks are to be saved, it will happen by unshackling our own hearts, minds, hands, and feet. Prayer will not save us because God will not do for us what we refuse to do for ourselves. Attempts to identify and unite with non-African groups when we are incapable of uniting with each other along cultural lines will render nothing to us but the same shame and scorn that we are experiencing today. Black folks seem to be the only ones on the planet who cannot seem to understand the principle of *group unity* and *community responsibility* for survival, which is the very reason why we are dying in record numbers. The young are dying faster than the old because we are killing each other. This is a certain road to extinction, since there will be no one to replace the dying elderly.

Scientific information on the development of various so-called races and cultures is provided in the next chapter. It explores the processes of human adaptation to environmental stresses which allowed *Homo sapiens* to develop different physical characteristics and cultures.

6. ENVIRONMENT, BIOLOGY, RACE AND CULTURE

> *The civilization of the twentieth century cannot be universal except by being a dynamic synthesis of all the cultural values of all civilizations. It will be monstrous unless it is seasoned with the salt of negritude. For it will be the savior of humanity.*
> --Leopold Sedar Senghor

Racial Variation

The prevailing theories of human biological variability is based on the view that distinctively different human groups developed as a result of (a) geographic separation; (b) environmental factors; and (c) successive admixtures or "blendings" of types through time (Joseph B. Birdsell (1981). There is *between-group variability* that deals with differences from one group to the next, as well as *between-individuals variability* that involves the extent to which individuals differ from each other.

The concept of race as a physical manifestation is first and foremost viewed by anthropologists as an adaptation to particular environmental and geographical elements. The concept of **geographical race** is accepted by most anthropologists today as a principle for viewing racial classification. It includes related concepts of **integrated race** as population history, and **race as adaptive group**. The concept of *integrated race* closes the gap between history and adaptation because it defines race as a collection of populations inhabiting some definable geographical area over tremendously long periods of time. As a result, populations would tend to resemble each other due to the exchange of genes among themselves more than with groups in other areas. Race as *adaptive group* is a concept which recognizes that defining characteristics (phenotypes) of a particular race developed by natural selection and spread to the limit of the group's range of physical and genetic possibilities.

The concept of *race as adaptive group* also acknowledges that racial groups were not isolated from each other, and that gene flow between them was determined by geography. The closer one group lived to another group, the more they came into contact with each other, and the higher the likelihood that genes would be exchanged as they interbred with each other. In other words, physical environments, geographical locations, and proximity of groups to each other have a direct impact on the physical appearance of human beings throughout the world. Julian Huxley introduced ideas about *gradual clinal variation* among human beings. Modern anthropologists came to recognize that Huxley was right; that practically all variation in the human species is clinal. It is continuous and gradual across geographic lines, and is neither discrete nor racial. The way we thought about "clustered traits" or **concordance of traits** when discussing human variation in the past was really wrong-headed (Johnston and Selby, 1978:274-5).

Figure-6 below shows that there are little or no effects of trait concordance within any single race (J. Hiernaux, 1964). In viewing physical traits, individuals at (1) would be very short and light-skinned, with very curly hair. Those at (2) would be short and dark with straight hair. Persons at (3) would be tall, dark with straight hair. **Skin color** within a group is viewed as distributed in a west (dark) to east (light). Stature is from tall (north) to short (south). **Hair Form** is distributed from straight (southwest) to curly (northeast) (Johnston and Selby, 1978:274-5).

Figure-6

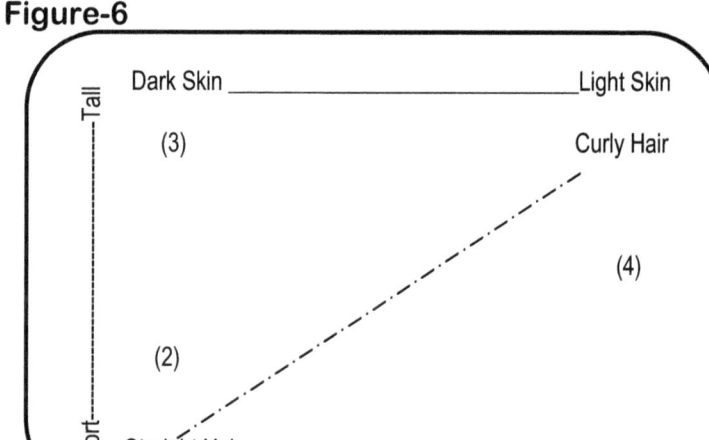

Modified *From Johnston and Selby, 1978:274-5*

Most anthropologists consider **Africoid, Mongoloid** and **Caucasoid** peoples as the three most distinctly different races that developed during the very earliest period of human evolutionary adaptations to the earth's different geographical environments. All of the other groups appear to be genetic admixtures or blendings of these three.

Birdsell (1981) travels backward in time as he discusses regional variations among living peoples that fall within a variety of natural patterns. He begins with North and South America's native inhabitants who crossed the Bering Strait from Asia to populate the Western hemisphere. They have the same physical characteristics, but through time developed less extreme forms than the Asians. For example, the fold of eyelid skin over the eyes is more extreme in Asians than in the New World natives. However, the yellowish skin tone and other physical characteristics of Native Americans and Asians are clearly grouped together, so anthropologists call all of them **Mongoloids.**

Another kind of population occurs as one continues across Eurasia to reach the European peninsula. The people called **Caucasoids** are characterized by highly de-melanated skin and many have light colored eyes. In passing from Eastern Asia to Europe there are no abrupt changes in physical characteristics. Rather, there are thousands of miles of gently graded characteristics where Asian and European groups lived close together and exchanged genes with each other.

At least three groups seem to be distinct admixtures, peoples who lived in close proximity to each other for very long periods of time and developed distinctive physical characteristics through genetic mixing. Continuing across Asia, the subcontinent of India is peopled by individuals called **Veddoids** whose hair and skin tones set them off from the other peoples of Eurasia. The Veddoids are clearly part Mongoloid, Caucasoid, and Africoid. The

Veddoids of India in turn made some genetic contributions to the **Aborigines** of northern Australia. The region that is now called the Middle East developed two groups called **Semites** who share genetic characteristics of Africans and Eurasians. "Semi-" means "half" and the word Semite refers to the people who lived close to each other at the intersection of Eurasia and Africa. Thus, the Hebrew and Arabic peoples comprise the two Semitic groups that developed and came to occupy the geographic region between Eurasia and Africa thousands of years before desertification caused the Sahara Desert to divide the northernmost part of the African continent (Birdsell, 1981).

Traveling south, a series of populations called **Africoid** with dark skin and various types of curled hair extended throughout the entire continent of Africa Birdsell (1981). They vary considerably, showing the world's greatest differences among themselves. In stature they range from the tallest humans in the world found in the open grassland country to the smallest ones of the Congo forest. Africoids also show the greatest variation in skin tone, ranging from the darkest in the world to a light, yellowish brown skin. Albinos are at the extreme end of Africoid skin tone possibilities. Theorists point to Africans' ability to produce albino offspring to further support the claim that African females carry the MtDNA of all humanity, from the darkest skin pigmentation to the lightest. Africoid people recognizably comprise many phenotypical variants of a single major human group.

"Out-of-Africa" theorists point to genetic scientists' discovery about the great variation in the MtDNA found in African women to further support the theory that humanity began in Africa. Africoid women are the only ones to carry the genetic makeup of every human being on earth. The less mixed they are with non-Africoids, the more likely they are to have the entire genetic "package" inherited from their prehistoric mothers from some three million years ago. Christopher Stringer and Robin McKie (1997) are two of the many prominent anthropologists who have added to the preponderance of archeological and DNA evidence supporting the "**Out-of-Africa**" theory and the "**African Eve**" hypothesis that modern humans arose from a single "**cradle of civilization**" in Africa, and that African women are the "**mothers of all humans.**" They provide a wealth of supporting scientific evidence that human precursors remaining in Africa after the first large group migrated out evolved into a second "Out of Africa" group. The second group became physically and intellectually modern humans—*Homo sapiens*—who then went on to re-colonize Eurasia. This group is viewed as the one that replaced so-called archaic humans 100,000 years ago. Stringer and McKie (1997) are joined by other theorists who trace all human ancestry back to a single African female ancestor, who is dubbed "Eve."

The use of race as a determining factor in judging the qualities of intellect, beauty, fitness, and capability of an entire group of people on the face of this planet is a relatively new development. It was only about 400 years ago that Eastern Europeans devised this scheme in order to conquer, occupy, and completely dominate the majority populations in the world. Once people were conquered militarily, Christian missionaries were given the job of alienating future generations of the children from their parents by totally denying them participation in their own language, religion, culture and traditions. The core of their re-education and mis-education schemes centered upon convincing these children that they were inferior to Whites. It is necessary to study the environmental and biological processes that created the so-called "races" to understand how superficial it is as a concept that attempts to predetermine the worth of human beings (Kaiwar (1989).

On one level, you might say that citizenship or nationality deals with such issues as voting rights and passports. Race, on the other hand, involves discussions of DNA, genetics, human adaptation, biology, and environment. It considers the *ecological niche* or *habitat* of particular *prehistoric* populations and leads to the question as to whether one's prehistoric ancestors evolved in a tropical or an arctic environment tens of thousands of years ago. Anthropologist Diop (1990:9) again adds clarity on the subject matter.

> There existed in the beginning, before the successive contacts of peoples and of nations, before the age of reciprocal influences, certain non-essential relative differences among peoples. These differences had to do with the climate and the specific conditions of life. The peoples who

lived for a lengthy period of time in their place of origin were moulded by their surroundings in a durable fashion. It is possible to go back to this original mould by identifying the outside influences which have been superimposed on it.

With African people we are literally dealing with millions of years of evolution and environmental adaptation, since Africans are by far the oldest human beings on earth and the parents of all humanity. Caucasians are the last group to develop and are the farthest distance away from the original model of humanity, civilization and culture that developed in Africa.

Science has proven that only African women carry the most highly complex MtDNA of every human being on earth. Caucasian women, on the other hand, have the most depleted form of MtDNA with the most recessive genetic traits of all human groups. Physical, cultural, and social differentiation developed within specific environments as a means of adapting to particular natural settings in ways that permit or even maximize survival. Without the ability to physically and culturally adapt to their immediate natural settings, the human species would have perished. Human genetic and phenotypic *adaptability* and *plasticity* on both group and individual levels, respectively, allowed changes in size, shape and even physiology.

Johnson and Selby (1978:249) discuss the three levels of adaptation. **Genetic adaptation** is a response to a specific environmental stress, and will be present in the group as a whole. For example, peoples in Ethiopia and the Andes live in altitudes above 10,000 feet. Large lung capacities and deep "barrel chests" are their genetic adaptation to the stress of reduced oxygen concentrations. **Physiological adaptations** are adjustments made by individuals in response to short-term stress. The stresses involved may be connected to nutritional intake, climate, altitude, and similar causes. **Developmental adaptation** refers to stresses that occur over very long periods in an individual's lifetime. Lactase tolerance, for example, is the result of populations that have been able to digest large amounts of dairy products for thousands of years. **Plasticity** is referred to as a response to some form of chronic stress. The ability to increase levels of pigment-darkening melanin within the melanocytes of the basal layers of the skin, as a response to high levels of the sun's rays, is exemplary of plasticity.

The phenomena of biology and culture are interactive as well as interdependent concepts that operate simultaneously with living organisms. Environmental conditions and stresses experienced by populations 40,000 or more years ago created the cultural traits that are manifest in contemporary populations. An examination of prehistoric environmental factors demonstrates the powerful influence they imposed upon human existence.

Anthropology has established a subdivision called **human ecology** to study the relationship between environment, human biology, and culture. *Figure-7* illustrates the three important areas of human adaptation. **Culture** represents all the learned patterned behaviors that are characteristic of human groups throughout the world. **Environment** refers to the physical habitat of all human groups and their relations with all other organisms in earth's environment. **Biology** refers to population biology, which includes rates of birth and death, matters of group health, and biological adaptation.

The above information demonstrates that what is referred to as race is merely a regional variation in *Homo sapiens* that is primarily adaptive in origin. It is the inherited observable **phenotype** (physical appearance) of a human being that developed during prehistoric periods in response to environmental and genetic factors. Thus, "races" are actually no more than physical differences that developed over a period of tens of thousands of years for the purpose of

Figure-7: Culture-Biology-Environment Interaction

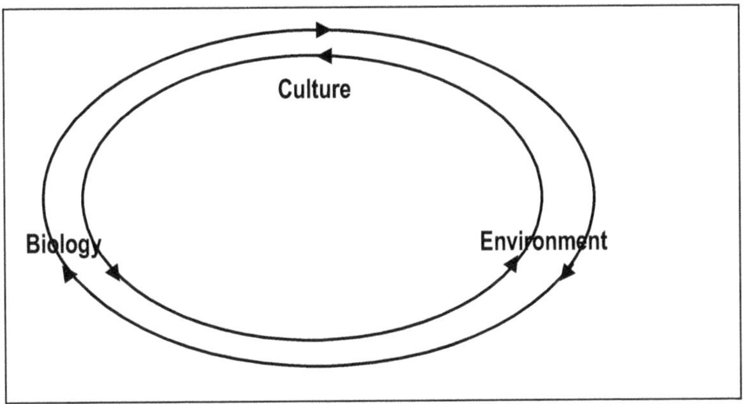

[Diagram showing Culture, Biology, and Environment connected in an elliptical cycle]

Modified From J.B. Birdsell's Human Ecology-Culture diagram, p. 5.

maximizing fitness to survive in local and regional habitats. The process of adaptation for the maximization of fitness occurred within the stresses and limitations of each environment.

As demonstrated above, human ecology is the study of the relationship between human beings and their environment. It also includes the study of how human beings affect and are affected by their environment. Human adaptation to environment increases the likelihood for survival and reproduction. When circumstances change individuals are likely to try ideas or behaviors that are different from those of their parents. There are two ways to discover the probability for successful behavioral change. One way is to experiment with various new behaviors. The other way is to evaluate the experiments of others.

Natural environments are not the only elements that present stresses to human beings. The next chapter deals with developmental adaptation to stresses caused by cultural and political oppression experienced over long periods of time.

7. CLASH OF VALUES, BELIEFS AND WORLDVIEWS

*You've been tricked! You've been had!
Lied to! Hoodwinked! Bamboozled!*
--El Hajj Malik El-Shabazz (Malcolm X)

*The first step. . . is to make the Black man
come to himself;
To pump life back into his empty shell;
To infuse him with pride and dignity;
To remind him of his complicity in the crime
of allowing himself to be misused and therefore
Letting evil reign supreme. . . .*
--Steven Biko of South Africa

Adaptation to Oppression

Human adaptation to various types of stress is a normal process that can maximize survival of the group or the individual. However, the adaptation can itself become a major stress, especially in regard to stress brought on by cultural, social, political, and psychological oppression. The longer the duration of an identified stress, the higher the probability that the adaptive response will become permanent. Institutional racism and discrimination are enduring problems in the United States, where institutionalized racist oppression presents an ever-present reality for African Americans and other people of color. Racist attitudes and practices, whether covert or overt, admitted or denied, are at the root of African Americans' identity crisis.

Clash of Cultures

The way in which tropical zones of Africa are directly related to the values, beliefs, world view and cultural modalities held by African people has been discussed earlier. Africans are heat-adapted people who developed and maintained the biogenetic features naturally selected to maximize survival in tropical environments. Thus, to understand African people it is necessary to examine their cultural modalities that developed within the tropical environments of Africa for more than 3.5 million years. Populations within Africa's richly vegetated tropical environments developed a *spiritual worldview*. That is, they believed in the reality of spirits and the spirit world. In accordance with this worldview, they also developed a *holistic belief system* that viewed everything in the universe as being interdependent and interrelated -- held together by a Divine Creator God who permeates and is the ultimate Force behind all creation.

Although Africans believe in a spiritual world view, their outlook on life is not one of supernaturalism. They balance their spiritual worldview with an intensely humanistic outlook, especially in the area of morality and ethics, according to Wiredu (1980:6), who argues: "I believe that this freedom from supernaturalism in our traditional ethic is an aspect of our culture which we ought to cherish and protect from countervailing influences from abroad."

Africans also have a *theist-communalist-harmonious value system.* This means that in addition to believing in the One God, they value group interests over individual interests, and they embrace the concept of universal harmony. These features are a part African culture and belief that are diametrically different from those of Western culture. Caucasian culture has a *compartmentally structured material belief system* that values individual interests more than group interests. Another huge difference between the two cultures is that Western culture holds to a material worldview that does not recognize Spirit as part of reality.

As I have pointed out for years in my workshops and seminars, modern Western cultures of Europe and America have developed a *material belief system and worldview* while every other culture in the world holds a *spiritual worldview*. These are two fundamentally irreconcilably different views of life and the universe that impact every phase and nuance of human existence. The fundamental differences between Western culture and the other world cultures lies in the acceptance or non-acceptance of a belief in the reality of Spirit. The spiritual worldview embraces the existence of realms of reality beyond the limited physical realms outlined by modern Western science. Some of the main differences are presented in **Figure-8** and **Figure-10**.

People who have cultures that are grounded in a spiritual worldview believe in the reality of a Divine Spirit or Divine Force that imparts its essence throughout the universe. For example, the African worldview holds that everything in the universe is comprised of spirit in either encapsulated or un-encapsulated form. This worldview continues to be held by Africans throughout the African Diaspora, including all the Americas plus the Caribbean. Marcus J. Borg (2004:63) discusses how the spiritual and material worldviews have been colliding in Western culture for the past 300 years. Berg adds another level of understanding on the subject by suggesting there is a "More" factor connected to the world of material and energy, "a nonmaterial layer or level of reality, an extra dimension of reality that is shared by all the religions of the world." . . . This conviction was until recently the "human unanimity."

As Borg suggests, world cultures unanimously hold this belief in the "More," the One Supreme Being, and call "It" by various names: God, Spirit, Olodumare, the sacred, the Force, Yaweh, Onyame, the Tao, Allah, Brama, Wakantanka, Atman, and so forth. Since God is almost unanimously conceptualized as pure spirit, it is not correct to impose a gender upon the Supreme Being. "It" is a more proper term of reference for Almighty God in discussions of God's attributes. Both feminine and masculine attributes of God are presented as a way of expressing the necessity for balance throughout the universe. These two *complimentary opposite energies* are viewed as forces of creativity that are fundamental to life itself throughout the universe.

Bernard Haisch (2006:40), in his book *The God Theory: Universes, Zero-Point Fields and What's Behind It,* describes the spiritual worldview as being shorthand for the supposition that reality includes both your own nature and your conscious being. As such, the spiritual worldview involves both tangible, physical matter and an immaterial "something." He believes that this immaterial "something" is "intimately and essentially involved in the existence of consciousness and life, and is ultimately traceable to a divine origin and purpose."

Haisch points out that the feud between modern Western science and spirituality is perpetuated by the Christian Church, with its history of intellectual repression, wars, deaths, and destruction. He also suggests that any scientific investigation of "Spirit" should be conducted in the same manner that other topics are researched. Practically speaking, ancient world cultures must have constructed their ideas about Spirit upon some truths that came to be known through experience. I agree with Haisch's argument that the truths must contain laws that are as fundamental as gravity or electromagnetism, but of a different order. It is up to us to find those laws, possibly by investigating amid the culturally-fertilized religious concepts that are still alive and active today.

As the oldest people on earth and most likely the first to conceptualize religious beliefs, Africans described the human soul as an immortal, undying, eternal entity that experiences multiple rebirth manifestations on earth. From that idea was drawn the mathematical concept and symbol of *Infinity* illustrated in ***Figure-9***. Africans believe that the human soul carries a portion of Almighty God's divine essence that occasionally leaves its heavenly abode in a series of earthly rebirths, and repeatedly returns to Heaven again in its spiritual state each time the human physical body dies. This belief links

Figure-8

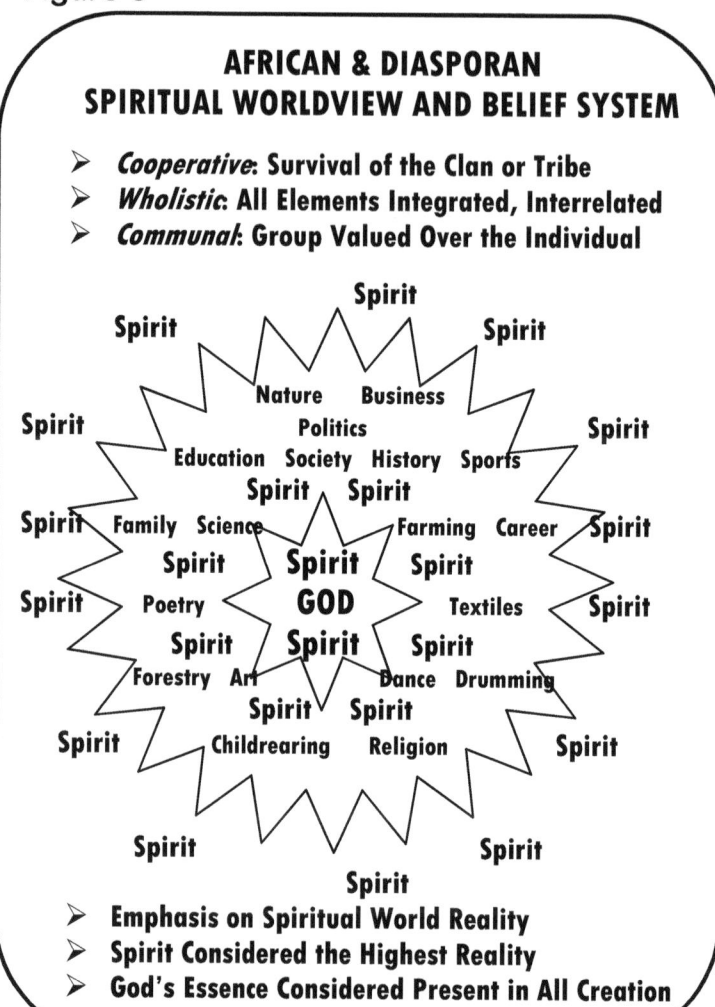

together three concepts: infinity, immortality, and eternity. All three concepts express never-ending existence.

The psycho-behavioral aspects of the European and the non-European worldviews are presented side-by-side in *Figure 11*. The European aspects are the same as the American ones, and the non-European aspects represent Africa, Asia, and the rest of the world cultures. Psycho-behavioral aspects of European and non-European cultures are presented in *Figure-12*.

Figure-9

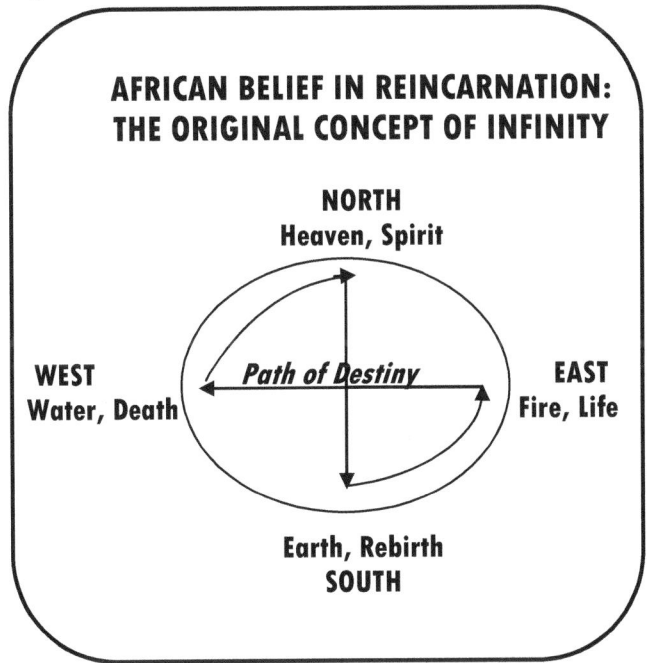

Southern and Northern Cradles of Civilization

Cheikh Anta Diop (1990:111), in his book entitled *The African Origin of Civilization,* set forth his "Two-Cradle" theory of civilization. He argues that two separate early "cradles" of civilization developed – the southern cradle and the northern cradle -- that were environmentally determined during the Ice Age. Stark cultural differences developed with features that still exist today. A sedentary lifestyle with farming became typical for the southern cradle, while the Eurasian plains, which were absolutely unfavorable to farming, were always the cradle of nomadism. Molded by their geographical differences, cultures that developed in each cradle were diametrically opposed to each other.

This information allows us to understand the difficulties non-Caucasians experience in trying to maintain survival or even a meaningful sense of wellbeing in Caucasian societies. Diop explains that the southern cradle was "embedded in the heart of Africa," while the northern cradle had deep roots in the Eurasian plains.

> The history of humanity will remain confused as long as we fail to distinguish between the two early cradles in which Nature fashioned the instincts, temperament, habits, and ethical concepts of the two subdivisions before they met each other after a long separation dating back to prehistoric times. The first of those cradles. . . is the valley of the Nile, from the Great Lakes to the Delta, across the so-called "Anglo-Egyptian" Sudan. The abundance of vital resources, its sedentary, agricultural character, the specific conditions of the valley, will engender in man, that is, in the Negro, a gentle, idealistic, peaceful nature, endowed with a spirit of justice and gaiety. All these virtues were more or less indispensible for daily coexistence.

Figure-10

EUROPEAN & AMERICAN MATERIAL WORLDVIEW AND BELIEF SYSTEM

- *Competitive:* Survival of the Fittest
- *Compartmental:* Separate Unrelated Elements
- *Individuality:* Individual Valued over the Group

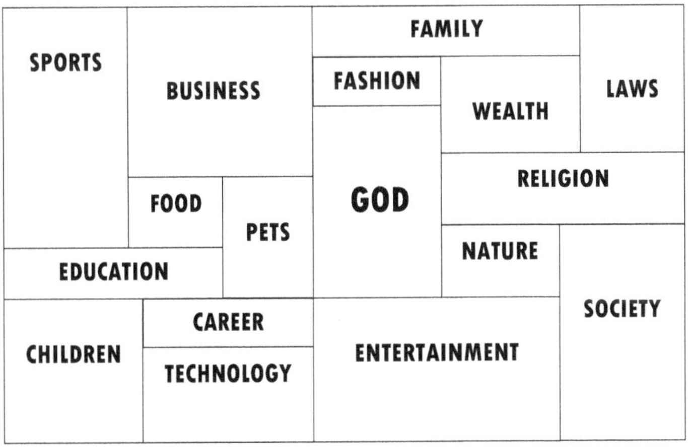

SPORTS	BUSINESS	FAMILY		LAWS
		FASHION	WEALTH	
	FOOD	GOD	RELIGION	
EDUCATION	PETS		NATURE	
CHILDREN	CAREER	ENTERTAINMENT		SOCIETY
	TECHNOLOGY			

- Exclusive Emphasis on Material World Reality
- Spirit Not Considered a Part of Reality
- God's Essence Considered Not Present in All Creation
- Thought, feeling, mind, and will can be explained in terms of physical laws

Figure-11

CULTURAL FEATURES

EUROPEAN
- Compartmental
- Competitive
- Individualistic
- Future time oriented
- Non-spiritual reality

NON-EUROPEAN
- Wholistic
- Cooperative
- Communalistic
- Past-present-future oriented
- Spiritual reality

Figure-12

PSYCHO-BEHAVIORAL ASPECTS

EUROPEAN
- Doing
- Xenophobia
- Differences-focus
- Linear, direct logic & thinking
- Conflict approach to change

NON-EUROPEAN
- Being
- Xenophilia
- Similarities-focus
- Circular, indirect logic & thinking
- Consensus approach to change

Just as the material conditions of the Nile River Valley were the point of departure for early African culture in the southern cradle, Diop explains that the same principle applies to early Eurasian culture in the northern cradle.

> By contrast, the ferocity of nature in the Eurasian steppes, the barrenness of those regions, the overall circumstances of material conditions, were to create instincts necessary for survival in such an environment. Here, Nature left no illusion of kindliness: it was implacable and permitted no negligence; man must obtain his bread by the sweat of his brow. Above all, in the course of a long, painful existence, he must learn to rely on himself alone, on his own possibilities. He could not indulge in the luxury of believing in a beneficent God who would shower down abundant means of gaining a livelihood; instead, he would conjure up deities maleficent and cruel, jealous and spiteful: Zeus, Yahweh, among others.
>
> In the unrewarding activity that the physical environment imposed on man, there was already implied materialism, anthropomorphism (which is but one of its aspects), and the secular spirit....All the peoples of the area, whether white or yellow, were instinctively to love conquest, because of a desire to escape from the hostile surroundings.

According to Diop (1990:112-113), once Eurasians made an initial contact with the African world to the south "where the living was easy, riches abundant, technique flourishing," invasions would not cease as they attempted by all means to escape from the harsh, hostile surroundings of their cold, unforgiving environment. Those who developed in the cold regions of the northern cradle remained nomads for a very long time. The practice of cremation grew out of nomadism, with the necessity of transporting the ashes of ancestors in small urns.

The matriarchal system developed as the base of social organization in Egypt and throughout Black Africa. Matriarchy is a basic trait of African agricultural civilization. The practice is a harmonious dualism, an association accepted by both sexes and even defended by men. Matriarchy is not a cynical triumph of women over men. It is characterized by the collaboration and harmonious flowering of both sexes, and by a respect for women in society. African women gained a kind of economic ascendancy in society that may be based on their discovery of agriculture. African matriarchy is still an active practice today as it was during antiquity Diop (1974:145).

Another indication of the honored place of women in African societies is that succession to the throne, traditionally, is often regulated by royal women. Also, female rulership is not considered unusual in Africa, evidenced by the large number of chiefs across the Continent, and the warrior queens who have mounted thrones. There was Hatshepsut of Egypt, Sheba of Ethiopia, a long line of Candaces in Meroitic Sudan, and Nzinga of Angola to name a few. These were fierce, unyielding warrior queens who led their armies on horseback and symbolized the national pride of the warriors they commanded and the people they ruled. Female chieftainship is still commonly practiced in traditional Africa today.

Since women can reproduce life and men cannot, African women are valued over men. Therefore, in Africa a man's family must pay a dowry or bridewealth to the woman's family upon their getting engaged. The size of the dowry depends upon the status of the young woman's family, as well as the skills, education, and character of the young woman herself. The dowry is like an insurance policy paid to her family to ensure that the prospective husband will treat his wife properly and provide for her. If he fails to do so, he loses his dowry and his wife because her family will simply come and carry their daughter back home, then marry her to someone else. This is possible because a woman always belongs to her family, and never belongs to the man that she marries. Diop argues that if the opposite seems true today in some parts of Africa it can be attributed to Islamic influence, which emerged in accordance with northern cradle cultural traditions. Colonization is another influence, whereby female leadership was absolutely ignored and denied by White invaders. After independence, African men decided they liked the oppressive changes Caucasians had forced upon women, and attempted to keep it that way.

Patriarchy was the Eurasian system of social organization, where men were the pillar of that kind of harsh, unyielding nomadic life. Women's participation in society was limited, primarily relegated to having children, doing household chores, and cooking. Recent findings conclude that some Eurasian women and children conducted net or snare hunting in addition to food gathering activities. Men hunted large game to provide most of the nutritional needs for survival. According to Diop (1974:113), the nomadic patriarchal principle was typical throughout the entire life of the Indo-Europeans, from the Greeks and Romans to the Napoleonic Code, to our day. It is the reason why women's participation in public life developed much later in Europe than it did in Africa.

Institutional Racism

It was Stokely Carmichael (aka Kwame Toure) who coined the term "institutional racism" to refer to racist attitudes and policies that are embedded within institutions such as universities, corporations, and public programs. He defined it as "the collective failure of an organization to provide an appropriate and professional service to people because of their color, culture, or ethnic origin." Richard R. Race discusses how institutional racism is detected in the processes, attitudes and behaviors that amount to discriminatory practices. From a practical standpoint, it is irrelevant whether racist practices occur through unwitting prejudice, ignorance, thoughtlessness, or stereotyping because they are all oppressive measures that disadvantage non-Caucasians and privilege Caucasians. According to Dr. Frances Cress Welsing (1991), Whites' *deep-seated sense of inferiority* causes them to erect institutional barriers that prevent the progress of people of color, this being the only way in which they can present the *illusion of superiority*.

Amos N. Wilson(1990:89) quotes Joel Kovel (1984) to discuss the aims of America's institutions:

Throughout our history, whites have created the institutions by which black people are forced to live, and which force them to live in a certain way, almost invariably so as to foster just that constellation of unworthy traits. From slavery itself to modern welfare systems, this has been the enduring pattern, reinforced in popular culture and education by a panoply of stereotypes along the same lines.

The result of these cultural manipulations has been to ensure to the black person a preassigned degraded role, no matter where he turned.

An illustration of how institutional racism works is presented in *Figure-12*. Society's dominant interested groups are White and racist. At the founding/creation of this country, beliefs in White supremacy, individualism, and capitalism were embedded into the policies and practices of America's institutions. Politicians and administrators were appointed and charged with maintaining those beliefs, policies and practices. Thus, institutions of education, law, marriage, economy, religion, politics, media, the arts, etc. all reflect the notion of White Supremacy, individualism, and capitalism. Thus established, the heads of institutions enforced these policies and practices through regulations sent to the respective governing agencies: local school boards; courts; churches; legislative branches; and so forth. Governing agencies have the power to control, limit, punish, and reward the activities of individuals and groups in accordance with established policies.

The model represents a self-perpetuating system in which change occurs as a result of public protest and lobbying, such that institutions are forced to modify or change established policies and practices for at least a small period of time. The scope of institutional control includes populations, images, knowledge, symbols, language, perception of reality, knowledge, standards of beauty, visual arts, social mores, performing arts, mating/marriage, childrearing, associations, relationships, etc.

The various forms of institutional racism include certain housing contracts, "redlining" in bank lending policies, racial profiling by security and law enforcement workers; the use of stereotyped racial caricatures such as: "Sambo," "Steppin' Fetchit," "Aunt Jemima" in literature and art; the under- and mis-representation of certain racial groups in the media; and barriers to employment or professional advancement based on race. It occurs in general health care as well as in health intervention services in minority communities. The fact that minorities are overrepresented in various disease categories, especially HIV/AIDS, is in part related to racism. The national response to the AIDS pandemic in minority communities has been slow because of a lack of funding and insensitivity to ethnic diversity in prevention efforts.

Oppression and Mental Illness

Dr. Na'im Akbar (1974), in his commentary on mental disorder among African Americans, blames social and political oppression for the rise in Black mental illness.

> The Afrikan-American has been the victim of both physical and mental oppression. He has endured

the atrocities of physical abuse and his mental efforts to cope have been subjected to intellectual oppression. Intellectual oppression involves the abusive use of ideas, labels, and concepts geared toward the mental degradation of a people. There is no area in which mental or intellectual oppression is more clearly illustrated than in the area of mental health judgments.

Figure-13

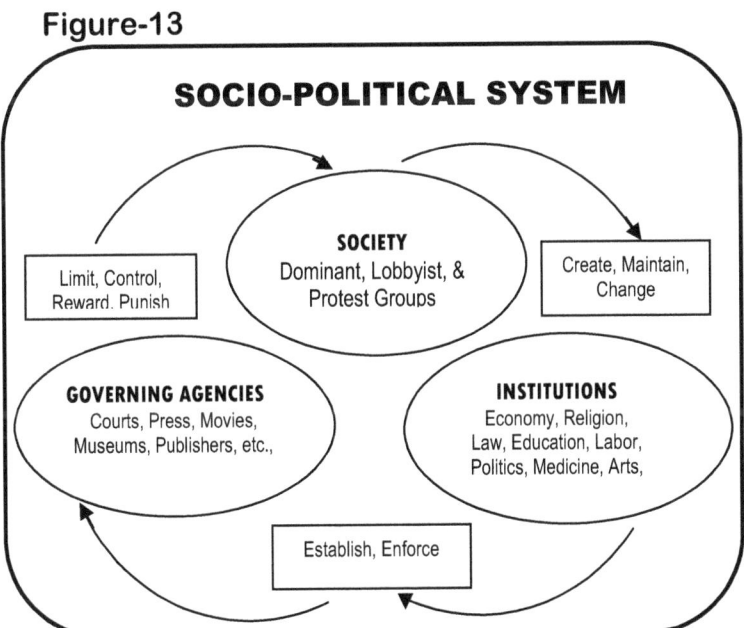

Olomenji (1996:71) uses Dr. Bobby Wright's term "mentacide" to describe African American mental disorders that manifest because of America's oppressive institutions and programs that aim to terminate Black people as a group. He defines mentacide as "the silent rape of a people's collective mind by penetration and perpetuation of alien culture, values, belief systems, or ideas." Thus, the term is viewed as the "deliberate and systematic destruction of an individual's or group's mind with the ultimate aim being the extirpation or elimination of that group. According to Olomenji, mentacide utilizes the institutions to universally project images, values, beliefs, and opinions that create illusions which Black people believe are real until it is too late. One example of these "illusions" that Olomenji speaks of is Black people's belief that they are citizens of the United States. He argues that the reality is that Black people are slaves in this country -- that they believe they are actually first-class citizens in America: Dr. Bobby Wright . . . defined enslavement as follows: "whenever the life-sustaining resources (food, shelter, water, etc.) of one group [the Blacks] are controlled by another group [the Whites, the Arabs]."

Some very troubling questions are asked by Olomenji (1996) about the future of Africans in America in the twentieth century: "Will Black people survive genocide by White America in the 1990s and beyond the year 2000? Who will win the battle for the collective Black mind? Are we Black people capable and willing to change our slave mentality? Do we as Black people have the collective will to fight the enemies of our National interest?" More than ten years after posing these questions African Americans are in an even worse position, and the same questions are being asked without any assurance that we will win this battle.

Black psychiatrists and psychologists are very concerned about the alarming escalation of African

American mental health issues. They commonly refer to the psychological warfare being waged against African minds and the strategies used to gain control over them. A part of this planned control over African minds is the recruitment and training of African American scholars, according to Akbar (1974). In his critique of the book *Black Rage,* written by Black psychiatrists Grier and Cobbs (1968), Akbar makes no attempt to disguise his disgust and dismay. The two authors had an opportunity to present an alternative perspective by Afrikan-American mental health scientists about Afrikan-American mental health conditions. Instead, these "accomplished psychiatrists presented a Caucasian social worker's handbook and guide to the neurotic Negro." The book focused on "how to understand the justifiable hatred of the Blacks."

Akbar points out their failure to address the importance of two essential variables in determining the adequacy of human behavior: "(1) the historical antecedents of determinants of that behavior; and (2) the effects of a functionally inhuman environment and conditions on the human being." He sharply notes the authors' failure to take into account Anglo American efforts to eradicate the very cultural features, beliefs, and behaviors that are critical to African American survival. Akbar further criticizes the book's failure "to address those issues on intellectual oppression which persist even when the more obvious conditions of physical oppression have been reduced.

Na'im Akbar (1996:31) further discusses how important it is for therapists to be knowledgeable of their patients' cultures and worldviews in order to bring critical insight and understanding to treatment and healing the person. He sets forth his theory of the "three components of being: physical, mental, and spiritual" that must be considered when treating Africans and Asians.

> The African views the person as spirit in his/her essence with the physical and mental components as tools of spiritual development. . . . Spiritual language and its intangible quality presents discomfort only for the heavily encumbered Western mind which is unable to comfortably conceptualize outside of the physical and observable. The very prominence of spiritual considerations in African American life should tell the observer that any science which precludes the spiritual is alien and irrelevant to understanding people of African descent and how they understand all forms of life.

African Americans are, indeed, suffering a real and tangible crisis because the values, beliefs, and worldview that support their survival, sense of wellbeing, and modes for advancement have been under attack for hundreds of years. They experience greater levels of stress and mental anguish as they increasingly take on Caucasian cultural norms. In other words, the more they adapt to racial oppression, the sicker they become.

Racial oppression is increasing everywhere, encouraged by people in the Bush administration. Fear among Black people abounds, as the nation witnesses the criminalization of ordinary citizens, especially those – Black or White – who dare dissent against government policies on any and every issue: the war in Iraq; the FCAT standardized test; the unregulated practice of placing steroids in foods; the privatization of water; law enforcement racial profiling; immigration; global warming; hurricane Katrina victims; gasoline prices; gay marriage; mortgage foreclosures; corporate abuses and scandals; war on terrorism; homeland security.

Ordinary, law-abiding citizens are targeted by the FBI, or some other branch of law enforcement if they speak out against abuses of civil and human rights of American citizens. These things are happening to Whites, so Blacks are understandably intimidated. African Americans were shaken to the core in the 1960s by all the public display of violence. We have always known about the brutality of Whites against Blacks. Thus, the assassination of Martin Luther King, Jr., Malcolm X, Medgar Evers and others were considered the norm. However, when John and Robert Kennedy were shot down like animals in the streets of America, events that were televised by CNN and presented to the entire world, it signaled just how far those in control of this government will go with their brutality to protect White privilege and maintain institutional racism.

Whether or not it is acknowledged, the American public in general and African Americans in particular have lived with the stressful reality of government-supported violence. In these days of Homeland Security, anyone's home can be victimized by warrantless searches; anyone innocent of any wrongdoing can be picked up as a suspected terrorist, sent to Guantanamo Bay, and held there indefinitely for no reason without an attorney or visitation.

The previous chapters establish a foundation of general information, historical record, and scientific data that directly relate to issues with which African Americans continue to struggle, and brutalities from which Black people continue to suffer. The information is presented to provide readers with a well-rounded depth of understanding as to how contemporary issues have developed over a long period of time. It presents a limited historical timeline, a cast of characters, and a record of events pertinent to African Americans' loss of cultural values, traditions, sense of identity, and ability to survive and advance in the face of overwhelming socio-political strategies aligned against us.

It would be a serious error at this point not to include documented historical data on the traditional role of women in African culture. Too many Black men have adopted a lot of alien cultural ideas about the place and role of Black women. Being the mother of all humanity and a key principal in the development of human civilization and religion, women of African heritage do not fit into the small boxes set forth by Hebrew and Arabic cultures. The following chapter focuses on the portion of African history that is replete with documented evidence of African women warriors.

8. AFRICAN WOMEN WARRIORS

*If you touch a woman
You have struck a rock.*
--South African proverb

*If you want to know who I am
I am daughter of Angola, of Keto and Nago.
I don't fear blows because I am a warrior.
Inside of samba I was born.
I raised myself, I transformed myself,
And no one will lower my banner, O, O, O.
I am a warrior woman daughter of Ogun and Yansa.*
--Song by Clara Nunes,
Brazilian singer

It has become commonplace for westernized and Islamized African men to view all African women as being assigned to the same limited roles as women in Caucasian and Muslim societies. African American men in particular are reluctant to research the roles played by powerful women warriors in traditional African culture, society, and history. Matriarchal warrior tribes and matrilineal tribal descent are themes found throughout Africa and its history. The tradition of female warriors has survived from ancient times into modern times, and is the central most defining cultural trait that separates African women from their Caucasian sisters. According to Abayomi Azikiwe (2007):

>...the role of African women within their societies during the ancient, pre-colonial and colonial eras

illustrate quite clearly that the assumptions around the strict divisions of labor and political power among traditional African nations depart significantly from those in Europe and Asia. The lives, contributions and accomplishments of these women also defy the stereotypical notions of the role of females within traditional African societies prior to the advent of colonialism and national independence.

Western media are largely responsible for presenting an image of African women as victims. Coverage on African women usually centers on issues of oppression, such as the Muslim influenced tradition of female circumcision in East Africa, "Islamic" extremism in West Africa, or rape in South Africa. This type of coverage presents a lopsided image of African women's lives.

Out of respect for our foremothers from three million years ago and coming forward, let me set the record straight. Only African women can boast of simultaneously having the softness of the nurturing mother of all humanity on one hand; the hardness of the armed general who leads armies into battle on the other hand; and everything else in between. The historical information presented in this chapter demonstrates the role of loving, protecting warrior played by African women throughout the entire African experience since time immemorial.

Only weak, insecure men are fearful of strong women. To their credit, men reared in traditional societies throughout African history have always been so strong and secure in their own manhood that they have not needed to attempt placing severe restrictions on African women. Such men are comfortable and proud in letting African women be *all* that they are capable of, with whatever the situation demands. Even if African men made such an attempt it would not work, because traditional African women are equally strong in their sense of womanhood. Ancient African wisdom has always informed us that when you conjoin the energies of one type of strength to the energies and strength of its complementary opposite, it results in a powerful spiritual creative energy that is far greater than the sum of its parts. The understanding and practice of this principle reside at the essential core of all African creative genius, productivity, and stability. Thus, the lack of this level of bonding between African men and women leads to social decline, cultural deterioration, and racial suicide. The highest level of such bonding can only be accomplished with African men and women because: (a) only they are the parents of all humanity; and (b) other races/cultures have different energies that lack the same level of compatibility. Even casual observation of African societies worldwide is enough to demonstrate the strength of this claim.

The Historical Tradition

The tradition of female warriors has been practiced throughout African history. According to Greek accounts, the earliest women warriors were African women from **North, Northwest, and West Africa**. Greeks referred to them as Amazons, and reported that the Amazons from **Dahomey** were all-female troops whose skills were so sharply honed that they served as royal bodyguards. The West African kingdom of Dahomey maintained a well-trained army of women in service of the king up through the late 19th century. This all-female army participated in fierce battles and was reported to be vastly superior to male soldiers in their fighting skills. Some of these women soldiers continued to sabotage the French even after Dahomey's official defeat by France at the end of the 19th century (Stanley B. Alpern, 1998).

In the mid-18th century, Ibo women in **southern Nigeria** shared combat duty with men, as did **Muslim Fulani** women in **northen Nigeria** during the 1820s. Many of these women warriors were also traditional priestesses. **Nupe** women warriors of northern Nigeria, called Isadshi-Koseshi, opposed Fulbe invasions time and time again. Fulbe men would raid the Nupe for cattle and slaves, especially women. Nupe women warriors would successfully fend off each raid attempt by the Fulbe men. The Nupe people are one of the ethnic groups that claims their original home was in Egypt.

Women warriors and chiefs have continued in traditional African society from the pre-colonial era until today. In 1929, thousands of **Igbo** women from the Bende District, Umuahia, Ngwa, and other places in Nigeria traveled to Oloko to stage an uprising in protest against the colonial government's plan to tax women, "the trees that bear fruit." The women also accused the Warrant Chiefs of restricting the role of women in the government. The uprising came to be called the "Igbo Women's War of 1929." It was organized and led by rural women of the Owerri and Calabar Districts. The protesting Ibo women bound their heads with ferns, painted their faces with ash, put on loincloths, and carried sacred sticks with palm frond wreaths. Thousands of women marched on the District Office, dancing, singing protests, and demanding change. This protest spread into a vast regional insurrection of some 2,000,000 protestors which mobilized demonstrations in three provinces. Women in the Aba region proceeded to attack and loot the European trading shops, stores, and Barclay's Bank. They even broke into the prison and released the prisoners. By the time the uprising ended, sixteen native courts were destroyed or burned down, and many Warrant Chiefs were forced to resign (Max Dashu, 2006).

It is important to discuss in some length the **Tuareg Berbers** from that part of the Sahara Desert which ranges from Mauritania into Morocco and Algeria and all the way to Egypt. Since ancient times, Tuareg women have continued to break two stereotypes: women as the "weaker" sex; and cloistered, veiled Islamic women. They have a **matriarchal society**, almost unbelievable in the context of what is *assumed* to be "Islamic." Chieftainship is hereditary through the female line. Inheritance is through the mother's side. Tuaregs are also **matrilocal**, so when a man marries out of his tribe he will move to the woman's tribe. A man may move up in society by marrying a higher status woman, but this rarely happens because women seldom marry below their station. On the domestic scene, women keep all the household keys in their possession (Lyn Webster Wilde, 2000).

All Tuareg women are considered as warriors, and have a great deal of respect and freedom. They are fond of showing off their "strength" by impromptu public wrestling matches. Tuareg women are so aggressive that the men prefer to choose non-Tuareg females as their concubines because they are "less capricious and overbearing." There is a common saying among Tuareg men, who claim: "If there were only women amongst us, we Tuaregs would vanquish the world" (Donald Campbell, 1928).

Tuareg women do not wear a veil. Instead, it is the men who modestly cover their noses and mouths with the end of their tagelmousses (several meters of gauze, wrapped around the head in a turban) after a certain age. These women further have equal, if not greater, rights to choose and to take as many lovers as they wish before marriage. This practice is said to increase their value, skill, and desirability as future wives (Campbell, 1928).

Tuareg men are still feared today for their ferocity and skill as warriors, and are highly respected as traders and businessmen. However, the men "veil" themselves and defer to their women because of cultural beliefs. They believe that the world has a great number of evil "spirits" that are eager to invade the body through any opening - especially the mouth and nostrils. Therefore, the men must cover and protect the entranceways to the body. Women, on the other hand, know the secrets of life. Only women can conceive and give birth; therefore, they have natural protection against these evil spirits (Wilde, 2000).

Female warrior queens were also the norm throughout the **central and southern regions of Africa**, as recorded in the historical accounts of the **Congo, Angola, Zimbabwe, and South Africa**, to name a few.

The female warrior tradition did not end when African women were brought into the Western hemisphere. History Professor Margaret Washington (2005) provides this report on Black women's activities before, during, and after the Civil War in America:

> During the antebellum era, black women abolitionists moved, in keeping with the urgency of the times, from quiet activism to militancy. Black women furthered the goal of emancipation during the Civil War by continuing their abolition work. Black women organized petition campaigns to Congress and the president; they sent food and clothing to the Union front lines for destitute blacks; and they went into Union-occupied areas to provide education for black refugees. After the Emancipation Proclamation was signed on January 1, 1863, black women abolitionists immediately began working on the next phase of their mission -- the task of uplifting their race as a free people.

Throughout the 1830s, black women in America engaged heavily in activism. They vowed to, "heed the enslaved mothers' cry for children torn away," and designated their dwellings as "free homes" for those fleeing bondage. One exemplary incident occurred in the summer of 1848 when African American women beat back a group of slave catchers. The incident was reported by *The North Star,* an African American paper in Cincinnati, on August 11, 1848. As the report goes, about eight or ten Africans who had escaped from southern plantations successfully made it across the Ohio River to freedom. However, southern slave catchers tracked them into town, intent on catching the Africans and returning them to the slave plantations to collect the bounty that was placed on their heads. No one expected the free African women of the town where the fugitive slaves were hiding to quickly emerge from adjoining houses and use their bodies as a barrier protect the fugitives. Women continued to quickly leave their houses and join the group until the Black Amazons were about equal in number to the slave hunters. Armed with shovels, tongs, washboards and rolling pins, these African warrior women placed their lives on the line by confronting the White slave catchers who carried revolvers, sword-canes and bowie knives. The strength and determination of the women to bar the slave catchers' entry into the town caused the besieged White men to turn around and give up their mission (Margaret Washington, 2005).

Many male abolitionists—Black and White--opposed a public role for female abolitionists. Some of the male opponents of women in abolitionist work held antifeminist views, while others feared backlash from the link between antislavery and the even more unpopular cause of gender equality. The "woman's issue" complicated quarrels among abolitionists regarding tactics in the religious and political spheres. The problems eventually led to confusion and a schism between the factions. The Garrisonians won control of the American Anti-Slavery Society in 1840, when opponents quit in protest of the election of a female officer (Margaret Washington, 2005).

African American female anti-slavery activists became role models for Anglo American women to assert themselves. Despite male opposition, thousands of White women braved public disapproval to participate in the early abolitionist campaign. Often veterans of moral reform activities, these women were inspired by religious principles and republican ideology. Like their African American counterparts, they encountered opposition within the movement. A few women attended the founding convention of the American Anti-Slavery Society in 1833, even though that society at first barred women members. Abolitionist women maneuvered around this by forming their own local organizations, which met at national conventions in 1837, 1838, and 1839. They also raised considerable amounts of money for the antislavery cause by sponsoring events such as picnics and bazaars (Margaret Washington, 2005).

The history of Maroon societies in the Caribbean documents a continuation of the African Amazon tradition, and a demonstration of African women's willingness and ability to conduct guerilla warfare. The word "Maroon" (*Marron* to the French;

Cimarron to the Spanish) loosely refers to Africans in Jamaica and Brazil during the seventeenth and eighteenth centuries that "returned or reverted to the wild." Marronage involved the process of slaves' flight from servitude to establish their own hospitable towns and hegemonies. Mavis C. Campbell (1988) discusses the kind of "Africanness" that existed in Maroon societies that transcended regional, ethnic or linguistic affinities. She quotes Roger Bastide, whose research on the Maroon societies in Brazil called "Quilombos" discovered a very similar situation. According to Bastide: "It would seem that in most cases, as in Palmares [Jamaica], we are dealing with 'tribal regression,' a kind of return to Africa." In Brazil the Quilombo settlements of runaway slaves began in the sixteenth century as soon as they began to import slaves into the country. Women warriors were always a significant factor, although the literature has always focused almost exclusively on the activities of male Maroons.

Warrior Queens and Warrior Priestesses

Warrior Queen **Majaji** led the Lovedu army in battle armed with a shield and spear. The Lovedu people were a part of the ancient Cushite Empire during their long war with Rome. The empire ended in350 A.D. when the Cushite stronghold of Meroe was finally overcome by Roman assaults. It is believed that this queen and general died on the walls of Meroe defending her people (http://www.geocities.com/jywansal/Afrikan Warriors .html).

There were several Egyptian warrior queens, all of who descended from the royal families of

Cush: **Ahotep; all seven Cleopatras; Arsinoe II and III.** These queens ruled Egypt and served as generals who led their armies and navies through Roman times (http://www.geocities.com/jywansal/ AfrikanWarriors.html).

A long succession of Ethiopian queens and military leaders named **Candace** also descended from royal families of Cush. The first Candace led an army mounted on war elephants and repelled Alexander's invasion of Ethiopia in 322 BCE. In 30 BCE Candace Amanirenas defeated an invasion by Patronius, the Roman governor of Egypt, and went on to sack the Greek colony of Cyrene. At that time Cyrene was the oldest and most important of the five Greek cities in the region now known as Libya (http://www.geocities.com/jywansal/AfrikanWarriors .html). Another Queen Candace led her armies in person to fight the Romans in southern Egypt during the 1st century B.C. The Romans were forced to retreat without entering Nubia. According to classical records, this particular Queen Candace was mannish and blind in one eye as a result of a war injury (www.swagga.com/queen.htm).

Queen Judith of the Ethiopian Falashas, attacked Axum in 937 AD. Axum was the sacred capital of Ethiopia. Judith killed all the inhabitants, including the descendants of Israelite King Solomon and Ethiopian Queen Makeda (Sheba). She then proclaimed herself queen, a move that struck dreads in the hearts of Ethiopian Christians. Queen Judith destroyed the Christian churches and killed thousands of people in the process. The Falasha Queen ruled unchallenged for around forty years (http://whenweruled.com/articles.hp?lng=en&pg=18). Falasha people are the Jews of Ethiopia who refer to themselves as *Beta Israel* (House of Israel). Falashas combine Judaism with traditional African beliefs and practices, so they do not adhere to mainstream Judaism. They claim to be descendants of the Israelites who migrated from Jerusalem to Ethiopia with Menelik, son of King Solomon and Queen Makeda (http://ww.questia.com/library/encyclopedia/falashas.jsp).

Through the tenth and eleventh centuries, a long succession of African Muslim Habe warrior queens ruled the Hausa states of modern day northern Nigeria: **Queens Kufuru, Gino, Yakumo, Yakunya, Walzana, Daura, Gamata, Shata, Batatume, Sandamata, Yanbamu, Gizirgizir, Innagari, Jamata, Hamata, Zama, and Shawata. Amina,** daughter of **Queen Turunku** of the Songhai people in mid-Niger, ruled the Hausa Empire centuries later. Amina personally led her army of 20,000 soldiers into battle. During her reign as queen from 1536 to 1573, she extended her nation's boundaries to the coast of the Atlantic Ocean, and founded many cities along the way (http://www.geocities.com /jywansal/AfrikanWarriors.html). Again we see a radical difference between African Muslim women and their Arabic female counterparts. It appears that even though Africans adopt Islam, they doggedly adhere to their mother culture, thus assimilating the two. Research needs to be conducted in this subject area.

Queen Moremi Ajasoro, a pre-colonial Yoruba woman of Nigeria, saved the Holy City of Ile-

Ife from invaders. She is a figure of high significance in the history of the Yoruba of southwest Nigeria. Moremi resided in Ile-Ife, a town that was being incessantly attacked by the adjoining Ugbo people. Droves of Ile-Ife citizens were being enslaved by the Ugbo. Moremi was a very brave and beautiful woman who exercised her wits and beauty in order to deal with the problem facing her people. Upon being taken as a slave to the Ugbo, Moremi used her beauty effectively and married the ruler of the Ugbo, thus becoming their queen. After she discovered the secrets of the Ugbo, Moremi escaped to Ile-Ife and revealed everything to the Yorubas, who subsequently defeated the Ugbo in battle. Moremi is still revered today throughout Yoruba society and is remembered in many folk tales, myths, and sculptures (en.wikipedia.org/wiki/Moremi).

Queen Mussasa was an Angolan warrior who reigned in the seventeenth century. She belonged to the Jaga ethnic group that made up two distinct but seemingly similar bands of warriors who bettled the Portuguese in the sixteenth and seventeenth centuries. Her nation was located on the Cunene river in what is now Angola. In her dual role as General and Queen, Mussasa led her soldiers into battle and expanded her empire greatly through military prowess. She was succeeded by her daughter, Tembandumba (Jessica A. Salmonson, 1991).

Another Angolan warrior was **Queen Mbande Nzinga (Zinga)**. She was the sister and advisor of the king of Angola and served as his representative in negotiating treaties with the Portuguese. When her brother died in 1624, Nzinga mounted the throne, swearing that no Portuguese would ever conquer Angola during her lifetime. She appointed women to all government offices, including her two sisters Kifunji and Mukumbo. The warrior queen and her largely female army inflicted terrible casualties on the Portuguese when they broke the peace treaty with Angola. In the process, she conquered nearby kingdoms in an attempt to build a strong enough confederation to drive the Portuguese out of Africa. True to her word, the Portuguese were unable to invade Angola until after Nzinga's death at the age of 81. It is suspected by some that Nzinga was behind the death of her brother because he was not strongly against the Portuguese. However, this is only a speculation in the absence of documented evidence (http://www.Geocities.com/jywansal/AfrikanWarriors.html).

Linga was warrior queen from the region of the Congo. She also led her army against the Portuguese in 1640. Women warriors were so common in the Congo that the Monomotapa Confederacy had standing armies of women (http://www.geocities.com/jywansal/AfrikanWarriors.html).

Because of the popularity of the movie, many people are familiar with the name of Queen **Nandi**, warrior mother of Shaka, King of the Zulu. Nandi battled slave traders and it was she who trained her son to be a warrior. When Shaka became King, he established an all-female regiment. These warrior women often fought in the front lines of Shaka's army (http://www.geocities.com/jywansal/Afrikan Warriors.html).

Mantatisi was a warrior queen of the baTlokwas in the early 1800s. She fought to preserve the tribal lands of her people during the wars between Shaka and Matiwane. She succeeded in protecting her people's land; however, when her son became king after she died, the baTlokwas people were defeated by Mahweshwe (http://www.geocities.com/jywansal/Afrikan Warriors.html).

Madame Yoko of the Kpa Mende Confederacy ruled her kingdom and led her army comprised of warriors from some fourteen tribes. The Kpa Mende Confederacy was the largest tribal group in nineteenth century Sierra Leone. At that time at least 15% of all the tribes in Sierra Leone were led by women. Today, women rulers make up about 9% overall. According to Linda R. Day (1994), both primary and secondary sources on the history of the Mende people repeatedly refer to influential women in political positions.

> For at least one hundred years, women have filled at least 10% of the 113 or so "paramount chief" positions in this region. [A] look at the region's history suggests that female chieftainship has evolved from deeply rooted indigenous institutions.

It is recorded in the pre-colonial history of the Mende that they had female chiefs and war leaders. Madame Yoko was such a powerful female chief who was also a prominent figure in the Sande Society for women, an organization that was a source of ritual authority and wealth in goods and loyal supporters. A traveling missionary reported in 1885 that Chief Yoko was so wealthy and powerful that she had three husbands who lived in three separate towns. The female chief's husbands and kinsmen were so appreciative of Yoko that they regularly showered her with gifts (Michelle Z. Rosaldo:1974:181).

The cultural and oral traditions of the Mende people indicate that they migrated from ancient Cush/Sudan between the second and sixteenth centuries. This is yet another group that traces its history back to the Nile River Valley civilization of Meroe in ancient Cush. Nineteenth century regional warfare led to many Mende people being captured and sold into slavery. The most notable instance was the case of Mende slaves aboard the Amistad, a historical event that has become highly publicized because of the movie *Amistad* (en.wikipedia.org/wiki/ Mende_people).

Empress **Menen Leben Amede** ruled Ethiopia in the nineteenth century. She commanded her own army and acted as regent for her son Ali Alulus. The warrior empress was wounded and captured in a battle in 1874. Her son paid the ransom for his mother's release, and she continued to rule until 1853 (http://www.geocities.com/ jywanza1/Afrikan Warriors.html.

She-Dong-Hong-Beh was a general of the Dahomey Amazons under King Gezo. She led an army of some 6,000 women warriors against the Egba fortress of Abeokuta in 1851. Only about 1,200 of the Amazons survived the extended battle because they were armed with spears, bows and swords, while the Egba had European cannons. In 1892 King Behanzin of Dahomey (now Benin)led his army of 12,000 troops against French colonists over trading rights. Some 2,000 Amazons took part in that battle. Despite the fact that the Dahomey army was armed only with rifles, against the French machine guns and cannons, the Amazons made a strategic attack that inflicted heavy casualties on the French. The women warriors engaged in hand-to-hand combat with the survivors, eventually forcing the French army to retreat (http://www.geocities.com /jywanza1/Afrikan Warriors.html).

Around 1898 Queen **Sarraounia** of Azna emerged as ruler of an animist group of Eastern Hausa that refused to become either Muslim or Christian. "Sarraounia" means queen or chief, and among the Azna people of Lougou and surrounding Hausa towns and villages, the term also refers to a lineage of female rulers who exercised both political and religious power. Queen Sarraounia led the Azna people in battle against the French colonists in 1899 with every resource available to them. While some nearby African kingdoms readily collaborated with the French in the hope of finally subduing the warrior queen and her kingdom, and others capitulated without a fight, Sarraounia mobilized her people and resources against them. Asna recources included military as well as magical elements, as they prepared to confront the French force which launched a fierce attack on her fortress capital of

Lougou. When her people became overwhelmed by the superior firepower of the French, Sarraounia and her fighters retreated tactically from the fortress and engaged the attackers in a protracted guerrilla battle. This eventually forced the French to abandon their project of subduing her. The 1986 film *Sarraounia* is based on her life.

Mukaya became both empress of the Luba people of Central Africa and general of the Luba army in the nineteenth century. Luba territory stretched along the rain forest from Zaire to northern Zambia. Initially, Mukaya fought alongside her brother Kasongo Kalambo. However, after he was killed in battle she assumed sole control of the empire and the army (http://www.geocities.com/jywanza1/Afrikan Warriors.html).

Nehanda Charwe Nyakasikana was a nineteenth century warrior priestess of the Zezuru people in the Shona nation of Zimbabwe. She was known among her people as a "svikiro," one who becomes possessed by ancestral spirits and gives advice based on that communication with an agent of the ancestors. Nehanda became a military leader when the British invaded her country. As a spiritual leader, she provided inspiration for the Shona revolt against the Rhodesian colonization of Zimbabwe. At first Nehanda promoted good relations between the Zezuru people and early European pioneers. However, the imposition of a "hut tax" and other tax assessments levied by the British in 1894 caused both the Ndebele and Shona people to revolt in June 1896. This became known as the "First Chimurenga" or "Second Matabele War." The rebellion was encouraged by traditional religious leaders, including Nehanda. She led a number of successful attacks on the English, but they eventually captured and executed her. The warrior priestess' heroism became a significant source of inspiration almost one hundred years later in the 1960s and 1970s nationalist liberation movement. Nehanda's name is now usually honored with the respectful prefixed title of *Mbuya*, or grandmother (Max Dashu).

Major General **Aderonke Kale** served as the highest ranking female officer in the Nigerian Army during the 20th century. She was a medical doctor by profession and worked in the Nigerian Army Medical Corps. (www.motherlandnigeria.com/women.html).

In 1900 Ghana, Ahsante Queen Mother **Yaa Ashantewa** galvanized the Ashante people and led a revolt against the British in continuous battles until her capture. This great African warrior Queen has been recognized by historians as a major contributor to African efforts to prevent the British from consolidating imperialism in Ghana, what was then known as the Gold Coast. Her story is woven throughout the history of Ghana. Yaa Ashantewaa opposed both the European commercial agents and their allies among the neighboring people of Kokofu. She eventually challenged the British colonialist courts that had been established in Kumasi after they deportation the Ashantehene (King) in 1896. In March of 1900 the British formally announced to the

Ashante Chiefs that the exiled leaders of the nation would not be allowed to return home and assume their rightful authority. The British then went too far by demanding that the Golden Stool, which is considered the soul of the people, be surrendered to them (www.swagga.com/queen.htm).

The chiefs held a secret meeting at Kumasi to discuss the British demands and the forced exile of their leaders, especially their King, the Ashantehene. Some wanted to make war on the white men and force them to bring back the Ashantehene. However, Yaa Ashantewa noticed that some of the other chiefs were afraid of going to war with the British, and wanted to beg the British Governor to bring back the Ashantehene King Prempeh. Then suddenly Yaa Ashantewa stood up and delivered these stirring words:

> Now I have seen that some of you fear to go forward to fight for our king. If it were in the brave days of, the days of Osei Tutu, Okomfo Anokye, and Opolu Ware, chiefs would not sit down to see thief king taken away without firing a shot. No white man could have dared to speak to chief of the Ashanti in the way the Governor spoke to you chiefs this morning. Is it true that the bravery of the Ashanti is no more? I cannot believe it. It cannot be! I must say this, if you the men of Ashanti will not go forward, then we will. We the women will. I shall call upon my fellow women. We will fight the white men. We will fight till the last of us falls in the battlefields.
> (www.swagga.com/queen.htm)

This speech inspired the men to take an oath to fight the white men until they released the Ashantehene. Led by Yaa Ashantewa, the Ashantis fought so fiercely that they kept the British hemmed up in the fort. However, about 1,400 British reinforcements arrived at Kumasi. Yaa Ashantewa and other leaders were captured and they also were sent into exile. Yaa Ashantewa's war was the last of the major wars in Africa led by a woman (www.swagga.com/queen.htm).

It should be pointed out that Yaa Ashantewa's actions were not an anomaly. There, have been many instances in Ashanti history when women have excelled in a public capacity. For example, in 1814 the Ashantehemaa **Adoma Akosua** was left in charge of the affairs of the Ashante nation while the Ashantehene Osei Bonsu went to the coast to visit his troops on the battlefield there. Another example is when the woman warrior Dwabenhemaa **Ama Seiwaa** took over as paramount chief of the Dwabeii in 1843 and bravely led her people back to Ashante territory from exile in Akyem Abuakwa in the south east of the Gold Coast after both of her sons died in succession (www.swagga.com/queen.htm).

African American Warrior Women

Hester Lane, a successful African American entrepreneur of New York City, used her home as an Underground Railroad station. Lane went so far as to travel South to purchase enslaved children whom she freed and educated (Margaret Washington, 2005). It was a common practice for Blacks to buy slaves whenever possible in order to set them free. In this manner, family members and friends who were freed from slavery by other Blacks gladly agreed to work for the purchasers in various capacities to repay the money that was spent on them so that even more could be set free. The literature is conspicuously silent on this voluntary, humanistic arrangement between Blacks.

Black activist **Mary Marshall's** Colored Sailors' Boarding Home was another busy sanctuary for runaway slaves. Marshall was determined that "No one who had the courage to start should fail to reach the goal." She and other Black women activists organized petition drives, wrote antislavery poetry, hosted traveling abolitionists, and organized fairs. By 1832, black women had formed the first female antislavery society in Salem, Massachusetts. They also held executive offices in biracial female antislavery societies in Philadelphia, Boston, and elsewhere (Margaret Washington, 2005).

In 1831, Black women activists in Boston, Massachusetts organized the African American Female Intelligence Society. This organization became a forum for activist **Maria Stewart.** She became the first woman to speak publicly against slavery. Stewart, a very spiritual woman, proclaimed that she was called by God to address the issues of black emancipation and the rights of black women. True to her warrior nature, Stewart boldly asserted: "We claim our rights as women and men, and we are not afraid of them that kill the body." She also published a pamphlet in *The Liberator* on behalf of black women and all enslaved Africans. Surprisingly, the men of Boston's black community censored

Stewart for her public expressions and forced her into silence. Following their sharp criticisms, she soon left Boston and never again spoke publicly. However, Stewart remained active through women's organizations and conventions. She joined other black women who held office, served as delegates, and otherwise participated in the biracial women's antislavery conventions in 1837, 1838, and 1839 (Margaret Washington, 2005).

The antislavery movement took a more progressive turn in the 1840s, when the American Anti-Slavery Society, founded by Anglo-American William Lloyd Garrison, welcomed women as officeholders and speakers. Most black women continued their quiet antislavery work, but some were outspoken. The first black woman to take the public stage for the American Anti-Slavery Society was **Sojourner Truth**. Born into slavery in 1797 among the Hudson Valley Dutch and emancipated in adulthood, Truth was already known as a preacher when she joined the Garrisonians in 1844. She made antislavery speeches throughout New England, and in 1845 gave her first address at the American Anti-Slavery Society's annual convention. Sojourner Truth was considered to be an archpacifist; however, by 1858 even she recognized that war with the South was inevitable if black people were to obtain their freedom.

Sojourner Truth lectured throughout the Midwest, where she confronted threatening pro-slavery (so-called "Copperhead") mobs. Sojourner Truth became known from Maine to Michigan as a popular and featured antislavery speaker. She and dozens of other African American women braved insults and threats of physical harm in order to serve as traveling lecturers and organizers. These public figures became important role models for women seeking to overcome societal barriers. Truth published a *Narrative* of her life, and used the proceeds to purchase a home and to finance her abolitionist work (Margaret Washington, 2005).

Another surge of radicalism occurred in 1850 with the passage of the ***Fugitive Slave Law*** which decreed that any citizen could be enlisted in the service of a slaveholder to capture an enslaved person. That law nullified any and all individual civil rights that states guaranteed their citizens, including those formerly enslaved. The *Fugitive Slave Law* literally brought warrior woman **Harriet Tubman** on the scene in American history. Tubman was a thirty-year-old self-emancipated African citizen of Maryland when she began defying the Fugitive Slave Law. She began leading enslaved men, women, and children out of the South. There were slave catchers lurking everywhere, and even with a price on her head, Tubman made more than thirty excursions into the South and safely conducted her charges through the Northern states and on to Canada. During the Civil War, Harriet Tubman offered her services as a spy for the Union Army (Margaret Washington, 2005).

Mary Ann Shadd (Cary) was a twenty-five-year-old freeborn schoolteacher when the Fugitive Slave Law was passed in 1850. Following in the footsteps of her father, whom she described as a "chief breakman" on the **Delaware Underground Railroad**, Shadd soon moved to Canada and established herself as a militant abolitionist, an influential emigrationist, and the first black woman editor of the *Provincial Freeman Newspaper*. (Margaret Washington, 2005).

In 1854, twenty-eight-year-old **Frances Ellen Watkins (Harper)** was another Black activist who joined Sojourner Truth on the Garrisonian lecture circuit. Watkins traveled throughout the Midwest, sometimes with Sojourner Truth, and spoke eloquently of the wrongs inflicted upon her people, selling her books of poetry at antislavery lectures and using the proceeds to support the Underground Railroad. In 1858, Watkins joined black male leaders in Detroit and led a large group of angry citizens in storming the jailhouse. The group attempted to remove from protective custody a black "traitor" to their cause, who intended to expose the operations of the Underground Railroad (Margaret Washington, 2005).

Born into a well-connected Baltimore family, Watkins was a poet and a teacher. Although Frances Harper was not born into a slave family in 1825 in Baltimore, Maryland, she nevertheless suffered from the oppressive slave laws and rampant discrimination of the time. Watkins was greatly bothered by the inequities and sufferings that her people had to suffer under the slave laws and resolved to take part in the effort to abolish slavery. She used her gift for language as lecturer in the

Anti-Slavery movement in the 1850's. Watkins moved to Philadelphia to be in a location which was considered the "station" of the Underground Rail Road. In Philadelphia she frequently met with fugitives from slave plantations and listened to their horrific tales of suffering and wrong. Their experiences intensely increased her sympathy in their behalf (Margaret Washington, 2005).

Caroline Loguen is another African American warrior woman. As the wife of Syracuse, New York abolitionist Reverend Jermain Loguen, Caroline Loguen answered many a midnight knock at the door by fugitive slaves during her husband's frequent absences. At one time, she and her sister successfully fought off slave catchers attempting to enter her home in pursuit of "fugitives." The Underground Railroad remained the "heart's blood" of black resistance in America. Black women abolitionists played a vital role in this work. Most often they were the ones who intercepted refugees; who provided them with food, clothing, shelter, health care, and spiritual and psychological comfort; and who directed them to the next station. It almost became commonplace for Black women to physically confront slave catchers and kidnappers who were often right on the heels of the fugitives.

Caribbean Warrior Women

According to folk history, Nyabinghi ("Nanny") was both a warrior queen and a warrior priestess of the Akan or the Ashante people of Ghana, born some time in the 1860s. She is also called Queen Juhmusa or Tahtahme. Accounts of this warrior queen who, as a free woman, voluntarily traveled from Ghana in West Africa to become a leader of enslaved Africans in Jamaica. She entered Jamaica for the express purpose of freeing Africans from the brutal slave plantations and establishing independent colonies where they could live free and peaceful lives. This act was not unreasonable, considering that the majority of slaves taken to Jamaica may have come from Ghana. Historical accounts of this woman who became the most famous of all leaders of the Windward Maroons in Jamaica have largely been ignored by historians who have restricted their focus to male figures in Maroon history. Biographical information on Queen Nanny is somewhat vague, because she is mentioned only four times in written historical texts. Even then, Queen Nanny is usually mentioned in somewhat derogatory terms by male historians. However, amongst the Maroons themselves this woman leader and priestess is held in the highest esteem (Max Dashu, 2006).

Queen Nanny is held up by Maroons as the most important figure in Maroon history. She is credited with being the single figure that united the Maroons across Jamaica, and played a major role in preserving African culture and knowledge. As the spiritual, cultural and military leader of the Windward Maroons, her importance stems from the fact that she guided the Maroons through the most intense period of their resistance against the British, between the years 1725 and 1740. Queen Nanny is said to have married to a man named Adou, but had no children. The warrior queen died in the 1730's.

At this point, the book turns to subjects directly related to African culture, philosophy, and traditions. The following chapter presents commonly held African values that have been present within African societies across the Continent for thousands of years. African American elders of fifty years and older will recognize and recall a lot of the information from this point forward as once being the social norm in their lifetime, when Africanity/Blackness stood for pride, dignity, and discipline.

9. COMMONLY HELD AFRICAN VALUES

*I thank you God for creating me Black.
White is the colour for special occasions,
Black is the colour for every day.
And I have carried the World
since the dawn of time.
And my laugh over the World,
through the night, creates the day.*
      --Bernard Dadie, Ivory Coast

Traditional African Values and Beliefs

The entire thesis of this book is that the state of African American mental health and social decline can be improved if African Americans can somehow begin to lose their unfounded sense of self-loathing and belief in White supremacy. I realize that in order for African people to get out of a destructive set of alien cultural values it is necessary to provide them with the ones they lost that ensured their survival and advancement.

Being born in Africa does not make someone an expert in African culture, the same as being born in England does not serve as a sole qualification for a person to teach English grammar. Many Continental Africans will argue that Africa is so culturally diversified from one ethnic group to another that it is impossible to speak of African culture as a unified continental entity. I strongly suspect that this argument has been taught to them by our colonizers in order to keep us divided. Since many of us are willing to accept their opinions uncritically, very often no thought is given to investigate the truth or factuality of their statements or to subject such statements to critical analysis.

It stands to reason that if we can discuss the common features of Middle Eastern, Asian, and Western cultures, it is certainly possible to discuss those found in "African culture." By the same token, if we find that the primary features of English culture are maintained in its colonies in America and Australia, we can discuss the same phenomenon in regard to Africans throughout North America, Latin America, and the Caribbean. This cultural phenomenon is what binds together Africans in the three Americas and the Caribbean with Africans on the Continent.

Dr. Kwame Gyekye (1987:191-192) has apparently been confronted by Africanists who contend that they see no affinities among the cultures of Africa.

> On the intellectual level the works of such eminent Western anthropologists as Rattray, Herskovits, Forde, Fortes, Evans-Pritchard, Radcliffe-Brown, Lienhardt, and Goody, which generally deal with specific ethnic groups in Africa, have produced the impression, which was not intended by their authors, that the institutions and practices of the ethnic groups in Africa are very different from one another. The reason is that none of these authors, through either a lack of interest in other ethnic

groups or a consciousness of his own limitations, tried in any significant way to relate his own observations and conclusions to those of other scholars, where they were available.... Consequently, such works fail to convey the impression that African cultures can be examined from a continental perspective.

A painstaking comparative study of African cultures leaves one in no doubt that despite the undoubted cultural diversity arising from Africa's ethnic pluralism, threads of underlying affinity do run through the beliefs, customs, value systems, and sociopolitical institutions and practices of the various African societies.

Gyekye's comparative examination of some of the most prominent authors' works leads him to assert that some of the most substantial underlying cultural similarities commonly found among the various ethnic groups that were studied are in the categories of:

- Cosmological ideas;
- Social values;
- Traditional political systems;
- Social institutions;
- Religious outlook;
- Moral injunction.

I recently worked on a grant with the assistance of Dr. Kwasi Wiredu, during which time we came up with anidea of the four defining features of traditional African culture. While these few values listed below accurately represent some core features of African culture, they are by no means exhaustive. I have expanded that short list by the first one mentioned below.

- Existence and power of a hierarchy of spiritual beings headed by the One God;
- Non-dogmatic approach to religion
- Humanistic (non-supernaturalistic) principles of morality and ethics
- Respect for age, wisdom, and knowledge;
- Concern for the wellbeing and health of the community.

Some of the core values and commonly held features of African culture will be repeated in the work of various Africanist scholars. At the risk of appearing redundant, such repetitions are included to demonstrate that these scholars are in agreement with each other. In his book, *Philosophy and an African Culture,* Wiredu (1980:7-8) cites Antebam's inventory of ten "common aspects of African life and culture":

- The idea of the existence of One Great God as an integral member of society as distinct from the Western and Christian idea of God staying aloof in Heaven;

- The belief in the perpetual existence of life, in which there is a cycle of pregnancy, life, death and a period of waiting in a universal pool of spiritual existence with a subsequent state of reincarnation;

- The belief in the idea that man is born free from sin and the idea that he remains so until he becomes involved in some polluting circumstances in life;

- The idea of beauty of thought, speech, action and appearance as a basic and necessary prerequisite for appointment to the high office of state;

- The [importance of] producing a child . . . in marriage;

- The importance of marriage as a criterion of social status; the principle of age as a vital criterion of wisdom;

- The tendency to stress, in all forms of art, the quality of significance [i.e. art for *life's* sake] as a criterion of beauty and virtue as opposed to… the slogan art for art's sake;

- Spontaneity of self-expression [the lack of] which is the greatest weakness of modern Western diplomacy;

- The peculiar conception that it is improper and obscene to say thanks soon after one has been offered food by a neighbor.

Cheikh Anta Diop's (1990:195) work set forward in *The Cultural Unity of Black Africa* is well known. He posits that the matriarchal family, the creation of the territorial state, the emancipation of woman in domestic life, xenophilia, cosmopolitanism, social collectivism, a material solidarity of right for each individual. However,

African solidarity is not a scientific solidarity that is lacking in human warmth. Diop further states that:

> In the moral domain, it shows an ideal of peace, of justice, of goodness and an optimism which eliminates all notion of guilt or original sin in religious and metaphysical institutions.

According to Diop (Op.cit.), these features of African culture differ radically from Western culture, as confined to Greece and Rome, because they are the foundations of all Western culture. Thus, European and American cultures are characterized by the city-state, xenophobia, individualism, moral and material solitude, and disgust for existence. He goes on to say that:

> An ideal of war, violence, crime and conquests, inherited from nomadic life, with as a consequence, a feeling of guilt and of original sin, which causes pessimistic religious or metaphysical systems to be built, is [their] special attribute....

It was said earlier that traditional African beliefs and values are cultural elements that bind together Africans on the Continent with those who were captured and scattered throughout the Western hemisphere. Just as some argue that there are no cultural affinities among African ethnic groups on the Continent, some also argue that it was extremely difficult for enslaved Africans to communicate and unite with each other because of linguistic and ethnic differences. My investigations do not lead to the same conclusions.

The Scattering: Linguistic Aspects

Yoruba people formed the largest West African ethnic group brought into the Western hemisphere during the Atlantic Slave Trade. The Yoruba from the southwestern region of Nigeria were the first and largest group, with royal house members among them. Included in this group were: Egguados, Ekiti, Fee, Yeza, Eyba, Oyos, Ajuon, Cuevano, as well as the Sabulu from western Yorubaland in the Dahomey territory. They all spoke languages belonging to the Niger-Kongo branch of the Kongo-Kordofanian linguistic group, according to Oba Ecun (1989:13).

The second largest groups were brought from Calabar in southeast Nigeria, which included: Equi and Ibidros, who speak languages from the Benue-Kongo linguistic subfamily. Gregerson (1977:6) includes Bantu languages in this group. Ibo people also came from this area, and their language is from the Caggua-Kongo linguistic subfamily. Other groups who proceed from this area were the Abaja, Bucamos and Obas (Ecun, 1989:13).

The third most important group came from several countries along the western coast of Africa: Sierra Leone (Grain Coast); Cote d'Ivoire (Ivory Coast); Ghana (Gold Coast); plus Togo, Dahomey, Benin, Nigeria, and Cameroun (Slave Coast. The Ashante and Fante spoke a dialect derived from Tigii, while the Dahomey Fons and the Minas Popas spoke a dialect partly based on the Eggue (Ecun, 1989:13).

All of the above languages belong to the Kongo-Kordofanian linguistic family, which means they shared the same phonological, morphological, syntactical, and grammatical features, as well as some lexical features (Borishade, (1994:1).

After examining the linguistic structures of Niger-Kongo languages of West Africa and comparing them with the structural features of the vernacular language spoken by African Americans, I discovered that so-called "Black English" is actually a continuation of Niger-Kordofanian languages (Borishade, 1994). Thus, the term "Black English" is legitimately referred to as a Creole language: an English lexicon used within a Niger-Kongo grammatical structure with all its attending phonology, morphology, and syntax.

Cohesion: Cultural, Religious, and Social Factors

Based upon the fact that the overwhelming number of West Africans that were brought into the Western hemisphere belonged to the same Niger-Kordofanian language family, I disagree with the claims of scholars who focus on what they believe were overwhelming communication problems among the multitude of different African ethnic groups. The enslaved Africans would have had no more difficulty with each other's languages than Europeans and Americans have with any of the Latin-based languages within the Indo-European linguistic family. We are aware of the close similarities among English, French, Spanish, and Italian, for example. The fact is overlooked that all, except a very few, of the enslaved Africans belonged to the same broad

Niger-Kordofanian language family that stretches from West Africa all the way to Central Africa (Borishade 2006, 1994, 1993; Gregerson 1977; Dunn 1976).

Besides the linguistic factor, there are six additional reasons that support my contention that the diverse enslaved ethnic groups would have been able to communicate with each other and form cohesive societies over a relatively short period of time. First, large numbers who belonged to the same homogeneous ethnic groups were transported at the same time, and did not all arrive in the Americas in heterogeneous crowds. This group would essentially have had no communication problems (Ecun 1989:13-14; Borishade 2006; Gregerson 1977:7).

Second, many of the slaves were multilingual. Anyone who has lived in Africa knows that it is a common practice for African children from different ethnic groups to learn each other's languages as they play together. Another point along this line is that African adults of various ethnic groups have always intermarried. Further, Africans with different ethnic backgrounds learn each others' languages in the process of conducting business. These practices existed among Africans in the past, and continue today (Borishade 1993).

Third, West African ethnic groups shared the same broadly defined culture and religious beliefs. Prominent Africanist scholars who have examined African religious beliefs and culture from one ethnic group to the other across the Continent have concluded there is really only one broadly distributed

African religion with multiple variations of ethnic liturgies, much like the multitude of Christian denominations. Amazing uniformity has always existed in the theological structure, cosmology, ontology, worldview, and philosophy throughout African societies, as reported by scholars like Mbiti (1969), Wiredu (1980), Gyekye (1987), Mudimbe (1988), and Diop (1990).

Fourth, the groups brought into the Western hemisphere shared the same distinct decision-making style that draws upon age-old proverbs and religious mythologies. Enslaved Africans drew from their shared mythologies for solutions, survival, and agreement by consensus (Mbiti, 1969; Wiredu, 1980; Borishade, 1993; Thompson, 1984).

Fifth, every African is a religious carrier, with their religion and mythology deeply embedded in their hearts and minds, then manifested in behavior. These elements occupy every aspect of life and expression: oral histories, rituals, music, dance, sculpture, and religious personages. Thus, a multitude of enslaved African ethnic groups already had religious cohesion among themselves. In fact, Yai (2001) discusses the globalization of African religion that spread throughout West and Central Africa long before European contact (Borishade, 2006).

Finally, leadership personnel and institutional infrastructures were already established in accordance with lineage, gerontocracy, nobility, chiefdoms, secret societies, priests, and religious specialists. Leaders' roles and contributions to the people acquired greater significance proportionate to the gruesome ordeals that were forced upon them. Membership in African secret societies often cut across ethnic lines. Women and men with proven leadership skills, intelligence, and social commitment received special education and training in traditional universities and organizations as civic and political leaders. In addition to the world-renown West African universities that flourished for hundreds of years prior to European contact, there were the traditional university systems within organizations like the Ogboni, Poro, Sandi, Chi-Wara, and Gelede societies. It is not reasonable to think that such proven, pre-established, institutionalized leadership simply went ignored or disappeared. On the contrary, these leaders would have been recognized and sought out during the brutalizing experiences of slavery because of their intellect, knowledge, and skills. Spiritually gifted religious specialists, in particular those who were masters in the healing arts, similarly would have been put to service for the same reason (Borishade, 2006).

  Evidence supporting the claim that relatively easy communication and cohesion were possible among the various enslaved African ethnic groups is found in the oral and written history, religious beliefs, cultural traditions, social institutions, and linguistic elements of Diasporan African groups today. Despite the obstacles, enslaved Africans would have been able to reorganize and communicate across ethnic groups. Their determination to do so would certainly have gained impetus from the dire nature and conditions of their situation. They managed to continue their religious beliefs and cultural features by cleverly using the deceptive strategy of dissimulation. Instead of becoming "good Christians" or "good Catholics," Africans deliberately used Catholic iconography and infrastructure to camouflage the fact that they were still practicing African religion and worship. Over time, African and Catholic religions combined into a syncretism, whereby the names of Catholic saints that were attached to the African deities, as well as some of the Catholic beliefs and practices, became permanently synchronized (Borishade, 2006).

Many of the same cultural values and beliefs that have always been commonly shared by Africans on the Continent were likewise shared by African Americans up to the 1960s. Loss of this knowledge has resulted in a loss of cultural identity as well as social fragmentation and decline.

The above processes that took place among Africans brought into the New World are the cultural elements that bind together Africans on the Continent with those who were captured and scattered throughout the Western hemisphere. We remain linked by our genetics, culture, languages, and history. Therefore, it is up to us to continue the legacy begun by our ancient ancestors tens of thousands of years ago.

The next chapter provides more details on why the Yoruba culture of West Africa are of central importance to African American identity, character development, and survival.

10. SIGNIFICANCE OF YORUBA CULTURE

*We should go down to the grassroots of our culture,
Not to remain there, not to be isolated there,
But to draw strength and substance therefrom,
And with whatever additional resources of strength
and material we acquire, proceed to set up a new form
of society raised to the level of human progress.*
--Sekou Toure of Guinea

Why the Yoruba?

Discussing the Yoruba people is critical because many of the enslaved West African ethnic groups that were scattered throughout the Western hemisphere belonged to the same religious global village as the Yoruba, according to Dr. Olabiyi B. Yai (2001:3). According to him, many of the West African ethnic groups had shared some of the same deities long before European contact and prior to the slave trade. Oba Ecun (1989:13) is another Africanist scholar who notes that the Yoruba were the largest ethnic group contributing to the Diasporan African population throughout the Americas and the Caribbean. This means that the history of African American, Afro-Latin American and Caribbean people in the Diaspora is an extension of Yoruba history that stretches all the way back more than 10,000 years to ancient Nile River Valley civilizations.

The ancestral home of the Yoruba and Diasporan Africans, by extension, was ancient Kush (Sudan) in the Nile River Valley where they, along with the people of Nubia (Ethiopia) and Kemet (Egypt), created the first and greatest civilizations the world has ever known. Their history and accomplishments form the foundation upon which all studies of African people and civilization can be grounded going all the way back to ancient times. Therefore, referring to them is based upon the same premise used by Europeans and Americans when they discuss the ancient Greek culture as the basis and foundation of all Western civilization. In similar fashion students are taught that England is the starting point for studying Anglo-American history, and textbooks on the founding of the United States begin with the history of England with America as one of its colonies.

The Kushite capital Meroe was a central city of international acclaim for its outstanding educational institutions and religious traditions. Yoruba civilization flourished in ancient Kush/Sudan until relatively recent history. Around A.D. 636 there was a massive Arabic invasion into Kemet and surrounding regions. Africans chose to suddenly flee from their ancestral homelands rather than convert to Islam. Millions of Africans, including the Yoruba, fled from northeast Africa as the Arabs conquered one territory after another. As a result, northern African territories became occupied and dominated by Arabic people rather than the Africans who developed and built those civilizations. The stelae, statues, hieroglyphs, and other forms of artwork clearly show that African people left images of themselves.

The Yoruba are one of the African groups that helped to lay the very foundations of African religious beliefs, civilization and culture that have thrived for some 10,000 to 12,000 years. Their history includes the development of the three great kingdoms of West Africa, as well as being captured and scattered throughout the Western hemisphere. Therefore, the history of African American, Afro-Latin American, and Caribbean people is a continuation of Yoruba history.

African History

If you have no history, you have no future. It is the *total history* of a society or race of people that informs them of who they are, what their mission and goals should be, the direction in which they should be headed, what they should be doing while headed in that direction, and what they are supposed to accomplish once they arrive there. Thus, past, present and future are inseparable because the past creates and informs the present while it inspires and guides the future.

First Golden Age

Let's take a "thumbnail" review of the total history of Africa that particularly relates to African Americans, Latin Americans, and Caribbeans. The *First Golden Age of Africa* began at least 3.5 million years ago when African women and men gave birth to all humanity, sent their children off to populate the entire world, and successfully brought humanity through the evolutionary period. Their next step was to establish civilizations in which knowledge and learning began to flourish. This led to the pharonic era of Africa.

Africa's *First Golden Age* did not belong to Kemet (Egypt) alone, but was shared by Nubia (Ethiopia), Kush (Sudan), and other African nations farther south in sub-Saharan regions. In fact, John Henrik Clarke (1988:2) presents evidence that it was the African nations farther south that were the originators of the early culture of Kemet. By 6000 B.C.E.E., Kemet, Nubia, and Kush had all become organized nations with complex systems of government, and had developed the first and greatest educational, scientific, and medical centers in the ancient world. By 6000 B.C.E.E. they had already revolutionized architecture by constructing stone pyramids. The first golden age ended around 1550 B.C.E.E.

Semitic people were about 3,000 years behind Africans in civilization building. It was around 3,000 B.C.E.E. when they first began to establish large city-states around the Mesopotamia region. The cities of Ur, Lagash, and Eridu are known from Hebrew history found in the Bible. During the first 3,000 years of Africa's *First Golden Age* when Africans had established great civilizations with achievements in science, mathematics, astronomy, surgery and medicine, Semites were nomadic and semi-nomadic sheep herders, living in tents. The abundant references to tents in the Old Testament are linguistic cultural markers for Hebrew people that indicate nomadic and semi-nomadic lifestyles with housing that can be quickly dismantled and moved to another location.

Europeans were even farther behind Africans than the Semites. Around 6000 years ago Europeans were still immersed in the Neolithic stage of development. Neolithic means "new stone age," which began in Greece around 7000 B.C.E.E. and continued until 1700 B.C.E.E. Neolithic culture lasted between 7000 and 3000 B.C.E.E. in southeast Europe, and from 4500 to 1700 B.C.E.E. in Northwest Europe. The two technologies that define Neolithic culture are agriculture and pottery.

A.W.R. Whittle's (1996) book, *Europe in the Neolithic: The Creation of New Worlds,* uses archaeological evidence to refute the literature that presents glowing narrative about the swift advancements made by Europeans during the Neolithic era. The strength and credibility of his scholarship in the subject has created radical changes in the writing and interpretative approaches over the past ten years. Whittle argues that Neolithic society in Europe was deeply

> rooted in the values and practices of its forager predecessors right across the continent. The processes of settling down and farming were piecemeal and slow. Only gradually did new attitudes emerge, to time and the past, to the sacred realms of ancestors and the dead, to nature and the concept of community.

Even prior to 6000 B.C.E.E., Kemet, Nubia, and Kush had already developed organized nations with complex systems of government with educational, scientific, and medical centers in the ancient world. These accomplishments were already established when Europeans were struggling to emerge from the practice of hunting and gathering in the period roughly between 7000 and 1700 B.C.E.E. By 1500 B.C.E.E. when Africa was entering her Second Golden Age of civilization, Europe was still stuck in the Neolithic Age just beginning to develop sedentary societies with agriculture an animal husbandry. According to Whittle, Europeans had still not even acquired a strong concept of community because of their centuries-long practice of foraging in nomadic and pastoral lifestyles. The European practice of cremating their dead compliments their longstanding nomadic lifestyle whereby people were constantly on the move.

Second Golden Age

Ancient Nile culture began to flourish around 3,800 B.C.E., the period of the Old Kingdom when Egypt attained its first continuous peak of civilization in complexity and achievement. This was the first of three so-called "Kingdom" periods, which mark the high points of civilization in the lower Nile Valley. The Old Kingdom is most commonly regarded as spanning the period of time when Egypt was ruled by the Third Dynasty through to the Sixth Dynasty (2686 BC – 2134 BC). This was the period in which Osiris and Isis ruled Egypt.

Osiris became a beloved figure because of the many things he did for the benefit and advantage of mankind in general, according to Egyptologist E.A. Wallis Budge (1973:9-11). Osiris was greatly devoted to the arts of agriculture. He taught the people to plough and to sow, and to raise crops of wheat and barley, and Isis showed them how to make bread from the grains. He was also the first to teach men to plant grape vines, and to make and preserve wine. Osiris became revered because he traveled about the world teaching mankind to plant vines and to sow wheat and barley. He traveled by way of the coast of Arabia into India, where he built many cities, including Nysa. Osiris then brought his army through the Hellespont into Europe. He left Isis to rule Egypt when he decided to spread his rule around the world. He returned only after civilizing the entire earth. He found that Isis ruled wisely and his kingdom was still in perfect order.

The words of Diodorus of Sicily are in agreement with Budge:

> Now the Ethiopians ... were the first of all men. ...The Egyptians are colonists sent out by the Ethiopians, Osiris having been the leader of the colony ... Osiris ... gathered together a great army, with the intention of visiting all the inhabited earth and teaching the race of men how to cultivate ... for he supposed that if he made men give up their savagery and adopt a gentle manner of life he would receive immortal honors. ...", and that Osiris then went from Egypt and Ethiopia to Arabia, Greece, and India.

This African king became a benefactor of the whole world by finding out which food was suitable for mankind, such that after his death he gained the reward of immortality, and was honored as a deified ancestor, or deity. Osiris was given another name at this point, Onnophris, meaning the "good one." In his role as the fourth divine pharaoh, this was Osiris's name.

Osiris also spread the African religion of *Ifa,* now recognized as the religion of the Yoruba, among all mankind. The religion of *Ifa* is probably the source of all human religions, including the Rig Veda, Shinto, Taoism, Judaism, Stoicism, and Christianity. The divination system of *Ifa* is probably the source of other divination systems such as *I Ching*, and *Tarot* (Frank D. Smith, Jr.).

Thus, it is supported by history and archaeology that Egypt was settled by Ethiopians who were sent to establish a similar government. The people of Ethiopia, Sudan, and Egypt built the first temples and laid down fair laws for their people. All of this history is related to the history of Africans in the Diaspora.

Africa was in her *Second Golden Age* of prosperity and achievement during the height of the pharonic period of ancient Kush, Nubia, Kemet and the building period of the Great Zimbabwe. It was the reign of Pharaoh Ahmose I in Kemet's Eighteenth Dynasty in 1550 B.C.E. that ushered in the second golden age of Africa. Ahmose was responsible for driving out the Hyksos invaders from

Kemet after they had occupied it for about 120 years.

Although Kemet stands as the symbol of this second golden age, the accomplishments and glory of that second period were shared by nations farther to the south. During this period Africans perfected their education system. They were highly skilled in mathematics, astronomy, science, medicine and surgery, and they shared these advancements with sub-Saharan Africans as well as non-African civilizations.

During the *Second Golden Age* of Africa, around the 10th to the 9th century B.C.E., Kushite and Nubian kings brought Kemet her last age of grandeur and social reform. As a world power, Kemet reached unprecedented heights of leadership in education and the sciences, as well as the way in which it cared for its people. Africa's *Second Golden Age* ended in 332 B.C.E.E. when the Greeks invaded Kemet, led by Alexander the Great (Clarke, 1974:3).

After Kemet, the next great African civilization was built by an Egyptianized people in the region called Nubians. Nubia was conquered and colonized by Kemet in the fourth millenium BC. This allowed Kemite civilization to be diffused southward, where a new African kingdom called Kush was built up in the floodplain around the Nile's third cataract. The capital city of Kush was Kerma and it served as the major trading center for goods travelling north from the southern regions of Africa.

Kush attained its greatest power and cultural energy between 1700 and 1500 B.C.E.E. When Kemet was invaded and dominated by the Hyksos it allowed Kush to come out from under the rule of Kemet and flower as a distinct culture. This period ended when the New Kingdom kings of Kemet overcame the Hyksos and regained sovereignty of their country. Kemet reconquered Kush and once again brought it under Kemite rule. When Kemet's New Kingdom collapsed in 1000 BC, Kush rose again as a major power by conquering all of Nubia, giving Kush control of Nubia's wealthy gold mines.

Following the reassertion of their independence in 1000 BC, the Kushites moved their capital city farther up the Nile to Napata. Nile River Valley people were, for the most part, the same people who had spread throughout the region. This may be the reason why the Kushites by and large considered themselves to be Egyptians and the proper inheritors of the pharonic titles and traditions. They organized their society along the cultural lines of Kemet, assumed all the Kemite royal titles, and their art and architecture were based on Kemite architectural and artistic models. Kushite pyramids were smaller and steeper. They introduced other innovations as well, but the Napata culture does not on the surface appear much different than Kemite culture. It is a magnificent historical irony that the Kushites later invaded and conquered Kemet. The Napata kings formed the twenty-fifth pharonic dynasty in the eighth century; this dynasty came to an end with the Assyrian invasion of Kemet in the seventh century B.C.E.

For several centuries after 590 B.C.E., the Kushite kingdom developed as an independent state, while Egypt experienced Persian, Greek, and Roman domination. The pharonic tradition of Meroe in Kush raised stelae that record the achievements of each reign. They erected pyramids to contain the tombs of their rulers. The ruins of Kushite palaces, temples, and baths attest a highly educated and civilized people with a centralized political system and a well-managed irrigation system. By the first century B.C.E. they began using script for their language and stopped using hieroglyphs. The Kushite language has never been fully deciphered. Some scholars have found evidence that metallurgical technology may have been transmitted westward across the savanna belt to West Africa from Kush's iron smelteries.

The Assyrians, and later the Persians, forced the Kushites to retreat farther south, thus closing off much of the contact that the Kushites formerly had with Kemet, the Middle East, and Europe. When Napata was conquered in 591, the Kushites moved their capital to Meroe (pronounced meh'-ro-way), a more secure location right in the heart of the Kushite kingdom. Being relatively isolated from the Kemite world, what is now referred to as the Meroitic Empire turned its attention to the sub-Saharan world. While it still continued the cultural traditions of pharonic Kemet, the Meroites/Kushites began to develop newer forms of culture and art, influenced by traditions found in sub-Saharan Africa. In turn, pharonic traditions began to appear among many sub-Saharan groups, especially those of West Africa. A slow but steady migration began from

Meroe into West Africa and continued for thousands of years. Historical accounts reveal that the people who migrated from Meroe continued Africa's legacy of high civilization and accomplishment forward until present history. Today Kush, the ancient home of the Yoruba, is called Sudan. Many of today's West African groups can be traced back to ancient Meroe by using genetic, archaeological, historical and linguistic evidence (Borishade).

Yoruba civilization flourished in Meroe until more recent history. Following the death of Muhammad in 632 A.D., there was a massive Arabic expansion into Egypt and surrounding regions. Tens of thousands of Africans chose to flee from their ancestral homelands rather than convert to Islam at the edge of a sword. As a result, northern African territories became occupied by Arabic people who continued to expand Islam. The stelae, monuments, hieroglyphs, and other forms of artwork clearly show that ancient Egyptians were African people who left images of themselves. Moreover, the Egyptian language was African, as was the religion.

Third Golden Age

The *Third Golden Age* of Africa occurred during the rise of the great Sudanic empires of West Africa; Ghana, Mali and Songhai with their three great internationally renown Sudanic universities in Gao, Jenne and Timbuktu. These empires were renowned as educational centers with many schools and universities. Scholars and students from other parts of Africa, Asia, and the Middle East beat a path to the doors of these universities for the privilege of being taught by brilliant male and female African scholars.

The Sudanic universities at Gao, Jenne and Timbuktu taught courses in philosophy, medicine, law, government, astronomy, math, literature, ethnography, hygiene, logic, rhetoric, grammar, geography, music, and poetry writing. Those universities operated right up until around the 15th century, shortly before the Atlantic slave trade began in full swing. When Arabs swept through West Africa on an Islamic jihad they dismantled all the universities, took possession of the books, and sent both the books and the captured African scholars into Arabia. Arabic knowledge took a sudden leap forward as a result of African knowledge entering Arabia.

Fourth Golden Age

The late Dr. John Henrik Clarke has written about the three Golden Ages of Africa mentioned above. I am going on record by discussing the *Fourth Golden Age of Africa*, a development which has not heretofore been considered in the total scheme of African history

In my opinion, the *Fourth Golden Age* of Africa began with the international activities of three Yoruba descendants who had been captured during the Atlantic Slave Trade and transported from West Africa into Brazil. Three freed Afro-Brazilian women left Brazil in the late 1800s, returned to West Africa, and began the *Lagosian Cultural Renaissance*. The women's express purpose for traveling back to Africa was to conduct in-depth studies into traditional

African religion, of which Africans enslaved in Brazil had retained only a small portion. The women stopped first in Sierra Leone then traveled to Nigeria where they stayed for a long time studying, updating, polishing, and re-articulating traditional Yoruba religion. These women returned to Brazil, where their mere presence and teachings spread like wildfire and Africanized millions of non-Africans throughout much of Latin America. This was an amazing development, since proselytizing is not done in African religion.

The Lagosian Cultural Renaissance was responsible for endorsing African racial purity and causing Yoruba religion to become a world religion from the 1890s forward. This international movement involved Continental Africans as well as people of African descent from all over the Caribbean and Latin America. They canonized an emergent internationally inspired Yoruba culture and articulated an updated version of the religion that made Yoruba culture the exemplar of African racial dignity and religious knowledge worldwide.

The region of Bahia is where the knowledge and practice of African religion and culture has been preserved ever since in Brazil. Over the years, Brazilians from the Bahia region have continued the tradition of ongoing study. They travel annually to the *Holy City of Ile-Ife* in Nigeria to gain more knowledge under the tutelage of traditional high priests in the religion of Ifa. They do this every year in order to return home to Bahia with higher levels of religious knowledge to offer their initiates.

African religion does not proselytize like the Christianity and Islam. If you do not seek it, it is not offered or discussed. Even when someone asks for it, an African priest or priestess studies someone a long time before taking the person on as an initiate. In Brazil and the rest of the Caribbean, Latin Americans apparently found something in African religion so marvelous and of such a high level of spirituality and knowledge that they adopted it as a religion and way of life for all time. The strength of the religion was such that Latin Americans carried it right up into the Catholic Church, where over time the Church was forced to accept it. Latin American Catholicism will never be the same as a result of the African religious influence.

Among all the African ethnic groups brought into the western world during the slave trade, it is the religion of *Ifa* held by the Yoruba people that has been preserved and practiced more than others. To date, *Ifism* is practiced throughout the African Diaspora: the U.S.A., Haiti, Jamaica, Brazil, Cuba, Puerto Rico, Belize, Mexico, and other locations that are a part of the *African Diaspora* (locations throughout the western hemisphere that now have African populations). The original Yoruba names for Almighty God and the Divinities have remained unchanged in the Western hemisphere for more than 400 years. The Yoruba language, religious traditions, songs, and incantations have also been preserved intact.

The name for the Yoruba religion has changed in different locations throughout the African Diaspora, however, along with the syncretization of

Ifism with Catholicism. Afro-Latin and Caribbean peoples found it convenient to use the Catholic religion to mask their continued participation in African religion. The convenience factor resides in the fact that the Catholic theological structure is almost identical to that of tradition African religion. Thus, names of Yoruba deities were randomly exchanged with names of Catholic saints right under the noses of the priests without their having a clue as to what was going on until it was too late. Some of the most outstanding, convincing demonstrations of the retention of Yoruba religion by New World Africans are found in Haiti with the religion of *Vodoun*; in Brazil with *Candomble*; and in Cuba with *Santeria*. Afro-Cubans in particular retained all forms of the Yoruba divination system. In the U.S.A. African Americans practice either Yoruba *Ifism* proper, or *Santeria*. *Ifism,* or the religion of *Ifa* is the authentic Yoruba religion that has continued since ancient times.

Yoruba oral and written histories claim a noble ancestry and a great civilization that began about 10,000 years ago. Their legends speak of brilliant scholars, mathematicians, and scientists; noble leaders; powerful generals; visionary priests; and gifted artisans. Their poems and myths reveal a proud people with intelligent, gifted rulers who skillfully developed marvelous, progressive kingdoms. Based upon this rich history and cultural foundation, it is certainly appropriate to choose Yoruba cultural values as guidelines for African American personal development, mental health, and survival. These ideals are not unique with the Yoruba: they are common features throughout

Africa. However, it is the availability of historical and cultural records that allow Yoruba to be traced back to ancient times, more than the recorded events of all the other groups brought into the Diaspora.

Today, the religious beliefs, philosophy, culture, and values of those ancient African Ancestors continue to exist throughout all of Africa. Amazingly, some remnants of these cultural elements have been maintained by elderly African Americans. These cultural elements and social traditions form the foundation of what makes Africans feel like whole persons. Within these elements reside the means for upliftment, survival, and advancement. The memoirs and narratives of our enslaved African foremothers and forefathers are an enduring testament to the powerful intellect, survival skills, and strategies residing within indigenous African religious beliefs, values, and culture. These elements were survival tool kits that no one could take away; however, we gave them away in the 1960s.

The next chapter introduces some of the cultural values, moral concepts, philosophical principles, and liberal arts mastery that have been taught among the Yoruba and other African groups since ancient times. These principles form the fundamental basis of individual character development necessary for someone to be considered a positive member of society.

11. YORUBA MORAL CONCEPTS AND PHILOSOPHY FOR CHARACTER DEVELOPMENT

*Follow the customs of good conduct
or flee the country.*
--Yoruba proverb

Components of Good Character

Idowu (1994:157) lists and provides a detailed discussion of several components used by Yoruba to determine recognizable demonstrations of good character. He also quotes passages from the Yoruba literary corpus to provide examples of each component. A brief list of those components is as follows:

> ➤ *Female chastity before and after marriage*. It is also forbidden for a man to seduce another man's wife, on pain of paying a heavy penalty and having to face grievous consequences.

> ➤ *Hospitality, particularly toward strangers.* It is right to be hospitable because you can never tell when you yourself might be in need of hospitality. In the old days when food for sale was left by roadsides, a hungry traveler who had no money was permitted to partake

freely of the fruits or yams of a farm, provided he ate what was taken on the spot.

- *Opposition to selfishness.* The selfish person is held in contempt and regarded as not deserving of any help in time of difficulty.

- *Kindness involving generosity.* This is a great virtue because kind people have the unfailing blessing of Olodumare (Almighty God) and of men always.

- *Condemnation of wickedness.* The law of retributive justice operates in such a way as to return the reward of wickedness, not only upon the wicked, but also upon his offspring.

- *Truth and rectitude/uprightness.* The truthful and upright have the unfailing support and blessing of the divinities, while lying and falsehood are considered damnable.

- *Forbiddance of stealing.* In the old days, thieves were pilloried and then killed. Today the people who witness someone stealing will give a shout so that others nearby may join in chasing down the thief to beat him until the police mercifully arrive. Another practice in the old days was to leave articles of food for sale at cross-roads or by roadsides without anyone to watch them. Any traveler who wanted some of the food took what he wanted and left the payment on the stall. Neither the food nor money was stolen.

- ➤ **Condemnation of falsehood and covenant-breaking.** In the old days the lips of liars were removed and the person would be settled in a quarter of society by themselves. Such persons were employed as state executioners.

- ➤ **Reproof of hypocrisy.** A hypocrite is called "One who moves in zigzags" such that his or her character is unpredictable.

- ➤ **Protection of women.** It is the responsibility of Yoruba men to give protection to the women. When men and women walk together, the woman is allowed to go in front and the man walks behind to defend her in case of sudden danger. It is mean and immoral to outrage a defenseless woman.

- ➤ **Honor and due respect to old age.** This is the duty of every Yoruba person. The young must respect the elder because of their seniority as well as because of their riper and richer experience from which the young should profit. Youth are reminded that whenever a young person has a need or gets into trouble, it is an elder who comes to the rescue.

Dopamu and Alana (2004:155-171) present a similar list of components for good character in their discussion of Yoruba ethical systems. They also cite passages from the Yoruba literary corpus to exemplify each passage on morality, ethics, and the development of good character that need not be repeated here.

Central Importance of Iwapele

It is impossible to enter any discussion of Yoruba concepts of morality without first pointing out the central importance of the term *iwapele*. The term is extremely complex, such that its definition and role in Yoruba society and belief system introduce several other concepts. Dopamu and Alana (2004:155-171) argue that the Yoruba religion has applications for the contemporary world:

> The Yoruba concept of *Iwa* (character) has a universal application... The sum total of this is that anyone that has *Iwa* (Character) will always think of good actions that will be of benefit not only to himself/herself but also to the society and members of the society to which he/she belongs.

Wande Abimbola's (1975) massive work entitled *"Yoruba Oral Tradition: Poetry in Music, Dance and Drama"* provides insight to the principle of *Iwapele* as a social ideal by focusing on its two interpretations. I borrowed from his work extensively in my doctoral dissertation, *The Study of African American Sermonics and Protest Rhetoric in Relation to the Yoruba Concepts of **Oro** (Hoo-ro) and **Iwa** (1993)*. According to Abimbola, the original lexical meaning can be interpreted as "the fact of being, living, or existing." He explains that the term can mean either "existence" or "character." Rowland Abiodun's (1987:67) article "African Art Studies: The State of the Discipline," explains that "the noun *iwa* is formed by adding the prefix *i* to the verb *wa* (to exist, to be)." The idiomatic meaning of *Iwa* brings in the concept of *Iwa-pele* as good character.

One can also refer to ***Iwa buburu*** as "bad character." Then there is *Iwa-lile* which literally means "hard character." It refers to a person who is difficult and uncompromising. This is explained further by Idowu (1994:156) who borrows from the Yoruba literary corpus to discuss a character named Aniwonikun. The name literally means *He who has gall or malignancy in his bowels.*

> The bad people, people of evil character, are they who fear needlessly, and it is their sin that causes them needless fear. One of the stories told to inculcate this lesson is that Aniwonikun, who was a person given to incessant but needless fear, all in consequence of a bad conscience:
>
> > *Leave him alone, let him run:*
> > *It is their character that chases them about.*
> > *So declares the oracle about Aniqonikun*
> > *Who fears incessantly day and night;*
> > *Will you but practice good character,*
> > *Will you but practice sound character,*
> > *Aniwonikun, and stop running about like a coward.*

Thus, *Iwapele* refers to moral behavior and good character. These two separate interpretations or meanings ("existence" and "character") merge, in that the latter represents the "essence of being" and one of the very fundamental aims of existence, especially within the context of harmonious social relations. With this same understanding that *Iwapele* incorporates meanings of both existence and character, Abimbola (1975:395) goes a step further by locating *Iwapele* within both social and spiritual contexts:

> The man who has *iwapele* (his emphasis) will not collide with any of the powers both human and supernatural and will therefore live in complete harmony with the forces that govern the universe.
>
> This is why the Yoruba regard *iwapele* as the most important of all moral values, and the greatest attribute of any man. The essence of religious worship for the Yoruba consists therefore in striving to cultivate *iwapele*. This is the meaning of the saying: *Iwa lesin*. (Iwa is another name for religious devotion).

Abimbola uses the above passage to demonstrate the extent to which the Yoruba consider *Iwa* as the correct way of representing oneself to others. In this regard, several additional attributes contribute to the concept of good character. He posits that "the importance placed on the principle of *Iwa* by the Yoruba shows that African traditional religions are based on deep moral values which sustain the beliefs of the adherents of those religions." By analyzing Yoruba mythology concerning *Iwa* and the many attending concepts, we can begin to recognize and understand the depth and complexity of the Yoruba belief system and traditional philosophy.

Abiodun (1987:67-68) further adds to our understanding of the two interpretations of *Iwa* (existence and character) by presenting a verse from the Yoruba literary corpus. The following passage also possibly demonstrates a strong pride in Africanity expressed by ancient Africans.

> *Orisanla d'aro meta*
> *O da kan ni dudu*
> *Od kan ni pupa*
> *O da kan ni funfun.*
> *Dudu ni o re mi*
> *O o gbodo re mi ni pupa.*
> *Dudu ni o re mi,*
> *O o gbodo re me ni funfun.*
> *Iwa mi ni o ko tete re*
> *Ni Kutukutu Obarisa.*
>   (Akinbiyi Akiwowo, pers. com., 1976.

> Orisanla prepared three dyes.
> He made one black,
> He made one red,
> He made one white.
> Make me black,
> Do not make me red.
> Make me black,
> Do not make me white.
> Dye me with my iwa first
> At the dawn of creation.

Abiodun's (1987:68) interpretation of this verse explains that these colors express both human existence as well as qualities. His explanation also provides insight into complexity of ancient Ancestors' sense of self-identity that suggests they viewed African culture and "blackness" as being intricately intertwined with high moral character in human existence and society. Of the three colors mentioned, black represents *Iwa* as both existence and character.

"Dye me with my iwa first" means "First give me existence" or "First create my being." The "black," "red," and "white" dyes represent the various possibilities of "character" that the individual can be endowed with at creation.

Also in this verse, we note that Orisanla, the creator-divinity does the "dying" (that is, the imbuing) with iwa (meaning either "being" or "character"). But most important, his work or product is above reproach in traditional Yoruba thought….

Abiodun (1975:73) adds further complexity to the concept of Iwa by explaining that "the integral relationship between *Iwa* (character) and *ewa* (beauty) derives from a Yoruba aphorism that declares *Iwa l' ewa*, that is 'Iwa is beauty.'" No matter the extent of a person's physical attractiveness, if devoid of *Iwa*, an individual is compared in physical likeness to a piece of wood found lying in the forest. This usage of *Iwa* pertains less to the superficial physical appearance of human beings and things and more to their deep essence in Yoruba culture and metaphysics. One can note the close linguistic affinity between the two terms and the inter-relatedness of the two interpretations.

Idowu (1994:154) brings in the communal aspect of determining which individuals represent the beauty of Iwa. Yoruba are highly spiritual people and morality is the very fruit of the religion. However, the humanistic approach to morality establishes members of the community as the *first* arbiters of who can be considered as a moral "person" fit for society. Individuals with bad character are shunned and kept out of certain social circles and activities. It is on a higher spiritual plane of existence that God as *final, ultimate* arbiter of human character is considered.

> To the Yoruba, man's character is of supreme importance and it is this which Olodumare judges. Thus the demands which Olodumare lays upon man are purely ethical. Man's well-being here on earth depends upon his character; his place in the After-Life is determined by Olodumare according to his deserts. Olodumare is the "Searcher of Hearts" Who sees and knows everything and whose judgment is sure and absolutely inescapable.

There are two attending concepts that are also intertwined and blended with *Iwa*, such that the three are viewed as inseparable. They are **ashe** and **itutu**. Ashe represents the power to make things happen by the force of **Nommo**, the spoken word. *Ashe* manifests authoritatively in prophecy and predictive grace. Thompson (1984:5-16) informs that *itutu* is mystic coolness, a psychological and spiritual quality that imparts a gentleness and generosity of character. *Itutu* enriches the sense of certainty conferred by the blending of *Iwa* and *ashe*. It does so through the human capacity for sagacity; intelligence, wisdom, fair-mindedness, and mental balance demonstrated through the exercise of good judgment and sobriety. According to Thompson, *Itutu* imparts a level-headedness that is expected to increase with age as one gains breadth and depth of life experiences.

The Fourteen Principles

Fourteen principles within the body of Yoruba philosophy are held to be of utmost importance in human development from childhood to what I refer to as "godhood" in African terms. All of the following terms are connected with the concept of *Iwa*. The first seven listed below are explained by Abimbola (1975:393-394).

1. Iwapele represents good character and moral behavior. Inner or spiritual beauty is an indication of good character. Practice and development of moral behavior form the foundation for inner beauty and spirituality. This principle shines forth as the manifest light of the Divine. Good character is prized by the Yoruba more than anything else in life because without it you will lose everything: home, wealth, loving spouse, good friends, respect, children, etc.

2. Suuru means patience. A person of good character must also have patience in order to consider things well and arrive at a just and honest solution (Abimbola, 1984:415). Patience is grounded in religious faith and an understanding of universal laws, cycles and principles. The fact that all things change over time is one of the immutable Universal Laws. Whatever situation exists today is guaranteed to be reversed some time in the future. However, it is critical that one's integrity remains constant despite these cyclical life experiences. This positive, philosophical outlook is the reason why it is difficult to drive African people to such despair that they commit suicide. Africans understand that if life continues, circumstances will change for the better.

3. Otito represents truth or truthfulness. Truthfulness is a quality that promotes trust and confidence. These qualities in turn support social bonding between individuals. This principle represents a spiritually inspired motivation toward honesty with oneself and with others. Traditional African culture frowns upon liars. There is a proverb which states that "*every liar is a murderer.*" Elders who understand human nature teach that a habitual liar will one day steal. If it is successful the first few times, stealing becomes habitual. A habitual thief will eventually break and enter people's homes. It is guaranteed that one day the thief will kill the owner in an attempt to escape. In other words, one thing leads to another.

4. Inurere literally means having a healthy mind or goodwill toward others. Extending a positive attitude toward others follows the *Golden Rule* of treating others as one wishes to be treated. This openness and sense of fairness embraces others within a circle of redeeming goodwill. This principle promotes good health and healing for individuals and relationships. It is proven that healthy thoughts and healthy relationships promote health and wellbeing in individuals.

5. Ikonimora means having a warm attitude toward others. This is interpreted as gentleness, kindness, generosity, and caring about others. If it is not contained within oneself, it cannot successfully be extended toward others. Practice of this principle has a stabilizing effect upon society because its members voluntarily take responsibility for each others needs in a communal atmosphere of concern and sharing. This quality offers tolerance and redeeming goodwill even to individuals who oppose you. A lifelong habit of kindness toward others guarantees that someone will help you when in need. Your own good works in life are like putting aside money in a savings account. There will always be something there from which you can draw. This principle is connected with the Universal Circle of human existence. The positive or negative energies and circumstances that we create for others are turned back upon ourselves. In other words, our acts circle back around to us fourfold at some future time.

6. Ife represents love. A love for others begins with love for oneself then extends outward. It requires a positive self-image, self-acceptance, and self-esteem, irrespective of your personal shortcomings and imperfections. Love and acceptance of others in spite of their flaws is an outgrowth of self-love, self-regard, and self-acceptance. Knowledge of yourself, your people, your culture, and your total history provides necessary elements for loving and accepting yourself, even in the midst of cultural and political oppression.

7. Ibowafagba refers to respect for elders. This is considered to be a central quality for a happy, prosperous life. Children are never equal with parents. Whenever young people have a serious problem it requires an elder to help resolve it. Elders provide an entire world into which babies are born. They make sacrifices for the young. Many elders devote their lives that others may live. Therefore, they deserve respect. Respect for elders results from understanding the spiritual significance of hierarchical structures of the universe. Even badly flawed mothers should be respected because they allowed their children to enter the world through them at a time when they were unprepared or unable to mother them properly. Respect is another quality that begins from within. Self-respect flows from a life of demonstrated ethical and moral responsibility. An attitude of disrespect toward others is a signal that an individual lacks respect for self.

8. Itutu expresses having a mystic coolness, self-discipline. This is the way in which a person of character represents herself or himself to another person. Self-control, self-confidence, character, good-will, generosity, and patience make up *mystic coolness.* Someone who hides negative attitudes behind a calm veneer cannot claim *Itutu* because the nature of such a person's heart is hot at all times, and not cool. Thus, *mystic coolness* goes far beyond superficial postures of looking and acting cool while secretly holding hot, angry, negative thoughts toward others. Generosity is a vital component of *coolness.*

The act of giving to others is considered an embodiment of good-will, character, and composure. *Mystic coolness* also represents an internal quality that demonstrates long-term personal development as well as an enduring commitment to and involvement with community. It represents a positive outlook on life, an awareness of the responsibility to use one's mystic powers for good, for positive interpretations of experience, and for an expectation of positive future outcomes. This principle also involves how you present yourself in public. If your outward appearance is untidy, unattractive, and antisocial, it cannot be cool for the very reason that your heart is made hot with the very knowledge that your presentation is offensive. *Mystic coolness* also requires patience. Impatience and always being in a hurry to do things at the risk of not doing them well indicates a lack of maturity, intellectual focus, and self-discipline

9. Ashe is the power to make things happen. Human beings have the ability to create through the spoken word. Personal and spiritual growth are essential qualities because individuals with highly developed character are able to speak positive things into existence. The power of *ashe* is expected to increase with age, but that is only possible if an individual leads a life of moral thoughts and ethical behavior.

10. Ifarabale: Abiodun (1987:77) explains that *ifarabale* is another concept connected to *Iwa* that literally means "calming or controlling the body; letting reason rather than emotion control; not losing one's composure. Abiodun (1987:78) presents Yoruba proverbs that exemplify the value that Yoruba place on calculated patience in achieving a set goal: *Alagbara ma mero baba ole,* means "A thoughtless strong man is worse than a lazy man";

Asuretete ko roye je, aringbere ni I moyee dele, "He who walks slowly [acts intelligently] will bring the title home, while he who runs [acts recklessly] misses the chance of enjoying a title."

An attending assumption within ifarabale is the important role played by *ori*. In *ifarabele, ori* (the head) rules the rest of the body. Emphasis on the head addresses the high premium that Yoruba place on intelligent action. *Ori* has at least three interpretations: the head as the seat of reason; the inner head; and the spiritual head or Destiny. Yoruba people venerate the *ori-inu* or "inner head," viewed as a personal spirit that guides an individual's destiny.

Abiodun (1975:77) says that Ifarabale is a prerequisite to the successful expression of *oju-inu*, which means "inner eye" or insight, a special kind of understanding of a person, thing, or situation, and is not usually derived from an obvious source. If a person is "hot-headed," and given to acting out emotionally without forethought, that individual will not develop the wisdom and insight that can only come from the practice of emotional control.

11. Aduro gangan represents straightness and stability. This type of straightness represents straightforwardness and honesty. It symbolizes the upright, vertical position that aligns human beings with the Divine Forces of the universe, such that individuals can receive Divine Guidance. Alignment includes an attitude of submission to a Higher Power. Note the fact that for an African woman to straighten her back is a sure signal that she is ready to take action on a situation, especially when dealing with a child's unruly behavior. If the back straightening is accompanied by direct, unblinking eye contact and a pointed finger, children recognize that this means trouble.

12. ***Imoju-mora*** has several general translations, according to Abiodun (1987:80-83): (a) sensitivity to the need of the moment; (b) ability to adapt and change without being formally told to do so; (c) propriety; and (d) measure. He explains that the manifestation of *imoju-mora* can occur only after all the other qualities of *iwapele* are called into play. One who demonstrates this quality is said to possess ***ori-pipe***, which literally translates ad "complete head." This means that such a person possesses an intelligent and creative mind with which to patiently and accurately judge the extent of positive action or creative innovation possible while appropriately remaining within the parameters of tradition.

Thus, *imoju-mora* is a quality of alertness and perhaps spiritual readiness, meaning that one is spiritually ready to make moral decisions and to perform ethical acts when called by Destiny to participate in life's events. In this case it can mean the constant, inspired motivation to be an instrument for the greater good of society. In a sense this principle includes what I refer to as "historical mindedness." That is, you never know when life will call for you to step into history by performing an act or service, however important or insignificant it might seem at the moment.

13. *Irele* deals with humility and respect. One should have respectful humility in the presence of those with higher status. *Irele* represents a belief that the spiritual and physical universes have hierarchical structures. The term also implies a submission of self to Higher Powers that rule human existence and all of life. The principle does not include a submission to individuals and social structures that practice immorality, injustice, and brutality. In this instance the Divine Mandate is to oppose such individuals and social structures.

14. *Oju-inu* deals with divine vision as well as insight. This principle represents someone with wisdom who is able to "see" or predict future outcomes of present activities. Development of *oju-inu* is possible by gaining knowledge, wisdom, and understanding through a life of faith and emotional control, and behavioral discipline. The primary reason that elders are highly respected is because their knowledge, wisdom, and understanding combine with their spiritual gifts, allowing them to "see" and understand more than others. A proverb states that "an elder can see more lying down on the ground than a young person can see while up in a tree."

The Seven Virtues

The Virtues discussed below are taught to African children as guides for their development into maturity. The term "virtue" refers to the excellent qualities of an individual's character that are so highly developed that it is almost perceived as a tangible, potent force or energy field that involuntarily emanates from the person. The teachings themselves are very ancient, reaching back in time to the African Mystery Schools of Kush/Sudan, Nubia/Ethiopia, and Kemet/Egypt. Some of the Virtues below repeat concepts that are presented in the Yoruba Principles. This indicates that ideas in the teachings are pervasive features of African culture, expressed differently from one ethnic group to another.

1. Control of thoughts is the first step in personality development and maturation. Thoughts become attitudes, and attitudes influence behavior. Children do not understand the full nature of consequences. In African culture even thoughts are things that can be manifested in our reality and hurt others. We know that wherever the head is, the body will follow with action. Therefore, it is necessary that parents and others teach the young to control their thoughts. Spiritually, this requires placing one's heart and mind under the control of Divine Forces.

2. Control of actions is a result of self-control over one's thoughts. *Control of actions* represents self-discipline and self-control. Individual self-control can be achieved, but the control of others is not possible. Once this is understood, gentleness and tolerance can develop. Social order and peace are considered as both essential and sacred elements. A society can have neither social order nor peace when uncontrolled individuals are running around disturbing everyone.

3. Fortitude, Steadfastness of purpose means having the inner strength and the focus to complete projects and ventures once they are started. It also involves the strength and determination to be an instrument for creative goodness from beginning to end, despite powerful appeals not to carry through with worthwhile ventures and missions. Commitment to creative goodness is the most important project in an individual's life because it supports development from a physical animal existence to that of a spiritual human entity with knowledge, wisdom, and understanding through diligence.

4. Temperance and Identity with spiritual life and higher ideals signal a conscious willingness to behave in harmony with the Divine Rhythms of the Universe under the spiritual guidance of Divine Forces within human communities. In this instance, the community is probably the most important element, because human beings are social beings. Survival is not possible without the support of one's community. Therefore, the qualities of temperance and high ideals are important factors that promote a sense of wellbeing and calmness in oneself and others.

5. Evidence of having a mission in life is a long-term process and a demonstration that one has a higher purpose in life. It includes a commitment to family and community. A person with a sense of mission has a strong sense of identity, history and place in life. Such a person envisions a lifetime of contributions for the common good of family, community, and humanity in general. A strong sense of mission makes minor setbacks in life seem insignificant because painful experiences are interpreted as learning opportunities. Yoruba believe that an individual's mission is selected by the person while still in Heaven prior to being conceived in the mother's womb. Ideally, each mission is selected specifically because of the lessons that the particular soul feels a need to learn. Amusing stories abound, however, about people who chose their destinies in a hasty or haphazard manner.

6. Freedom from resentment when wronged or persecuted means not being enslaved by one's own emotional impulses and long-term resentments. There is a belief that all situations occur for a Divine Purpose, irrespective of whether they are positive or negative. When negative experiences are viewed from this perspective they transform into opportunities for personal and spiritual development. This approach to life allows an aggrieved person to take charge of a situation. Choosing not to respond in kind to the angry, mean-spirited, destructive acts of others frees one from their control and manipulation. Holding on to painful memories of past wrongful acts by others long after gaining freedom from such persons' influence becomes an exercise in self-punishment. Thus, letting go of resentments is self-liberating. It is important to understand that this moral principle deals with self-discipline. It does not mean that one should submit to abuse of any kind, nor does it translate as a belief that suffering is a necessary component for character development and spiritual growth.

A deep spiritual aspect of this virtue lies in the Yoruba belief that an individual chooses her/his own Divine Destiny or "Head" before leaving Heaven to be conceived and reborn on earth. Every important aspect of one's birth situation and life is chosen as a means for one's soul to learn particular lessons and to accomplish certain goals while on earth. Therefore, there is no reason to harbor resentments toward negative persons and oppositional situations that were designed as tests for spiritual advancement. When faced with adversity this approach to life causes individuals to simply pause, assess the situation from various perspectives, and take control of the phenomena. This process always leads to self-empowerment, an increase in religious faith, and a discovery of hidden meanings in life.

7. Fidelity, Confidence in one's ability to learn and to do represents a belief that one can master advanced skills, higher education, knowledge, wisdom, and understanding that serve to enrich one's existence. Faith in one's own ability to progress in life is critical for self-development. Awareness of having a Divine Mission in life provides a strong sense of purpose, direction and motivation while striving for educational and personal advancement.

The Seven Liberal Arts
The Liberal Arts involve intellectual development, the acquisition of knowledge, education, and community activism. In addition to mastering the *Fourteen Principles* and the *Seven Virtues*, individuals have the added responsibility of becoming educated in the *Seven Liberal Arts*.

Development of these intellectual skills is accompanied by a responsibility to engage in uplifting and problem-solving community activities. Someone who is highly skilled in the *Liberal Arts* has the potential and the responsibility to be a living witness of Divine Transformative Power in the lives of human beings and in human societies. Therefore, you are expected to share knowledge, skills, and anecdotes of past victories over adversity.

1. Grammar. Mastery of the standardized grammatical structure and system of rules in language is necessary if one is to gain recognition and credibility. Every language has rules, even Creole languages like Ebonics (Black English). It is necessary for African Americans to be flexible, multi-dialectical code-switchers. Knowledge of Standard English and standard Ebonics provides such flexibility and proficiency in academics, business, and the community. The same advice applies to other languages, as well.

2. Oratory. The ability to move human emotions with the power of the spoken word is the highest art form in African culture because it involves the mystical power of human *Ashe.* Spoken words have the power to bring things into existence. Words are able to change human hearts, human societies, and the human condition. They have the mysterious ability to heal and to harm, to create as well as destroy. Words can set social events and circumstances in motion when spoken. Lofty oratory has the power to spiritually motivate human beings to achieve great feats that become recorded in history and legends. Orators must always speak with a high level of maturity, responsibility, morality and ethics because the Divine Law of the Circle returns to us fourfold whatever healing or harm that we send out through our words.

3. Logic and Philosophy. These arts create wisdom that can transform one into a living witness to the scientific, analytical, intellectual capacities that have been gifted to human beings. Studies in logic develop mastery in the process and principles of deductive reasoning and objective thought that provide clarity and understanding. Philosophy speculates on the existence of God, the creation of the world, human destiny, the place of human beings in the universe, the human condition, the causes, laws, and principles of the universe that govern material and spiritual realities. Logic and philosophy further question the meaning and nature of God, Spirit, the universe, nature, life, and human qualities.

A student of general philosophy has the benefit of being able to study people, life, and situations from various objective perspectives. Development of this knowledge requires a great deal of maturity, discipline and practice. Knowledge and practice of the philosophical approach in one's life enhances an individual's ability to appreciate and respect people who are from different backgrounds, cultures and religions. Philosophy helps to remove imagined, unwarranted fears and apprehensions related to the unknown aspects of human existence and the universe.

4. Geometry. This branch of mathematics deals with the properties, measurement, and relationships of points, lines, angles, surfaces, and solids. Geometry gives an individual knowledge of transcendental space. It further develops skills in inductive methods that give insight into problems of physical space. Geometry defines, compares, and measures squares, triangles, circles, cubes, cones, spheres, etc. In some instances geometric designs carry symbolic messages, as found in crop circles and the mathematic fractals of African and Native American artistic designs. Since ancient times African people have believed in the sacred nature of symbols such as the circle, the square, the triangle, and the cross. Scientists studying the Pyramids in Egypt discovered that the "foot" as a unit of measure first appeared in Africa, used by Egyptians as a secret construction unit. The "foot" was adopted by Europeans thousands of years later.

5. Arithmetic. Knowledge of mathematics, transcendental space, computations, and numerical problem solving develops mastery in the world of commerce and everyday living. Mathematics is used to learn about the physical world because mathematical principles are the foundation upon which all of Creation exists. Physical nature and natural processes throughout the universe become more understandable when they are expressed mathematically in terms of measurable properties, i.e. shape, quantity, and form.

It is impossible to understand scientific realities and the structure of our physical universe without having a fundamental grasp of arithmetic.

For example, scientists have known for some time that the same patterns are reproduced in accordance with what is referred to as the mathematical "golden ratio" in all levels of the cosmos. In other words, all matter throughout the universe is constructed in accordance with the same mathematical formula, from the largest scale of universe-level macrocosm down to the smallest sub-atomic particle and metaphysical-level microcosm.

Ancient Africans were highly skilled mathematicians. Study of the complexity of Egyptian pyramids at Giza reveals that several mathematical designs of the structures coordinate with time, speed, and distance of the motions of the earth, sun, and moon against the zodiac. The three pyramids also perfectly replicate the star system called "Orion's Belt." Therefore, the designers of the Giza complex of pyramids clearly were masters of astronomical mathematics thousands of years before this knowledge appeared historically.

6. Astronomy. Study of the planets and other celestial bodies and calculation of their dimensions, distribution, motion, composition, and evolution provides greater understanding of the size, structure and nature of the universe in which we are a part. It further allows for an accurate conception concerning earth in relation to the other planets and the place of human beings in the universe. The study of the heavens was a necessary precondition for the development of science. It is said that African women who are initiated into the university system of traditional culture are so highly trained in astronomy that they are knowledgeable of how the various planets effect discrete functions of the human body.

7. *Music, Drumming.* On one level these arts involve the organization of rhythms, harmony, and melody. On the other, they strongly emphasize social and spiritual harmony. Harmony is the central concept of music, involving the pleasing combination and interaction of several parts of a whole. Music creates harmony among members of society and between workers and their labors. Drumming and music form a bridge between visible and invisible realms, as well as lower and higher realms of existence. They further link visible instruments with invisible voices and intentions. Drumming and music bridge the visible material world of human beings with the invisible spiritual worlds of the Creator, the Divine Forces, and the Ancestors.

The three sets of integrated principles outlined above are key factors in spiritual growth and personal development. They are the essential sources and the deep wellspring of right thinking, right conduct, empowerment, and leadership in African culture. It is important to remember that self-discipline, knowledge and intellectual mastery always result from practice. An individual can be born with certain gifts, but mastery is gained by years of tutoring and practice.

12. DEVELOPMENT FROM CHILDHOOD TO GODHOOD

Everybody loves a fool,
But nobody wants one for a son or daughter.
--West African proverb

Traditionally, Yoruba people expect individuals to pursue personal and spiritual growth from the earliest stage of childhood to that of *godhood*. This expectation stems from their belief that Almighty God bestowed upon human beings the power of *ashe*: the mystical *power-to-make-things-happen*. It literally means: "So be it;" "It may happen;" or "It must happen." This term especially applies to the mystical power of the spoken word with its ability to *speak- things-into-existence*. Yoruba view *ashe* as a morally neutral complex of powers that has the ability to give and to take away, to heal and to kill, according to the purpose and the nature of the person speaking.

Ashe is considered to be divine force incarnate. Persons of high social status possess the greatest endowments of this power, beginning with the king. The king or queen is said to be the second of the gods. The spoken words of master priestesses and priests, the diviners, the most important chiefs, and the powerful elderly women have the capability of invoking spiritual beings and predicting future events. Belief that human beings possess this potentially dangerous mystical power is the basis of the importance Yoruba people place upon **good character and moral behavior**. Each stage of development outlined below is expressed in Diasporan terms in order to increase understanding. The information describes the process of spiritual development within a traditional African humanistic system of morality and ethics.

Mbiti (1969:206) discusses this humanistic aspect of morality that exists within the African spiritual worldview:

> "Most African peoples accept or acknowledge God as the final guardian of law and order and of the moral and ethical codes. Therefore the breaking of such order, whether by the individual or by a group, is ultimately an offence by the corporate body of society. For example, before the Gikuyu sacrifice and pray for rain, they first enquire from a diviner or seer why God has allowed such a long drought to come upon them.

Mbiti (1969:214) argues that African morality represents "dynamic ethics" rather than "static ethics" as found in the organized religions, because "dynamic ethics" define what a person *does* rather than what he *is*. In this sense "the essence of African morality is that it is more 'societary' than 'spiritual'; it is a morality of 'conduct' rather than a morality of 'being'." Thus, the traditional African outlook does not perceive a need for God to make a ruling on wrongful or evil acts. According to (Gyekye, 1987:135-138), people use their own intellect, insight and understanding of the moral issues involved when making judgments. Moral "goodness," moral discipline and ethical behavior are human expectations that support and promote social welfare and wellbeing, social harmony, and social cohesion. Individuals are morally good if their actions and behaviors are in the interest of society's common good. Thus, someone's "goodness" is decreed by people in the community where the person lives, and not by some supernatural being. It takes the people in the community to say that someone or something is good. This social dynamic is one whereby each individual exists within a reciprocal relationship with the community where expectations of moral behavior, responsibility, and support are the norm.

The above discussion provides insight into the traditional African concept and definition of good character and moral behavior. Although Africans strongly believe in the reality of Spirit and view Almighty God as the final and supreme arbiter, the traditional outlook is intensely humanistic. Any discussion or reflection on human morality will be based upon human welfare. Something is not good because God approves of it. Rather, God approves of something because it is good in the first place. Dr. Kwasi Wiredu (1980:6) of Ghana explains that what is morally good is "what befits a human being; it is what is decent for man – what brings dignity, respect, contentment, prosperity, joy, to man and his community. And what is morally bad is what brings misery, misfortune, and disgrace." He argues that:

> this freedom from supernaturalism in our traditional ethic is an aspect of our culture which we ought to cherish and protect from countervailing influences from abroad.

Gyekye's words (1987:42) support my argument in favor of African people worldwide adhering to African philosophical thought and standards of morality:

> My conclusion is that modern African philosophy must not – and cannot – dispense with a full-fledged inquiry into concepts in African traditional philosophy. Such an inquiry would provide an adequate basis for making judgments about African cultural values and their relevance for the contemporary world. Moreover, I believe most of the traditional concepts and values have, generally speaking, not relaxed their grip on modern African life and thought. Thus, a modern African philosophy would comprise the conceptual responses to the problems and circumstances of modern African societies as well as interpretation, criticism, and clarification of concepts in African traditional thought. The latter is necessary in order to provide continuity in philosophical orientation, at any rate in respect of some core philosophical concepts and values.

Wiredu (1980:6) goes farther to reveal the aesthetic connection between moral behavior and beauty: What is good is conceived to be what is fitting (*nea efata*, in Akan); and what is fitting is what is beautiful (nea *eye fe*)." His linguistic information reveals parallels between the Yoruba and the Akan conceptualization of moral character being perceived as a thing of beauty (i.e. *iwa* and *ewa*).

Wrongdoing and evil carry different definitions in African culture. Human beings in African society also determine which category applies, so again it is not left to a supernatural agency. Africans' reference to "ordinary" evil is categorized more in line with wrongdoing when a person commits a social transgression against someone and causes an "ordinary" amount of pain and suffering. However, the higher level of "extraordinary" evil refers to an act so great and so heinous that it brings shame, pain, suffering, disaster, and misfortune to an entire community, such that it brings on the wrath of the supernatural powers. This type of evil is remembered and referred to long after the death of the person who committed it.

The higher order of moral evil often involves taboos, things that the community abominates such as: lying; suicide; cruelty against women; adultery; incest; having sexual intercourse in the bush; rape; accusations of sorcery, magic and witchcraft; murder; stealing things dedicated to the deities or ancestors; having sex with a woman pregnant by another man; disobedience of children etc. These are things that should *never* be done under any circumstances because of the gravity of the consequences within human society, and not because the acts were hateful to any supernatural beings (Gyekye, 1987:135-138; Mbiti, 1969:209). Whether an immoral act is of a high order or a low one, every act of wrongdoing causes pain and harm to someone in the family and the community. It is impossible to develop spiritually if you are in the habit of harming others in any way. Wiredu (1980:6) admonishes that the *community* is the first arbiter of

> what is good behavior and what is bad, what is praiseworthy and what is blameworthy. We are given a choice. To acquire virtue, a person must

practice good deeds so that they become habitual.

Idowu(1994:154) is another Yoruba scholar who turns us again to the centrality of *Iwa* in any discussion of individual character and its conceptual connection with spirituality:

> ...Morality is summed up in Yoruba by the word *Iwa* which can be translated by the English word "Character". Iwa, according to the Yoruba, is the very stuff which makes life a joy because it is pleasing to God. It is therefore stressed that good character must be the dominant feature of a person's life. In fact, it is the one thing which distinguishes a person from a brute. When the Yoruba say of someone. . . "He acts the person", "He behaves as a person should", they mean that he shows in his life and personal relations with others the right qualities of a person. The opposite description is "He is not a person, he merely assumes the skin of a person". That means that the person is socially unworthy; in consequence of his character he is not fit to be called a person, even though he goes about in the semblance of one.

This entire discussion relates to the African spiritual worldview because human beings are comprised of a physical body, a mind with intellectual capacities, and a portion of God's spirit that imparts life, health, wellbeing, and power in accordance with the moral level of your thoughts and your ethical behavior.

Traditional Yoruba expectations for the lifelong process of spiritual development from childhood to godhood are outlined in more modern, Diasporan terms as follows:

BIRTH
➢ No discipline, No independence

CHILDHOOD
➢ Discipline through external controls

PUBERTY
➢ Discipline through external and internal controls

➢ Minimal independence

➢ Increasing family and social expectations

ADULTHOOD
- Discipline through internal controls
- Wisdom, knowledge, and understanding
- Guardian of cultural values, social ideals
- Enforcer of discipline
- Increasing financial independence
- Increasing family and social responsibilities
- Semi-involuntary community service and contributions

ELDERHOOD
- Greater degree of discipline is demonstrated through internal controls
- Higher level of wisdom, knowledge, and understanding demonstrated
- Increasing ability to bring clarity out of confusion
- Ability to remain *cool* in the heat of adversity
- Increasing role as guardian of cultural values, social ideals, discipline, morality and ethics
- Greater financial independence
- Increasing family and social responsibilities
- Voluntary commitment to community service and contributions

WARRIORHOOD*
- All attributes of Elderhood
- Spiritual commitment to the struggle for social justice and harmony
- Spiritual commitment to the resolve social and political issues
- Spiritual commitment to fight, even to die for the group or the Race
- Spiritual commitment to assist the needy

GODHOOD
- All attributes of Warriorhood
- Spiritual capability to transform negative and adverse situations with positive energies
- Power to speak things into existence
- Power to make things happen

13. FROM MIS-EDUCATION TO RE-EDUCATION AND LIBERATION

> *History is a clock people use to tell their historical, cultural, and political time of day. It's a compass that people use to find themselves on the map of human geography. History tells them where they have been, where they are, and what they are. But most importantly, history tells a people where they still must go and what they still must be.*
> --John Henrik Clarke

Miseducation

I am in strong agreement with Carter G. Woodson's (1933:xii) opinion that the educational systems in Europe and America have been "worked out in conformity to the needs of those who have enslaved and oppressed the peoples whom they once colonized. He says that the educational systems perpetuate

> an antiquated process which does not hit the mark even in the case of the needs of the white man himself. If the white man wants to hold on to it, let him do so; but the Negro, so far as he is able, should develop and carry out a program of his own.

We see the truth of Woodson's words in the American government's process of "dumbing down" its students for the past thirty years. There have been attempts to completely do away with the

Department of Education, and funds that should be spent on education are siphoned off to support the U.S. government's "Disaster Capitalism" that is a strategic component of America's addiction to war and its all-out efforts to control the entire world from Earth into outer space.

Even in the process of advocating for Africa-centered education for Africans worldwide, the nagging reality of our situation is that many, if not most Africans who have been educated in European and American school systems are the very ones who will raise the most stringent objections to Africanizing the curriculum. Woodson addressed the problem by saying:

> Negroes who have been so long inconvenienced and denied opportunities for development are naturally afraid of anything that sounds like discrimination. They are anxious to have everything the white man has even it is harmful. The possibility of originality in the Negro, therefore, is discounted one hundred per cent to maintain a nominal equality.

Dr. Asa Hilliard (1997:35) claims that Africans worldwide have become like a computer without a program, a spacecraft without a homing device, a dependent without a benefactor. He states the point succinctly and emphatically:

> There is something dreadfully wrong with an education/socialization process that leaves us ignorant of our past, strangers to our people, apes of our oppressors, and creatures of habitual, shallow thought, and trivial values. Therefore, there must be an independent African effort to

guarantee that our children and our communities develop the perspectives, purposes, skills and the knowledge to function in ways that enhance our survival and development.

I cannot state strongly enough that African survival depends upon reconnecting with the central elements and components of traditional African philosophy so that it once again becomes the very core of everyday life and practice. Dr. Hilliard's (1997:xx) excellent book asks the question "Whether to be African or not to be?" As he says, "Everything else we do flows from this basic point. We are either African or we are nothing; whether we are on the Continent or in the Diaspora."

Paulo Freire (1966) in his book entitled *Pedagogy of the Oppressed,* discusses the need for oppressed peoples to use education as an instrument of liberation and a means for educational revolution. Some people may be put off by the word "revolution" because it brings to mind social strife involved in the process of unshackling and transforming the minds of African peoples. For such persons I need only cite the words of several leaders and scholars who faced the same challenge. Frantz Fanon (1967) wrote "Each generation must, out of relative obscurity, discover its mission, fulfill it, or betray it. Eldridge Cleaver reminds us that "If you are not part of the solution, you are part of the problem." Malcolm X (El Hajj Malik El Shabazz) raises the discussion to another level by bringing in the concept of racial destiny: "A race of people is like an individual man; until it uses its own talent, takes pride in its own history, expresses its own culture, affirms its own selfhood, it can never fulfill itself."

It is my strong belief that races of peoples have a Divine Purpose for being on this earth, similar to individuals. What is the Divine Destiny of African people? Why are the plethora of African philosophers worldwide not pondering and writing on the subject? Perhaps it is because we are so busy studying and aping Caucasians and their culture that we spend no time studying our own.

As a result of our slave mentality and behavior, the wealth of Africa leaves the Continent daily on foreign ships and resides within foreign banks, while the masses to whom the wealth belongs suffer from want. As a result of choosing slavery as our zone of comfort, the wealth of African Americans is squandered daily on meaningless consumer goods that do not support either health or education. Without a deep analysis and understanding of one's own culture, there is no respect for the culture, no vision emanating from it, no sense of cultural purpose, and no way of fathoming the existence of African Destiny. Asa Hilliard (1997:xx) sets forth the problem succinctly:

> Either we see ourselves as members of a family, that is an ethnic family, or we do not. Families nurture, socialize and protect their members. Either the family is structured and stable for power or it is not. Either the family has a vision of the future or it does not. Either the family has standards of value or it does not. Either the family remembers its heritage or it does not. Either we understand our geopolitical position or we do not.

Clearly, a re-education is needed that will help the reconnection and rehabilitation process necessary for healing to begin. I am convinced that this cannot be accomplished in the racist school systems that are controlled by officials and administrators whose duty it is to prevent the liberation of African minds. The reality of the situation is that most Africans are either unwilling or financially unable to form independent schools. Many of the charter schools are run by misguided church officials and members who are part and parcel of the mind-crippling pedagogy and curriculum inherent in the Western educational system. There is no vision, no deep insights, no critical thinking, and no significant intellectual creativity for the good of the community promoted in most of those schools.

Re-Education For and About Women

Now that I have researched African women warriors, I cannot help but testify just a little from the African woman's perspective. When we consider the practice of warriorhood among African women, the phenomenon is far greater and deeper than a mere show of physical strength. We see women who have given birth to society take up arms to protect the lives that they have brought into the world. Traditional African priests and royals understand the spiritual science and the mystical force behind standing shoulder-to-shoulder with their men in times of extreme endangerment of the people. Real, authentic warriorhood is a spiritual development, not just some brutish, mindless love of fighting and killing.

Without hesitation I argue that it is time for the masses of our under-developed African American males to grow up and stop emulating White men, Asian men, and Arabic men because those models of manhood are neither admired nor respected by African women who know that their God-given role in this world is not as a floor-mat. Our men are not fulfilling their roles as protector and provider. At the same time, they feel it is their place to define the role of women. In fact, many have the pimpish idea that women should provide for them. African Americans seek out the foreign theories and practices of male domination that allow them to oppress Black women.

If African men cannot and do not appreciate African women, they are not worthy of life. Only African women walked beside African men on this earth for millions of years when there was no one else but the two of us to populate this planet. Only African women stood by African men throughout history in good times and bad, through joys and sorrows. It is African women who gave you life. We carried you in our wombs, at our breasts, on our laps, and on our backs. Therefore, it is time for African men to demonstrate appreciation for all that African women have done for them out of love.

Perhaps the reason Black males are endangered is because they are not being good stewards of the gift God provided them in Black women. A well-known fact among the spirit-led Grandmothers is that an African male can *never* become a man without an African woman at his side. Now that we know more about the moral fiber and courage that are inherent in African women's DNA, we can understand the saying. African men are the *only* equals to African women, and vice-versa. If an African male's character, courage, morals, ethics, and lifestyle do not meet the high standards set by African women, his shortcomings should not be allowed to genetically weaken the DNA and threaten the survival of her future offspring. Going to women of other races and cultures is a "cop-out" that does nothing but lock a Black man within his own static immature state, whereby no Black woman respects him. What I am setting forth are survival strategies, not empty racist statements. If you believe I am wrong, then explain the deterioration of Black society and the high rate of infant mortality in this country.

Instead of strong, upstanding, respected women, African American men appear to want what the White slavemaster once had: African female sex slaves and prostitutes. A lot of Black women have standards set so low for themselves that are putting up with the boyish foolishness, thereby passing self-destructive ideas and lifestyles on to the next generation. This is why our children are messed up, confused, at risk, and dying faster the elders.

What gives me hope is that there are the sisters who will quote the conventional wisdom of B.B. King: "I'll drink muddy water and sleep in a hollow log" before letting anyone wipe his feet on me. No male is that important, and nothing on his body is that essential. If a man's beauty is not of the authentic, spiritual kind that emanates from inner strength of character, demonstrated in years of positive behavior and community contribution, let him take his cuteness elsewhere. Let the roughnecked females of low character and morals have the pimps, thugs and brutes.

We need to place more emphasis in the development of our girls. African culture is very practical and matter-of-fact on the subject of sex, sexuality, and courtship. Thus, Africans on the Continent are very honest about the nature of males. God placed a brain within the skull of every human being. However, it is in the nature of males to let that part of his anatomy that has no brain do his thinking for him. He will do and say anything to please "little no-brain head." That being the case, when we train our girls to set the highest standards for themselves, we automatically raise the standards of the boys who will do whatever is necessary to please and appease "little no-brain head." This works especially well when the boys know that their entire lives will be examined and judged before they can get close enough to even speak to a girl. When we raise the standards and expectations of our girls, we also elevate the race because women are every child's first teacher.

As a final note on the subject, if African American males refuse to measure up, then it is time for us to marry our nice, respectable daughters (and ourselves) to Continental Africans who know how to protect, provide, and treat them well. The above discussion may easily qualify as a rant, but it is a necessary one for which I do not apologize. *Amen!*

Re-Education in General

Asa Hilliard (1997:70-78) sets forth a chapter on *The Teachings of Ptahhotep* of ancient

Egypt/Kemet, the oldest complete text in human history. The teachings are briefly noted here to bring all the information presented earlier to full circle. Another reason for including these teachings is to show the continuation and consistency of traditional Yoruba philosophical doctrines and moral codes from the time of ancient Egypt until contemporary history. A third reason to present these teachings is to show the ancient African behaviors and expectations required of teachers as well as students.

The opening paragraph of the first lesson is beneficial to both students and teachers.

1. Ptahhotep requires God's permission to teach. Therefore, teaching is a divinely sanctioned spiritual task.

2. Experience is the high qualification.

3. Teaching is for *hearers* (a prepared, ready, receptive, focused student).

4. The teacher teaches "the words of the ones who *listened to the ancestral ways*, and one who *listened* to the Gods" (in a *spiritual and cultural curriculum*, the essential content of education that surpasses mere preparation for a job).

5. One *aim* of the teaching is to eliminate strife from among the people, to bring harmony, to bring order.

6. A second *aim* is so that the two shores, east and west banks of the Hapi (Nile), (metaphorically east and west bank refers to matters of life and death respectively), may *serve God.*

After Ptahhotep is given the Divine Permission to teach, he is told to *selectively* teach only the learner, hearer, listener, to behave in three ways:

1. The learner, hearer, listener is to *become a model* for the children of the great.

2. The learner, hearer, listener is to become obedient.

3. The learner, hearer, listener is to *be devoted* to the teacher.

A third *aim is to cultivate wisdom* because "No one is born wise." Three objectives of education and socialization include:

1. To impart Wisdom.

2. To demonstrate MDW NTR (good or beautiful speech). That is, have mastery, as well as conceptual and metacognitive understanding of the language.

3. To "*speak to posterity,*" meaning to teach the things that will benefit and enlighten those (generations) who follow.

4. To be mindful of the *cosmic obligation* of teachers to future generations.

Ptahhotep instructs teachers, learners and listeners to do the following:

1. Subdue *pride*, which blinds or clouds perception (Preventive).

2. Subdue *arrogance*, which also blinds or clouds perception (Preventive).

3. Aspire to *perfection* (Corrective, Creative).

4. Be open to all (Corrective, Creative).

Ptahhotep next says that a wise man will raise a child who is pleasing to God, just as he himself lives and teaches to please God. *Ptahhotep* also offers preventive and corrective advice on discipline.

1. *Provide for* the hearer/listener.

2. *Love* your "son" (student).

3. *Punish* disobedience.

4. *Punish Isfet* (disorderly or bad speech).

Ptahhotep tells us not to be impulsive. He says that we must study before speaking and speak only when we know something. He also says that our speech should be gentle and non-provocative. Above all, we are admonished to speak *MAAT* (truth). By now you should be able to see parallels in the teachings of Ptahhotep and those of the Yoruba.

1. Be deliberate and thoughtful, reflective.

2. Know first, and then speak.

3. Use non-provocative speech.

4. Speak MAAT (truth).

Ptahhotep provides characteristics that define a wise person. This is important because those who demonstrate wisdom are models toward which learners and listeners strive. According to Ptahhotep, the wise person:

1. Feeds the soul with what endures.

2. Is known by good actions.

3. Her heart and tongue match (so she is not a hypocrite).

4. Lips are straight when speaking (speaks and does MAAT).

5. His eyes are made to see *what will profit the offspring*.

6. Her ears are made to hear *what will profit the offspring*.

7. He acts with MAAT (Truth, Justice, Order, Reciprocity, Balance, and Harmony).

8. She is free of *Isfet* (Falsehood, Disorder, Injustice, Disharmony, Imbalance, Non-reciprocity).

From Ptahhotep's teachings we learn that hearing and listening go together, but are not the same. The student seeks hearing because:

1. Hearing means accurate *perception.*

2. Hearing enters the hearer, meaning that there is a habit of accurate perception. The hearer is an *active listener* (with an attitude that Is open to learning: the prerequisite posture for learning).

3. Hearing well is (a result of) *speaking* well (because the speaker sends a clear message that the student can reiterate correctly).

4. Hearing well is *useful* to the hearer (because the speaker imparts relevant information).

5. Hearing is *best* of all.

6. Hearing is *beloved of God.*

7. Hearing is a matter of *conscience* (heart) (an aptitude for MAAT, a rejection of Isfet).

8. Hearing, when one loves to hear, means that one *acts* on what is heard. *Behavior changes.*

It is very difficult for Africans in the Diaspora to reconstruct much of the West African methods for education and socialization of the young because we have lost the knowledge of the social infrastructures. The life stage and other socialization processes are traditionally conducted in secret. Thus, the initiated "insiders" know what happens, but do not talk about it. "Outsiders" who talk about such things usually do not really know the processes. However, archaeologist Bassey Andah (1988) is a native Nigerian who has had the privilege of studying the socialization process closely in his home country. His outline of these processes are presented to demonstrate just how much socialization and enculturation knowledge Diasporan Africans have lost, making us easy prey for oppressive manipulation.

1. Rites:
   For validation
   For emphasizing stages of development
   For orientation, from ancestor to ancestor

2. Ritual Circumcision
   For sacrifice
   For transformation

3. Initiation Schools (male and female)
   In the holy places
   Ritual dance changes, etc.

4. *Age Grading*
   For bonding
   To teach the value of unity

5. *Family Council (elders)*
   For arbiters, buttresses, and guardians for the young
   For linking and bonding generations
   For group identity
   For mobilizing power

6. *Feasts and Ceremonies*
   For loyalty to the group
   For the acceptable release of tension

7. *Group History and Tradition*
   For unity
   For continuity
   For social stability

8. *Spirituality*
   For theological, cosmological, and philosophical systems
   For elements in day-to-day affairs

Andah notes that his observations are consistent with those of other Africans across the Continent. Hilliard (1997:82) explains that these socialization processes are designed to transform a person from a creature who is consumed with merely satisfying her or his appetites into a spiritual being in the finite likeness of Almighty God. In other words, the human being is expected to develop into a "*spiritual person*" who strives for the final stage of *godhood* as a wise, powerful elder with the power of *ashe*.

Liberation and Survival

The Akans use the term **Sankofa** to symbolize the importance of not abandoning the defining elements of one's beliefs, culture, and humanity. *Sankofa* means "go back and retrieve the valuable thing that you have left behind." The term is symbolized by a bird with her head turned backward over her wing. This means that her mind has already turned, so her physical turn is imminent. When the *Sankofa* bird is shown in flight with an egg in her mouth, the symbolic significance is even greater. The egg symbolizes a new creation that is about to be "birthed" into the world. However, it cannot be born until she returns to the place from where she came to retrieve the vitally important thing that she forgot, left behind, or rejected. For Africans in the Diaspora, the egg symbolizes African culture and traditions that we thought were too pagan, outmoded, or unsophisticated for our "modern" lives. I believe with all my heart and soul that Africans worldwide must be *hearers and listeners* for the lesson taught by the *Sankofa* bird because she points the way toward liberation, autonomy, survival and optimal empowerment. We will never gain liberation at the hands of our enslavers. Likewise, we will never liberate ourselves as long as we remain locked within our enslavers' culture.

The socialization process outlined by Andah explains why African children do not suffer from identity confusion and identity crisis. All their lives the entire community uses a complex combination of social mores and infrastructures, rites, feasts and ceremonies to teach them who they are and what is expected of them. During puberty rites around ages eleven to thirteen, age-sets of girls and boys are separated and taken from their homes to a remote location. The adolescents remain there for some proscribed period of time to undergo extensive education and training in every role and responsibility that they are expected to fill as adults. Both boys and girls are taught leadership skills. Adolescents enter the puberty rites as girls and boys and they leave as adults who are expected by the entire community to develop from *adulthood* to *godhood* during the course of their lives.

From the information presented earlier, we can see that the entire community guides children through each life stage with the help of social infrastructures, rites, festivals, and traditional institutions referred to as secret societies. The education and training of children is tightly structured and controlled by family members, spiritual mentors, community leaders, friends, and neighbors who all act and speak in one accord. Thus, the social environment that surrounds African children is far more structured and formal than what we imagine in America. We have lost the nurturing, supportive social infrastructures that exist among both traditional and modern Africans.

I turn again briefly to what is pointed out by Native American Nationalists who have fought hard to either maintain or regain their lost social infrastructures. They discuss the central importance of the four themes if African Americans truly seek a cultural strategy for survival. I agree that it is imperative that we develop in the following manner: (a) a strong sense of tribe; (b) a commitment to nationalism; (c) a regained sense of connection with nature and all of life; and (d) either an Africanized interpretation of our religious beliefs, or a return to African religion itself.

The traditional African processes for socialization and enculturation bring us into a more complete understanding of the saying: *"It takes a village to rear a child."* Our present understanding of the "village rearing each child" has deteriorated to mean that each person should occasionally look out for our neighbors' children in an unstructured manner. We can now more accurately comprehend the African dictum for proving human existence: *"I am because we are, and since we are, therefore I am."* In other words, each individual is a composite of the family and the community because they all actively contribute some element that represents the best and highest of themselves into each child. This is done for every child from birth to adulthood, to ensure positive growth and development. This level of community involvement endures for a lifetime. Therefore, each individual recognizes that his or her *entire being* as well as place, status and roles within a nurturing community are what provide meaning to her or his existence. Individuals are never alone because the community participates in each person's life from birth to death.

How starkly different the African dictum for existence is from the Western "Cartesian" dictum that states: "I think, therefore I am." The Western mind believes that ultimate relevance resides in the individual. The individual is essentially disconnected from other human beings by reason of personal interest, to the extent that she or he feels that the interactions and opinions of others are irrelevant. This is often verbalized by the expression: "It is *my* life and *my* business, so *I* do what *I* want." We often hear the opinion that decisions are left only to "me, myself, and I," without regard to the opinions and interests of family or society.

On the contrary, the life of every African individual on the Continent is deeply rooted in an ongoing involvement with family and community. This can be seen clearly, now that we have compiled information on traditional Yoruba philosophy and moral codes, the teachings of Ptahhotep, and the socialization and enculturation processes. We also note that children and students are required to be *obedient active hearers and listeners*, so as to learn the ways of wisdom and live a long and happy life. Likewise, adults are required to play a vital role in society; to be role models for the young; and to be active agents in maintaining codes of ethics, social norms and social stability.

In African society, a *person* is someone whose behavior *demonstrates awareness* that s/he carries a spark of divinity as a gift from Almighty God in the form of spiritual and mystical power. Therefore, each individual is required by God to become a productive *person* in society. A *person* in African terms is viewed as someone who practices good character, moral thoughts and ethical conduct, in order to some day reach the level of *godhood* in a ripe old age. Development of the spiritual and mystical powers that are indicative of human *godhood* is dependent upon personality and character development.

It can also be noted from the enculturation and socialization processes outlined above that development into what I refer to as *human godhood* can only be accomplished within a communal context. It is a traditional African concept that I have expressed in the African American vernacular.

The pursuit of *godhood* is synonymous with the pursuit of *goodness* which is demonstrated daily in moral behavior, to the extent that a person's behavior is viewed by the community as a thing of *beauty* to be admired by all. This is the only way an individual can be acknowledged and honored as a *person*, in the true and full African sense of the word. The process begins with individuals who are *hearers and listeners* of sound moral and spiritual instructions that are practiced daily over an entire lifetime. These are lifesaving instructions; advice that is meant to improve the quality of life and sense of wellbeing of individuals and communities.

In Africa, if an individual is not a participant in the lifelong process of individual development and community support, that individual's *personhood* will not be recognized by family or anyone else in the community. Any discussion of womanhood or manhood becomes moot if the community determines that someone is a brute that merely wears the *skin* of a person. In such an instance, the family takes the first line of attack in disciplining such an individual. Personal disgrace brings disgrace upon one's entire family and sometimes the community as well. For this reason, families try to settle serious offenses from spilling out into the community, because then an entire community might get involved once a family fails at containment and settlement.

It must be emphasized in the strongest terms that *good character* is the primary prerequisite toward earning the title of *person*. When rehabilitation is necessary, intervention begins from the outside-in. Once intervention begins, the process of transformation occurs from the inside-out. Individuals must become committed to a spiritual and behavioral transformation toward positive, spiritual cultural values. Everything around an individual changes once the person becomes committed to the process of long-term positive change. Right thinking, honesty, moral and ethical behavior and respect for others - especially elders - form the bases of good character.

African culture expects every individual to demonstrate moral conduct and goodness irrespective of age, sex, or status. Human goodness includes those things that bring peace, harmony, happiness, dignity, respect, and a long happy life. Thus, what is described as being good are activities that support and promote the common good of the family and community. *Persons* are individuals who work toward the stability and welfare of society as well as themselves. This is the secret to survival, success, and longevity, because the universal law of retributive justice is cyclical. It provides community support to those who have worked in behalf of the community. Someone will always come to your rescue in a time of trouble because you have earned it.

Within these pages are some of the primary beliefs, values, and principles found in Yoruba philosophical thought, presented for the purpose of healing African minds that have been programmed for destruction. These are some of the most ancient and authoritative African cultural and social ideals in the entire world, and they are time-tested standards of right thinking and moral conduct that African people in general have maintained for at least 10,000 years.

I am convinced that African survival and advancement requires shedding the ill-fitting borrowed garment of Western culture and re-clothing ourselves in the more suitable raiment of *African cultural consciousness*. At this juncture of our history, when tens thousands of us are dying daily worldwide, we need to say to ourselves: "We have tried everything else, so why not return to the spiritual and cultural source of our existence?" If African teachings and wisdom were able to lift other world cultures from barbarity, they should certainly be able to benefit the people who originated them. Traditional African values and ideals account for the remarkable strength and resiliency of African people, who are the parents of all humanity. The moral assumptions and expectations in African philosophy have been stabilizing forces in African civilizations throughout the entire history of humanity on this planet.

The intellectual imperatives and scientific inventions of ancient African Ancestors resulted in the building of magnificent civilizations with technologies that today's so-called modern world with all its technology is incapable of duplicating. The architecture of ancient Ethiopia, Sudan, Egypt, and Zimbabwe are proof of African genius. Further proof of our genius is found in indigenous knowledge of science, mathematics, medicine, astronomy, etc. that has been held since ancient times. We African scholars need the courage to occasionally step out of the dead, ivy-covered walls of Western academia where our ultimate aim is to impress each other with ten-syllable words spoken in smooth, quiet, dispassionate tones. Almost all the scholarly books that reveal the amazing discoveries of African knowledge of the highest order in mathematics, medicine, astronomy, etc. are written by Europeans.

Africans worldwide are knowledgeable of the achievements attributed to people in every culture except our own. Instead, we present creative excuses for not researching our own history and cultural achievements. The Africanist scholars who do take up the responsibility of such research are considered by most to be engaged in useless work. This is a shameful development. Why should anyone on earth respect us as a people when we do not have enough respect for ourselves to study our own culture? Surely African education should have some ultimate goal for an individual that is higher than merely getting a foreign corporate or university job, or a government position. If we do not begin developing a unified vision for Africa, the continent will be lost.

Somehow we forgot that just because something is new it does not mean that thing is good. We are late in discovering that the new ways into which we have assimilated and acculturated destroys us from the inside-out. Once a person's "*head*" or mind is compromised, the person's entire being comes under attack from within. It is impossible for someone to survive or lead a sane, balanced, normal life in either the physical sense or the spiritual sense, once that happens.

Archeology and history demonstrate that Western culture is relatively new. Instead of learning from people in ancient societies, Europeans and Americans killed them. In the process, they destroyed entire civilizations that were far more advanced in science, astrology, mathematics, medicine, philosophy, and knowledge than they were. This wanton destruction has resulted in what I refer to as the *Dark Ages of Modernity* where technology is passed off as civilization. Make note that the root word *civil* refers to human relations and how well one can get along with others. It is a contradiction in terms for a nation to call itself a civilization when it is addicted to high-tech warfare.

Africans need to begin glorifying ourselves, what we have accomplished, and what is ours just as the rest of the world does. The educated among us should get down to the business of compiling and publishing the precious ancient knowledge and wisdom held by our aging indigenous priests and visionaries. Vast libraries of knowledge are lost each time one of them passes on. We must establish independent institutions to retrieve lost African histories; to examine and discuss African culture; to document ancient knowledge of science, mathematics, astronomy, and medicine; and to further develop African philosophical and religious thought. If African knowledge was good enough to raise other cultures up from gross barbarity, surely it is capable of elevating the people who originated it. Africans have wasted many generations glorifying others. We are worthy of being lauded, so it is time for us to glorify ourselves. Failure to do so will ensure continued mental illness, decline, disrespect, and untimely death. Failure to do so will cause us to completely lose the African continent.

Malcolm was correct by stating that we have been tricked, lied to, hoodwinked, and bamboozled. However, there is no excuse for ignorance of African history and hatred of one's own race and culture today. If Africans do not know their history by now, it is a chosen ignorance, because information is everywhere about the tens of thousands of years of African contributions to humanity and to world. Resistance to such healing, self-affirming information may be indicative of an individual compulsion toward self-destruction.

The African values, teachings, and moral codes presented in this book are not completely foreign to Africans in the Diaspora, nor are they completely removed from us. It is only since the 1960s that we almost completely stopped rearing our children by them. Some of this is the result of children giving birth to children before maturing enough to learn the history, philosophy, and codes of conduct available within the culture. You cannot teach what you do not know; so the children of each successive generation of teen parents have become worse off than the generation before it.

This generational decline is a first in the entire history of African people. However, knowledge of these African cultural components continues to reside within the memories of African American elders. Our elders can testify to the sustaining power of their cultural ideals and traditions that combined with their religious faith to sustain them through generations of racial oppression, suffering and grief. That fact alone is a testimonial about the ability of these spiritual and philosophical principles to be applied in such a way as to support survival and promote advancement.

Many culture-conscious African Americans despair over the apparent disdain and disrespect that Continental Africans have for indigenous knowledge, religion, and culture. However, we recognize that they too have been brainwashed into a self-deprecating belief in White supremacy. African American cultural nationalists actually pity the Continentals who are so filled with self-loathing and ideas of White supremacy that they scorn people who have the good common sense to value their own African cultural heritage rather than that of their oppressors.

Caucasians have used missionary education to enslave the minds of African children for many generations. Time spent abroad in European and American universities serves as the final stage of White mind control. African cultural values have become co-opted to a point of no return by many foreign educated Continental Africans, such that they, like their Diasporan sisters and brothers, have become alienated from themselves. However, Continentals have the advantage of being able to return home to become re-immersed in the culture, while it is an expensive affair for Diasporans.

On the flip side, Continental Africans look upon Diasporan Africans with puzzlement and scorn when the latter go to great pains to adopt ancient traditions. They cannot fathom why someone born in America would go so far as to travel to Africa for such cultural and spiritual re-immersion. They do not realize that on this side of the Atlantic Ocean we understand that they are throwing away life-sustaining precious gems; therefore, as fast as they discard them we are desperately scrambling in the rubbish heap to retrieve and preserve those cultural wisdom-stones.

Our Continental siblings leave Africa because their nations lack so many modern conveniences that are found in Europe and America. They then spend the best period of their lives abroad building up Europe and America, instead of Africa. A proverb states that "only a fool leaves his house because it needs repairs, only to go and build up another man's house." Even when they return home to Africa most Western educated Africans set themselves far above the indigenous people, instead of sharing skills and knowledge for their uplift. The educated elites put on airs to impress the Caucasians who hate all of us and consider us no more than educated monkeys. It increases Diasporan Africans' painful memory that many of our own sisters and brothers on the Continent grew rich by participating in the slave trade and even now prefer the company of Whites when they come to reside in America.

Understanding some of the historical circumstances allows Diasporan Africans to forgive. However, it is often a topic for discussion as to whether the present deterioration of Africa is a form of Divine Retribution because of African participation in the Atlantic slave trade. To date, little has been done to facilitate a return home. These statements are not made to hurl blame. However, the historical facts need to be aired so as to promote dialogue and healing between us. All Africans are still being manipulated by the "*divide and conquer, divide and rule*" strategy. We are the only ones who can put an end to it. The survival of Africans on both sides of the Atlantic depends upon our doing so. Africa's continued independence depends upon our doing so.

Hopes for our self-redemption remain high. The Yoruba say: "I will drink from my part of the river," when it comes to receiving the blessings that God intended for us to have. I believe in the *proven* power of God that operates through human beings to break into human history to right wrongs; straighten out crookedness; and to deliver justice where there is injustice. It is my fervent prayer that we Africans will finally emerge as God's earthly helpers, *working in our own behalf* before all is lost.

Millions of us have experienced despair and frustration caused by the cultural losses we have suffered. However, some of us have committed our lives to untiringly follow the light provided by our ancient Ancestors as we continue this journey to rediscover, retrieve, reclaim, and reinstate the intellectual, spiritual, and cultural "*Holy Grail*" of our heritage. I can think of no more appropriate closing for this book than the following poem:

MY SEARCH, MY SOUL, MY REBIRTH

My mind yearns for the knowledge
On the core of my existence
My mind cries to unveil the untold mysteries
The centuries of buried truths
Of my ancestry and my people
My mind understands that
being lost in a lie breeds despair
being lost in a lie breeds self hate
being lost in a lie breeds self destruction
being lost in a lie breeds contempt
for self
for my family
for my people
for all that I should love
for all I should adore
for all I should protect and uphold
MY soul, My soul
Now abides in this great abyss with conflicted identities
Conflicted with European and Asian ideologies of my
Who I am, Who I should Be
Conflicted with years of abuse and misuse
Conflicted with the notions of those who present
distortions and untruth

I arise to reclaim the teachings of IMHOTEP
I arise to reclaim the knowledge of MAAT
I arise to be revived
I arise to be renewed
I arise to be reborn in the newness of all
That is Righteous and True
"ASHE"

--Bernice Parker Bell

APPENDIX-1

Beyond Vietnam:
A Time to Break Silence
By The Rev. Martin Luther King
Riverside Church – New York City
April 4, 1967

[Please put links to this speech on your respective web sites and if possible, place the text itself there. This is the least well known of Dr. King's speeches among the masses, and it needs to be read by all]

http://www.ssc.msu.edu/~sw/mlk/brkslnc.htm

I come to this magnificent house of worship tonight because my conscience leaves me no other choice. I join with you in this meeting because I am in deepest agreement with the aims and work of the organization which has brought us together: Clergy and Laymen Concerned about Vietnam. The recent statements of your executive committee are the sentiments of my own heart and I found myself in full accord when I read its opening lines: "A time comes when silence is betrayal." That time has come for us in relation to Vietnam.

The truth of these words is beyond doubt but the mission to which they call us is a most difficult one. Even when pressed by the demands of inner truth, men do not easily assume the task of opposing their government's policy, especially in time of war. Nor does the human spirit move without great difficulty against all the apathy of conformist thought within one's own bosom and in the surrounding world. Moreover when the issues at hand seem as perplexed as they often do in the case of this dreadful conflict we are always on the verge of being mesmerized by uncertainty; but we must move on.

Some of us who have already begun to break the silence of the night have found that the calling to speak is often a vocation of agony, but we must speak. We must speak with all the humility that is appropriate to our limited vision, but we must speak. And we must rejoice as well, for surely this is the first time in our nation's history that a significant number of its Perhaps a new spirit is rising among us. If it is, let us trace its movement well and pray that our own inner being may be sensitive to its guidance, for we are deeply in need of a new way beyond the darkness that seems so close around us.

Over the past two years, as I have moved to break the betrayal of my own silences and to speak from the burnings of my own heart, as I have called for radical departures from the destruction of Vietnam, many persons have questioned me about the wisdom of my path. At the heart of their concerns this query has often loomed large and loud: Why are you speaking about war, Dr. King? Why are you joining the voices of dissent? Peace and civil rights don't mix, they say. Aren't you hurting the cause of your people, they ask? And when I hear them, though I often understand the source of their concern, I am nevertheless greatly saddened, for such questions mean that the inquirers have not really known me, my commitment or my calling. Indeed, their questions suggest that they do not know the world in which they live.

In the light of such tragic misunderstandings, I deem it of signal importance to try to state clearly, and I trust concisely, why I believe that the path from Dexter Avenue Baptist Church -- the church in Montgomery, Alabama, where I began my pastorate -- leads clearly to this sanctuary tonight.

I come to this platform tonight to make a passionate plea to my beloved nation. This speech is not addressed to Hanoi or to the National Liberation Front. It is not addressed to China or to Russia.

Nor is it an attempt to overlook the ambiguity of the total situation and the need for a collective solution to the tragedy of Vietnam. Neither is it an attempt to make North Vietnam or the National Liberation Front paragons of virtue, nor to overlook the role they can play in a successful resolution of the problem. While they both may have justifiable reason to be suspicious of the good faith of the United States, life and history give eloquent testimony to the fact that conflicts are never resolved without trustful give and take on both sides.

Tonight, however, I wish not to speak with Hanoi and the NLF, but rather to my fellow Americans, who, with me, bear the greatest responsibility in ending a conflict that has exacted a heavy price on both continents.

The Importance of Vietnam

Since I am a preacher by trade, I suppose it is not surprising that I have seven major reasons for bringing Vietnam into the field of my moral vision. There is at the outset a very obvious and almost facile connection between the war in Vietnam and the struggle I, and others, have been waging in America. A few years ago there was a shining moment in that struggle. It seemed as if there was a real promise of hope for the poor -- both black and white -- through the poverty program. There were experiments, hopes, new beginnings. Then came the buildup in Vietnam and I watched the program broken and eviscerated as if it were some idle political plaything of a society gone mad on war, and I knew that America would never invest the necessary funds or energies in rehabilitation of its poor so long as adventures like Vietnam continued to draw men and skills and money like some demonic destructive suction tube. So I was increasingly compelled to see the war as an enemy of the poor and to attack it as such.

Perhaps the more tragic recognition of reality took place when it became clear to me that the war was doing far more than devastating the hopes of the poor at home. It was sending their sons and their brothers and their husbands to fight and to die in extraordinarily high proportions relative to the rest of the population. We were taking the black young men who had been crippled by our society and sending them eight thousand miles away to guarantee liberties in Southeast Asia which they had not found in southwest Georgia and East Harlem. So we have been repeatedly faced with the cruel irony of watching Negro and white boys on TV screens as they kill and die together for a nation that has been unable to seat them together in the same schools. So we watch them in brutal solidarity burning the huts of a poor village, but we realize that they would never live on the same block in Detroit. I could not be silent in the face of such cruel manipulation of the poor.

My third reason moves to an even deeper level of awareness, for it grows out of my experience in the ghettoes of the North over the last three years -- especially the last three summers. As I have walked among the desperate, rejected and angry young men I have told them that Molotov cocktails and rifles would not solve their problems. I have tried to offer them my deepest compassion while maintaining my conviction that social change comes most meaningfully through nonviolent action. But they asked -- and rightly so -- what about Vietnam? They asked if our own nation wasn't using massive doses of violence to solve its problems, to bring about the changes it wanted. Their questions hit home, and I knew that I could never again raise my voice against the violence of the oppressed in the ghettos without having first spoken clearly to the greatest purveyor of violence in the world today -- my own government. For the sake of those boys, for the sake of this government, for the sake of hundreds of thousands trembling under our violence, I cannot be silent.

For those who ask the question, "Aren't you a civil rights leader?" and thereby mean to exclude me from the movement for peace, I have this further answer. In 1957 when a group of us formed the Southern Christian Leadership Conference, we chose as our motto: "To save the soul of America." We were convinced that we could not limit our vision to certain rights for black people, but instead affirmed the conviction that America would never be free or saved from itself unless the descendants of its slaves were loosed completely from the shackles they still wear. In a way we were agreeing with Langston Hughes, that black bard of Harlem, who had written earlier:

> O, yes,
> I say it plain,
> America never was America to me,
> And yet I swear this oath--
> America will be!

Now, it should be incandescently clear that no one who has any concern for the integrity and life of America today can ignore the present war. If America's soul becomes totally poisoned, part of the autopsy must read Vietnam. It can never be saved so long as it destroys the deepest hopes of men the world over. So it is that those of us who are yet determined that America will be are led down the path of protest and dissent, working for the health of our land.

As if the weight of such a commitment to the life and health of America were not enough, another burden of responsibility was placed upon me in 1964; and I cannot forget that the Nobel Prize for Peace was also a commission -- a commission to work harder than I had ever worked before for "the brotherhood of man." This is a calling that takes me beyond national allegiances, but even if it were not present I would yet have to live with the meaning of my commitment to the ministry of Jesus Christ. To me the relationship of this ministry to the making of peace is so obvious that I sometimes marvel at those who ask me why I am speaking against the war. Could it be that they do not know that the good news was meant for all men -- for Communist and capitalist, for their children and ours, for black and for white, for revolutionary and conservative? Have they forgotten that my ministry is in obedience to the one who loved his enemies so fully that he died for them? What then can I say to the "Vietcong" or to Castro or to Mao as a faithful minister of this one? Can I threaten them with death or must I not share with them my life?

Finally, as I try to delineate for you and for myself the road that leads from Montgomery to this place I would have offered all that was most valid if I simply said that I must be true to my conviction that I share with all men the calling to be a son of the living God. Beyond the calling of race or nation or creed is this vocation of sonship and brotherhood, and because I believe that the Father is deeply concerned especially for his suffering and helpless and outcast children, I come tonight to speak for them.

This I believe to be the privilege and the burden of all of us who deem ourselves bound by allegiances and loyalties which are broader and deeper than nationalism and which go beyond our nation's self-defined goals and positions. We are called to speak for the weak, for the voiceless, for victims of our nation and for those it calls enemy, for no document from human hands can make these humans any less our brothers.

Strange Liberators

And as I ponder the madness of Vietnam and search within myself for ways to understand and respond to compassion my mind goes constantly to the people of that peninsula. I speak now not of the soldiers of each side, not of the junta in Saigon, but simply of the people who have been living under the curse of war for almost three continuous decades now. I think of them too because it is clear to me that there will be no meaningful solution there until some attempt is made to know them and hear their broken cries.

They must see Americans as strange liberators. The Vietnamese people proclaimed their own independence in 1945 after a combined French and Japanese occupation, and before the Communist revolution in China. They were led by Ho Chi Minh. Even though they quoted the American Declaration of Independence in their own document of freedom, we refused to recognize them. Instead, we decided to support France in its reconquest of her former colony.

Our government felt then that the Vietnamese people were not "ready" for independence, and we again fell victim to the deadly Western arrogance that has poisoned the international atmosphere for so long. With that tragic decision we rejected a revolutionary government seeking self-determination, and a government that had been established not by China (for whom the Vietnamese have no great love) but by clearly indigenous forces that included some Communists. For the peasants this new government meant real land reform, one of the most important needs in their lives.

For nine years following 1945 we denied the people of Vietnam the right of independence. For nine years we vigorously supported the French in their abortive effort to recolonize Vietnam.

Before the end of the war we were meeting eighty percent of the French war costs. Even before the French were defeated at Dien Bien Phu, they began to despair of the reckless action, but we did not. We encouraged them with our huge financial and military supplies to continue the war even after they had lost the will. Soon we would be paying almost the full costs of this tragic attempt at recolonization.

After the French were defeated it looked as if independence and land reform would come again through the Geneva agreements. But instead there came the United States, determined that Ho should not unify the temporarily divided nation, and the peasants watched again as we supported one of the most vicious modern dictators -- our chosen man, Premier Diem. The peasants watched and cringed as Diem ruthlessly routed out all opposition, supported their extortionist landlords and refused even to discuss reunification with the north. The peasants watched as all this was presided over by U.S. influence and then by increasing numbers of U.S. troops who came to help quell the insurgency that Diem's methods had aroused. When Diem was overthrown they may have been happy, but the long line of military dictatorships seemed to offer no real change -- especially in terms of their need for land and peace.

The only change came from America as we increased our troop commitments in support of governments which were singularly corrupt, inept and without popular support. All the while the people read our leaflets and received regular promises of peace and democracy -- and land reform. Now they languish under our bombs and consider us -- not their fellow Vietnamese --the real enemy. They move sadly and apathetically as we herd them off the land of their fathers into concentration camps where minimal social needs are rarely met. They know they must move or be destroyed by our bombs. So they go -- primarily women and children and the aged.

They watch as we poison their water, as we kill a million acres of their crops. They must weep as the bulldozers roar through their areas preparing to destroy the precious trees. They wander into the hospitals, with at least twenty casualties from American firepower for one "Vietcong"-inflicted injury. So far we may have killed a million of them -- mostly children. They wander into the towns and see thousands of the children, homeless, without clothes, running in packs on the streets like animals. They see the children, degraded by our soldiers as they beg for food. They see the children selling their sisters to our soldiers, soliciting for their mothers.

What do the peasants think as we ally ourselves with the landlords and as we refuse to put any action into our many words concerning land reform? What do they think as we test our latest weapons on them, just as the Germans tested out new medicine and new tortures in the concentration camps of Europe? Where are the roots of the independent Vietnam we claim to be building? Is it among these voiceless ones?

We have destroyed their two most cherished institutions: the family and the village. We have destroyed their land and their crops. We have cooperated in the crushing of the nation's only non-Communist revolutionary political force -- the unified Buddhist church. We have supported the enemies of the peasants of Saigon. We have corrupted their women and children and killed their men. What liberators?

Now there is little left to build on -- save bitterness. Soon the only solid physical foundations remaining will be found at our military bases and in the concrete of the concentration camps we call fortified hamlets. The peasants may well wonder if we plan to build our new Vietnam on such grounds as these? Could we blame them for such thoughts? We must speak for them and raise the questions they cannot raise. These too are our brothers.

Perhaps the more difficult but no less necessary task is to speak for those who have been designated as our enemies. What of the National Liberation Front -- that strangely anonymous group we call VC or Communists? What must they think of us in America when they realize that we permitted the repression and cruelty of Diem which helped to bring them into being as a resistance group in the south? What do they think of our condoning the violence which led to their own taking up of arms? How can they believe in our integrity when now we speak of "aggression from the north" as if there were nothing more essential to the war? How can they trust us when now we charge them with violence after the murderous reign of Diem and charge them with violence while we pour every new weapon of death into their land?

Surely we must understand their feelings even if we do not condone their actions. Surely we must see that the men we supported pressed them to their violence. Surely we must see that our own computerized plans of destruction simply dwarf their greatest acts.

How do they judge us when our officials know that their membership is less than twenty-five percent Communist and yet insist on giving them the blanket name? What must they be thinking when they know that we are aware of their control of major sections of Vietnam and yet we appear ready to allow national elections in which this highly organized political parallel government will have no part? They ask how we can speak of free elections when the Saigon press is censored and controlled by the military junta. And they are surely right to wonder what kind of new government we plan to help form without them -- the only party in real touch with the peasants. They question our political goals and they deny the reality of a peace settlement from which they will be excluded. Their questions are frighteningly relevant. Is our nation planning to build on political myth again and then shore it up with the power of new violence?

Here is the true meaning and value of compassion and nonviolence when it helps us to see the enemy's point of view, to hear his questions, to know his assessment of ourselves. For from his view we may indeed see the basic weaknesses of our own condition, and if we are mature, we may learn and grow and profit from the wisdom of the brothers who are called the opposition.

So, too, with Hanoi. In the north, where our bombs now pummel the land, and our mines endanger the waterways, we are met by a deep but understandable mistrust. To speak for them is to explain this lack of confidence in Western words, and especially their distrust of American intentions now. In Hanoi are the men who led the nation to independence against the Japanese and the French, the men who sought membership in the French commonwealth and were betrayed by the weakness of Paris and the willfulness of the colonial armies. It was they who led a second struggle against French domination at tremendous costs, and then were persuaded to give up the land they controlled between the thirteenth and seventeenth parallel as a temporary measure at Geneva. After 1954 they watched us conspire with Diem to prevent elections which would have surely brought Ho Chi Minh to power over a united Vietnam, and they realized they had been betrayed again.

When we ask why they do not leap to negotiate, these things must be remembered. Also it must be clear that the leaders of Hanoi considered the presence of American troops in support of the Diem regime to have been the initial military breach of the Geneva agreements concerning foreign troops, and they remind us that they did not begin to send in any large number of supplies or men until American forces had moved into the tens of thousands.

Hanoi remembers how our leaders refused to tell us the truth about the earlier North Vietnamese overtures for peace, how the president claimed that none existed when they had clearly been made. Ho Chi Minh has watched as America has spoken of peace and built up its forces, and now he has surely heard of the increasing international rumors of American plans for an invasion of the north. He knows the bombing and shelling and mining we are doing are part of traditional pre-invasion strategy. Perhaps only his sense of humor and of irony can save him when he hears the most powerful nation of the world speaking of aggression as it drops thousands of bombs on a poor weak nation more than eight thousand miles away from its shores.

At this point I should make it clear that while I have tried in these last few minutes to give a voice to the voiceless on Vietnam and to understand the arguments of those who are called enemy, I am as deeply concerned about our troops there as anything else. For it occurs to me that what we are submitting them to in Vietnam is not simply the brutalizing process that goes on in any war where armies face each other and seek to destroy. We are adding cynicism to the process of death, for they must know after a short period there that none of the things we claim to be fighting for are really involved. Before long they must know that their government has sent them into a struggle among Vietnamese, and the more sophisticated surely realize that we are on the side of the wealthy and the secure while we create hell for the poor.

This Madness Must Cease

Somehow this madness must cease. We must stop now. I speak as a child of God and brother to the suffering poor of Vietnam. I speak for those whose land is being laid waste, whose homes are being destroyed, whose culture is being subverted. I speak for the poor of America who are paying the double price of smashed hopes at home and death and corruption in Vietnam. I speak as a citizen of the world, for the world as it stands aghast at the path we have taken. I speak as an American to the leaders of my own nation. The great initiative in this war is ours. The initiative to stop it must be ours.

This is the message of the great Buddhist leaders of Vietnam. Recently one of them wrote these words:

"Each day the war goes on the hatred increases in the heart of the Vietnamese and in the hearts of those of humanitarian instinct. The Americans are forcing even their friends into becoming their enemies. It is curious that the Americans, who calculate so carefully on the possibilities of military victory, do not realize that in the process they are incurring deep psychological and political defeat. The image of America will never again be the image of revolution, freedom and democracy, but the image of violence and militarism."

If we continue, there will be no doubt in my mind and in the mind of the world that we have no honorable intentions in Vietnam. It will become clear that our minimal expectation is to occupy it as an American colony and men will not refrain from thinking that our maximum hope is to goad China into a war so that we may bomb her nuclear installations. If we do not stop our war against the people of Vietnam immediately the world will be left with no other alternative than to see this as some horribly clumsy and deadly game we have decided to play.

The world now demands a maturity of America that we may not be able to achieve. It demands that we admit that we have been wrong from the beginning of our adventure in Vietnam, that we have been detrimental to the life of the Vietnamese people. The situation is one in which we must be ready to turn sharply from our present ways.

In order to atone for our sins and errors in Vietnam, we should take the initiative in bringing a halt to this tragic war. I would like to suggest five concrete things that our government should do immediately to begin the long and difficult process of extricating ourselves from this nightmarish conflict:

1. End all bombing in North and South Vietnam.
2. Declare a unilateral cease-fire in the hope that such action will create the atmosphere for negotiation.
3. Take immediate steps to prevent other battlegrounds in Southeast Asia by curtailing our military buildup in Thailand and our interference in Laos.
4. Realistically accept the fact that the National Liberation Front has substantial support in South Vietnam and must thereby play a role in any meaningful negotiations and in any future Vietnam government.

5. Set a date that we will remove all foreign troops from Vietnam in accordance with the 1954 Geneva agreement.

Part of our ongoing commitment might well express itself in an offer to grant asylum to any Vietnamese who fears for his life under a new regime which included the Liberation Front. Then we must make what reparations we can for the damage we have done. We most provide the medical aid that is badly needed, making it available in this country if necessary.

Protesting the War

Meanwhile we in the churches and synagogues have a continuing task while we urge our government to disengage itself from a disgraceful commitment. We must continue to raise our voices if our nation persists in its perverse ways in Vietnam. We must be prepared to match actions with words by seeking out every creative means of protest possible.

As we counsel young men concerning military service we must clarify for them our nation's role in Vietnam and challenge them with the alternative of conscientious objection. I am pleased to say that this is the path now being chosen by more than seventy students at my own alma mater, Morehouse College, and I recommend it to all who find the American course in Vietnam a dishonorable and unjust one. Moreover I would encourage all ministers of draft age to give up their ministerial exemptions and seek status as conscientious objectors. These are the times for real choices and not false ones. We are at the moment when our lives must be placed on the line if our nation is to survive its own folly. Every man of humane convictions must decide on the protest that best suits his convictions, but we must all protest.

There is something seductively tempting about stopping there and sending us all off on what in some circles has become a popular crusade against the war in Vietnam. I say we must enter the struggle, but I wish to go on now to say something even more disturbing. The war in Vietnam is but a symptom of a far deeper malady within the American spirit, and if we ignore this sobering reality we will find ourselves organizing clergy- and laymen-concerned committees for the next generation. They will be concerned about Guatemala and Peru. They will be concerned about Thailand and Cambodia. They will be concerned about Mozambique and South Africa. We will be marching for these and a dozen other names and attending rallies without end unless there is a significant and profound change in American life and policy. Such thoughts take us beyond Vietnam, but not beyond our calling as sons of the living God.

In 1957 a sensitive American official overseas said that it seemed to him that our nation was on the wrong side of a world revolution. During the past ten years we have seen emerge a pattern of suppression which now has justified the presence of U.S. military "advisors" in Venezuela. This need to maintain social stability for our investments accounts for the counter-revolutionary action of American forces in Guatemala. It tells why American helicopters are being used against guerrillas in Colombia and why American napalm and green beret forces have already been active against rebels in Peru. It is with such activity in mind that the words of the late John F. Kennedy come back to haunt us. Five years ago he said, "Those who make peaceful revolution impossible will make violent revolution inevitable."

Increasingly, by choice or by accident, this is the role our nation has taken -- the role of those who make peaceful revolution impossible by refusing to give up the privileges and the pleasures that come from the immense profits of overseas investment.

I am convinced that if we are to get on the right side of the world revolution, we as a nation must undergo a radical revolution of values. We must rapidly begin the shift from a "thing-oriented" society to a "person-oriented" society. When machines and computers, profit motives and property rights are considered more important than people, the giant triplets of racism, materialism, and militarism are incapable of being conquered.

A true revolution of values will soon cause us to question the fairness and justice of many of our past and present policies. n the one hand we are called to play the good Samaritan on life's roadside; but that will be only an initial act. One day we must come to see that the whole Jericho road must be transformed so that men and women will not be constantly beaten and robbed as they make their journey on life's highway. True compassion is more than flinging a coin to a beggar; it is not haphazard and superficial. It comes to see that an edifice which produces beggars needs restructuring. A true revolution of values will soon look uneasily on the glaring contrast of poverty and wealth. With righteous indignation, it will look across the seas and see individual capitalists of the West investing huge sums of money in Asia, Africa and South America, only to take the profits out with no concern for the social betterment of the countries, and say: "This is not just." It will look at our alliance with the landed gentry of Latin America and say: "This is not just." The Western arrogance of feeling that it has everything to teach others and nothing to learn from them is not just. A true revolution of values will lay hands on the world order and say of war: "This way of settling differences is not just." This business of burning human beings with napalm, of filling our nation's homes with orphans and widows, of injecting poisonous drugs of hate into veins of people normally humane, of sending men home from dark and bloody battlefields physically handicapped and psychologically deranged, cannot be reconciled with wisdom, justice and love. A nation that continues year after year to spend more money on military defense than on programs of social uplift is approaching spiritual death.

America, the richest and most powerful nation in the world, can well lead the way in this revolution of values. There is nothing, except a tragic death wish, to prevent us from reordering our priorities, so that the pursuit of peace will take precedence over the pursuit of war. There is nothing to keep us from molding a recalcitrant status quo with bruised hands until we have fashioned it into a brotherhood.

This kind of positive revolution of values is our best defense against communism. War is not the answer. Communism will never be defeated by the use of atomic bombs or nuclear weapons. Let us not join those who shout war and through their misguided passions urge the United States to relinquish its participation in the United Nations. These are days which demand wise restraint and calm reasonableness. We must not call everyone a Communist or an appeaser who advocates the seating of Red China in the United Nations and who recognizes that hate and hysteria are not the final answers to the problem of these turbulent days. We must not engage in a negative anti-communism, but rather in a positive thrust for democracy, realizing that our greatest defense against communism is to take offensive action in behalf of justice. We must with positive action seek to remove thosse conditions of poverty, insecurity and injustice which are the fertile soil in which the seed of communism grows and develops.

The People Are Important

These are revolutionary times. All over the globe men are revolting against old systems of exploitation and oppression and out of the wombs of a frail world new systems of justice and equality are being born. The shirtless and barefoot people of the land are rising up as never before. "The people who sat in darkness have seen a great light." We in the West must support these revolutions. It is a sad fact that, because of comfort, complacency, a morbid fear of communism, and our proneness to adjust to injustice, the Western nations that initiated so much of the revolutionary spirit of the modern world have now become the arch anti-revolutionaries. This has driven many to feel that only Marxism has the revolutionary spirit. Therefore, communism is a judgment against our failure to make democracy real and follow through on the revolutions we initiated. Our only hope today lies in our ability to recapture the revolutionary spirit and go out into a sometimes hostile world declaring eternal hostility to poverty, racism, and militarism. With this powerful commitment we shall boldly challenge the status quo and unjust mores and thereby speed the day when "every valley shall be exalted, and every mountain and hill shall be made low, and the crooked shall be made straight and the rough places plain."

A genuine revolution of values means in the final analysis that our loyalties must become ecumenical rather than sectional. Every nation must now develop an overriding loyalty to mankind as a whole in order to preserve the best in their individual societies.

This call for a world-wide fellowship that lifts neighborly concern beyond one's tribe, race, class and nation is in reality a call for an all-embracing and unconditional love for all men. This oft misunderstood and misinterpreted concept -- so readily dismissed by the Nietzsches of the world as a weak and cowardly force -- has now become an absolute necessity for the survival of man. When I speak of love I am not speaking of some sentimental and weak response. I am speaking of that force which all of the great religions have seen as the supreme unifying principle of life. Love is somehow the key that unlocks the door which leads to ultimate reality. This Hindu-Moslem-Christian-Jewish-Buddhist belief about ultimate reality is beautifully summed up in the first epistle of Saint John:

Let us love one another; for love is God and everyone that loveth is born of God and knoweth God. He that loveth not knoweth not God; for God is love. If we love one another God dwelleth in us, and his love is perfected in us.

Let us hope that this spirit will become the order of the day. We can no longer afford to worship the god of hate or bow before the altar of retaliation. The oceans of history are made turbulent by the ever-rising tides of hate. History is cluttered with the wreckage of nations and individuals that pursued this self-defeating path of hate. As Arnold Toynbee says : "Love is the ultimate force that makes for the saving choice of life and good against the damning choice of death and evil. Therefore the first hope in our inventory must be the hope that love is going to have the last word."

We are now faced with the fact that tomorrow is today. We are confronted with the fierce urgency of now. In this unfolding conundrum of life and history there is such a thing as being too late. Procrastination is still the thief of time. Life often leaves us standing bare, naked and dejected with a lost opportunity. The "tide in the affairs of men" does not remain at the flood; it ebbs. We may cry out desperately for time to pause in her passage, but time is deaf to every plea and rushes on. Over the bleached bones and jumbled residue of numerous civilizations are written the pathetic words: "Too late." There is an invisible book of life that faithfully records our vigilance or our neglect. "The moving finger writes, and having writ moves on..." We still have a choice today; nonviolent coexistence or violent co-annihilation.

We must move past indecision to action. We must find new ways to speak for peace in Vietnam and justice throughout the developing world -- a world that borders on our doors. If we do not act we shall surely be dragged down the long dark and shameful corridors of time reserved for those who possess power without compassion, might without morality, and strength without sight.

Now let us begin. Now let us rededicate ourselves to the long and bitter -- but beautiful -- struggle for a new world. This is the calling of the sons of God, and our brothers wait eagerly for our response. Shall we say the odds are too great? Shall we tell them the struggle is too hard? Will our message be that the forces of American life militate against their arrival as full men, and we send our deepest regrets? Or will there be another message, of longing, of hope, of solidarity with their yearnings, of commitment to their cause, whatever the cost? The choice is ours, and though we might prefer it otherwise we must choose in this crucial moment of human history.

As that noble bard of yesterday, James Russell Lowell, eloquently stated:

> Once to every man and nation
> Comes the moment to decide,
> In the strife of truth and falsehood,
> For the good or evil side;
> Some great cause, God's new Messiah,
> Off'ring each the bloom or blight,
> And the choice goes by forever
> Twixt that darkness and that light.

> Though the cause of evil prosper,
> Yet 'tis truth alone is strong;
> Though her portion be the scaffold,
> And upon the throne be wrong:
> Yet that scaffold sways the future,
> And behind the dim unknown,

Standeth God within the shadow
Keeping watch above his own.

―――――――――――――――

APPENDIX-2

OTHER FINDINGS BY PEW RESEARCH CENTER SURVEY

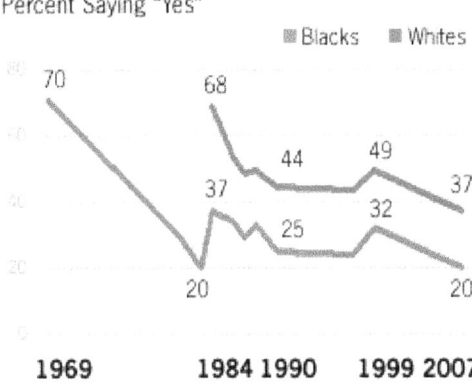

Are Blacks Better Off Now Than Five Years Ago?
Percent Saying "Yes"

- Asked whether blacks can still be thought of as a single race, given the increasing diversity within the black community, 53% of blacks say they can, but 37% of blacks say they cannot.
- Big gaps in perception between blacks and whites emerge on many topics. For example, blacks believe that anti-black discrimination is still pervasive in everyday life; whites disagree. And blacks have far less confidence than whites in the basic fairness of the criminal justice system.
- But there are also areas of agreement. For example, blacks and whites concur that there has been a convergence in the values held by blacks and whites. On the popular culture front, large majorities of both

blacks and whites say that rap and hip hop have a bad influence on society.
- Blacks and whites express very little overt racial animosity. As they have for decades, about eight-in-ten members of each racial group express a favorable view about members of the other group. More than eight-in-ten adults in each group also say they know a person of a different race whom they consider a friend.
- The most newsworthy African American figure in politics today - Democratic presidential hopeful Barack Obama - draws broadly (though not intensely felt) favorable ratings from both blacks and whites. But blacks are more inclined to say that his race will detract from his chances to be elected president; whites are more inclined to say his relative inexperience will hurt his chances.
- Three-quarters of blacks (76%) say that Obama is a good influence on the black community. Even greater numbers say this about Oprah Winfrey (87%) and Bill Cosby (85%), who are the most highly regarded by blacks from among 14 black newsmakers tested in this survey. By contrast, just 17% of blacks say that rap artist 50 Cent is a good influence.
- Over the past two decades, blacks have lost some confidence in the effectiveness of leaders within their community, including national black political figures, the clergy, and the NAACP. A sizable majority of blacks still see all of these groups as either very or somewhat effective, but the number saying "very" effective has declined since 1986.
- A 53% majority of African Americans say that blacks who don't get ahead are mainly responsible for their situation, while just three-in-ten say discrimination is mainly to blame. As recently as the mid-1990s, black opinion on this question tilted in the opposite direction, with a majority of African Americans saying then that

discrimination is the main reason for a lack of black progress.
- On the issue of immigration, blacks and whites agree that most immigrants work harder than most blacks and most whites at low-wage jobs. Also, blacks are less inclined now than they were two decades ago to say that blacks would have more jobs if there were fewer immigrants.

APPENDIX-3

QUANTITATIVE STUDIES ON AFRICAN AMERICAN IDENTY

Black Identity and Self-Esteem: A Review of Studies of Black Self-Concept, 1968-1978

J.R. Porter, R.E. Washington
Annual Review of Sociology, Vol. 5: 53 -74 (Volume publication date August 1979)

The National Survey of American Life: a study of racial, ethnic and cultural influences on mental disorders and mental health
James S. Jackson, Myriam Torres, Cleopatra H. Caldwell, Harold W. Neighbors, Randolph M. Nesse, Robert Joseph Taylor, Steven J. Trierweiler, David R. Williams
International Journal of Methods in Psychiatric Research 13(4):196 (2004)

The Self-Protective Properties of Stigma: Evolution of a Modern Classic
Jennifer Crocker, Brenda Major
Psychological Inquiry 14(3&4):232 (2003)

Race and Health Status as Determinants of Anger Expression and Adaptive Style in Children
Ric G. Steele, Vanessa Elliot, Sean Phipps
Journal of Social and Clinical Psychology 22(1):40 (2003)

Positive Self-Concept: An Equal Opportunity Construct
Bruce A. Bracken, M. Susan Lamprecht
School Psychology Quarterly 18(2):103 (2003)

Race and self-esteem: Meta-analyses comparing Whites, Blacks, Hispanics, Asians, and American Indians and comment on Gray-Little and Hafdahl (2000).
Jean M. Twenge, Jennifer Crocker
Psychological Bulletin 128(3):371 (2002)

Self-Esteem and Socioeconomic Status: A Meta-Analytic Review
Jean M. Twenge, W. Keith Campbell
Personality and Social Psychology Review 6(1):59 (2002)

Ten-Year Review of Rating Scales. III: Scales Assessing Suicidality, Cognitive Style, and Self-Esteem
Nancy C. Winters, Kathleen Myers, Laura Proud
Journal of the American Academy of Child & Adolescent Psychiatry 41(10):1150 (2002)

Ethnicity, gender and academic self-concept: A preliminary examination of academic disidentification and implications for psychologists.
Kevin O. Cokley
Cultural Diversity & Ethnic Minority Psychology 8(4):378 (2002)

Factors influencing racial comparisons of self-esteem: A quantitative review.
Bernadette Gray-Little, Adam
Psychological Bulletin 126(1):26 (2000)

Ethnically Correct Dolls: Toying with the Race Industry
Elizabeth Chin
American Anthropologist 101(2):305 (1999)

Black identity and drinking in the US: a national study
Denise Herd, Joel Grube
Addiction 91(6):845 (1996)

Self-concept of African-American male youth: Self-esteem and ethnic identity
Rosemerry R. Blash, Donald G. Unger
Journal of Child and Family Studies 4(3):359 (1995)

Impact of Affirmative Action on Beneficiary Groups: Evidence From the 1990 General Social Survey
Marylee C. Taylor
Basic and Applied Social Psychology 15(1&2):143 (1994)

Self-esteem among ethnic minority youth in Western countries
Maykel Verkuyten
Social Indicators Research 32(1):21 (1994)

Attributional style of African-American adolescents
Stephen B. Hillman, Paula Wood, Shlomo Sawilowsky
Social Behavior and Personality An International Journal 22(2):163 (1994)

Black and White Identity Formation; Studies in the Psychosocial Development of Lower Socioeconomic Class Adolescent Boys. Series on Psychological Disorders
Stuart T. Hauser
New York, John Wiley and Sons, Inc. (1971)

BIBLIOGRAPHY

Abimbola, Wande, ed. (1975). "Iwapele: The Concept of Good Character in Ifa Literary Corpus," *Yoruba Oral Tradition: Poetry in Music, Dance and Drama.* Ile-Ife, Nigeria: University of Ife.

Abiodun, Rowland (1990). "The Future of African Art Studies: An African Perspective," *African Art Studies: The State of the Discipline, Papers Presented at a Symposium Organized by the National Museum of African Art, Smithsonian Institution, September 16, 1987.* Washington D.C.: National Museum of African Art.

_____ (1987). "Verbal and Visual Metaphors: Mythical Allusions in Yoruba Ritualistic Art of Ori," *Word and Image* 3(3) July-Sept., pp. 252-270.

Akbar, Na'im (1992). *Chains and Images of Psychological Slavery.* New Jersey: New Mind Productions.

_____ (1985). *The Community of Self (Revised).* Tallahassee, Florida: Mind Productions & Associates.

Almaguer, T. (1994). *Racial Fault Lines: The Historical Origins of White Supremacy in California.* Berkeley, California: University of California Press.

Alpern, Stanley B. (1998). *Amazons of Black Sparta: The Women Warriors of Dahomey.* New York: New York University Press.

Ani, Marimba (Dona Richards) (1994). *Yurugu: An African-Centered Critique of European Cultural Thought and Behavior.* Trenton, New Jersey: Africa World Press, Inc.

Aptheker, H., ed. (1973). *The Education of Black People: Ten Critiques 1906-1960 by W.E.B. DuBois.* New York: Monthly Review Press.

Archive of War At Home (2007). "U.S. Domestic Covert Operations." http://mediafilter.org/MFF/USDomCovOps1.html.

Azevedo, Mario (1998). *Africana Studies: A Survey of Africa and the African Diaspora, Second Edition.* Durham, North Carolina: Carolina Academic Press.

Azibo, Daudi Ajani Ya (1996). *African Psychology in Historical Perspective and Related Commentary.* Trenton, New Jersey: Africa World Press, Inc.

Azikiwe, Abayomi (2007). *Pan African News Wire.* (panafricannews.blogspot.com/2007/11/africa-warrior-queens-gender-roles.html). Retrieved 2/17/08.

Bell, Bernice Parker (2008). "My Search, My Soul, My Rebirth." Unpublished Poem.

Ben-Jochannan, Yosef A.A. (1998). *Our Black Seminarians and Black Clergy Without a Black Theology.* New York: Alkebulan Books and Education Materials Associates.

_____ (1972). *Cultural Genocide in the Black and African Studies Curriculum.* New York: Alkebu-Lan.

_____ (1971). *Africa: Mother of Western Civilization.* Baltimore, Maryland: Black Classic Press.

Bernal, Martin (1987). *Black Athena: The Afroasiatic Roots of Classical Civilization, Vol. I.* New Brunswick, New Jersey: Rutgers University Press.

_____ (1991). *Black Athena: The Afroasiatic Roots of Classical Civilization, Vol. II.* New Brunswick, New Jersey: Rutgers University Press.

Birdsell, J.B. (1981). *Human Evolution: An Introduction to the New Physical Anthropology.* Boston: Houghton Mifflin Company.

Borishade, Adetokunbo (Winter 2006). "Analysis of the Haitian Rara Festival as Continuations of Yoruba, Fon, Arara, and Igede Traditions," *Journal of Intercultural Disciplines, Vol. VI,* pp. 111-152.

_____ (1999). *Classical African Values and*

Yoruba Philosophy for African American Intervention and Personality Development. Jacksonville, Florida: Sankofa Press.

_____ (1996). *Re-Aligning African Heads: Yoruba Curatives for Maafa-Related Ailments.* Jacksonville, Florida: Sankofa Press.

_____ (1994). "The Niger-Kordofanian Linguistic Bases of African American Ebonics: A Creole Language." *The Western Journal of Black Studies, 18*(1), pp. 1-10.

_____ (1993). *The Study of African American Sermonics and Protest Rhetoric in Relation to the Yoruba Concepts of Oro (Hoo-ro) and Iwa.* Unpublished Dissertation.

Boulding, Kenneth E. (1982). *The Image.* Ann Arbor, Michigan: University of Michigan Press.

Budge, E.A.W. (1928). *A History of Ethiopia, Nubia and Abyssinia (According to the Hieroglyphic Inscriptions of Egypt and Nubia, and the Ethiopian Chronicles).* London: Methuen & Company, Ltd.

Campbell, Dugald (1928). *On the Trail of the Veiled Tuareg.* Philadelphia, Pennsylvania: B. Lippincott Company.

Campbell, Joseph (1987). *The Masks of God: Primitive Mythology.* New York: Penguin Books.

Campbell, Mary E. (2007). "Thinking Outside the (Black) Box: Measuring Black and Multiracial Identification on Surveys," *Social Science Research 36*(3), pp. 921-944.

Carruthers, J. (1995). *MDW NTR: Divine Speech, a Historical Reflection of African Deep Thought from the Time of the Pharaohs to the Present.* London: Karnak House.

Chinweizu (1987). *Decolonizing the African Mind.* London: Sundoor Press.

Civil Rights Era (2006). *African American Odyssey.* (http://memory.loc.gov/ammem/aaohtml/exhibit/aopart9.html)

Clarke, John Henrik (1995). *Who Betrayed the African World Revolution? And Other Speeches.* Chicago, Illinois: Third World Press.

_____ (1993). *African People in World History.* Baltimore, Maryland: Black Classic Press.

_____ (1991). *Africans at the Crossroads: Notes for an African World Revolution.* Trenton, New Jersey: Africa World Press.

_____ (May 1988). "Africa: The Passing of the Golden Ages."

Cleaver, Eldridge (1968). *Soul On Ice.* New York: Dell Publishing.

Comer, James P. and Alvin Poussaint (1992). *Raising Black Children.* New York: Penguin Books U.S.A.

Cone, James H. (1999). *Black Theology and Black Power.* Maryknoll, New York: Harper & Row.

Copeland, Miles (1970). *Game of Nations.* New York: Simon and Schuster.

Cruse, Harold (1987). *Plural But Equal: Blacks and Minorities in America's Plural Society.* New York: William Morrow and Company.

_____ (1967). *The Crisis of the Negro Intellectual.* New York: William Morrow and Company.

Dashu, Max (2006). "Suppressed Histories Archives: Female Liberators" (http://www.suppressedhistories.net/articles/warriors.html). Retrieved 2/17/08.

_____ (2000). "Racism, History and Lies: Some Doctrines of Racial Supremacy as Classically taught in Euro/American Institutions, Textbooks and Media." (http://www.suppressedhistories.net/articles/racism_history.html). Retrieved 1/17/08.

Day, Linda R. (1994). "The Evolution of Female Chiefship during the Late Nineteenth-Century Wars of the Mende," *The International Journal of African Historical Studies,* 27(3), pp. 481-503.

DeVolney, C.F. *The Ruins of Empires.* New York: Peter Eckler Publishers.

Delaney, Martin R. (1991). *The Origin of Races and Color: With an Archeological Compendium of Ethiopian and Egyptian civilization.* Baltimore, Maryland: Black Classic Press.

Deloria, Vine (1969). *Custer Died for Your Sins: An Indian Manifesto, (Civilization of the American Indian).* New York: McMillan.

Diop, Cheikh Anta (1990). *The Cultural Unity of Black Africa: The Domains of Patriarchy and Matriarchy in Classical Antiquity.* Chicago, Illinois: Third World Press.

_____ (1981). *Civilization or Barbarism: An Authentic Anthropology.* Brooklyn, New York: Lawrence Hill Books.

_____ (1974). *The African Origin of Civilization: Myth or Reality.* Westport, Connecticut: Lawrence Hill & Company.

Dopamu, P.Ade, Nike S. Lawal, and Matthew N.O. Sadiku, eds. (2004). *Understanding Yoruba Life and Culture.* Trenton, New Jersey: Africa World Press Inc.

Drake, St. Clair (1970). *The Redemption of Africa and Black Religion.* Chicago, Illinois: Third World Press.

DuBois, W.E.B. (1972). *The World and Africa: An inquiry into the Part Which Africa Has Played in World History.* New York: International Publishers.

Ember, Carol and Melvin Ember (1996). *Cultural Anthropology, Eighth Edition.* Upper Saddle River, New Jersey: Prentice Hall.

Fanon, Frantz (1967). *Black Skin White Masks.* New York: Grove Press, Inc.

Freire, Paulo (1968). *Pedagogy of the Oppressed.* New York: Seabury Press.

Frobenius, Leo (1980). *Voice of Africa.* New York: Arno Press.

Glick, Brian (1989). "COINTELPRO in the '60s," *War at Home.* Boston, Massachusetts: South End Press.

Gregerson, Edgar (1977). *Language in Africa: An Introductory Survey.* New York: Gordon and Breach.

Gyekye, Kwame (1987). *An Essay on African Philosophical Thought.* New York: Cambridge University Press.

Hacker, Andrew (1992). *Two Nations: Black and White, Separate, Hostile, Unequal.* New York: Ballantine Books.

Hare, Nathan (1991). *The Black Anglo-Saxons.* Chicago, Illinois: Third World Press.

Herskovits, Melville J. (1990). *The Myth of the Negro Past.* Boston, Massachusetts: Beacon Press.

Hicks, David and Margaret A. Gwynne (1996). *Cultural Anthropology, Second Edition.* New York: Harper Collins College Publishers.

Hilliard, Asa G. III (1997). *SBA: The Reawakening of the African Mind.* Gainesville, Florida: Makare Publishing.

Horney, Karen (1950). *Neurosis and Human Growth: The Struggle Toward Self-Realization.* New York: W.W. Norton.

Idowu, E. Bolaji (1994). *Olodumare: God In Yoruba Belief.* New York: A & B Books Publishers.

Jackson, John G. (1970). *Introduction to African Civilizations.* Secaucus, New Jersey: Citadel Press.

Jahn, Janheinz (1961). *Muntu: An Outline of the New African Culture.* New York: Grove Press, Inc.

Johnson, Francis e. and Henry Selby (1978). *Anthropology: The Biocultural View.* Dubuque, Iowa: William C. Brown Company Publishers.

Kaiwar, Vasant (1989). "Racism and the Writing of History, Part I)." *South Asia Bulletin, 9*(2), pp. 32-56.

KaMau, Kheper Ka Ra (Dana Dennard) (1998). *The Re-Ascension of the Black Man's Mind: Coming Forth by Ra.* Tallahassee, Florida: Aakhet Press.

Karenga, Maulana (1987). *Introduction to Black Studies.* Los Angeles, California: Kawaida Publications.

King, Martin L. King, Jr. (1967). "Beyond Vietnam: A Time to Break Silence." A speech delivered at Riverside Church.

Keto, C. Tsehloane (1989). *The Africa-Centered Perspective of History: An Introduction.* Blackwood, New Jersey: K.A. Publications.

Lawal, Nike S., Matthew N.O. Sadiku and Ade Dopamu (2004). *Understanding Yoruba Life and Culture.* Trenton, New Jersey: Africa World Press Inc.

Mailer, Norman. *The White Negro.* San Francisco, California: City Lights Books.

Massey, Gerald (1995). *A Book of the Beginnings, Vol. II.* Baltimore, Maryland: Black Classic Press.

Mbiti, John S. (1991). *Introduction to African Religion, Second Revised Edition.* Oxford and London: Heinemann International.

_____ (1969). *African Religions & Philosophy.* Oxford and London: Heinemann International.

McMillen, Neil R. (1971). *The Citizens' Council: Organized Resistance to the Second Reconstruction, 1954-1964.* Urbana, Illinois: University of Illinois Press.

Metz, Helen Chapin, ed. (1991). "Kush, Meroe, and Nubia," *Sudan: A Country Study.* Washington, D.C.: Federal Research Division of the Library of Congress.

Mitchell, Henry H. (1975). *Black Belief: Folk Beliefs of Blacks in America and West Africa.* New York: Evanston, San Francisco, London: Harper & Row.

Mintz, Sidney (1970). Foreword in Norman Whitten, Jr. and John F. Szed. *Afro-American Anthropology.* New York: Free Press.

Mudimbe, V.Y. (1988). *The Invention of Africa: Gnosis, Philosophy, and the Order of Knowledge.* Bloomington and Indianapolis, Indiana: Indiana University Press.

Murray, Henry A., ed. (1960). *Myth and Mythmaking.* Boston, Massachusetts: Beacon Press.

Obenga, Theophile (1996). *A Lost Tradition: African Philosophy in World History.* Philadelphia, Pennsylvania: The Source Editions.

_____ (1992). *Ancient Egypt and Black Africa: A Student's Handbook for the Study of Ancient Egypt in Philosophy, Linguistics and Gender Relations.* Chicago, Illinois: Front Line.

Oberman, Irina (May 26, 2006). "Europe Conquered," *Stanford Review.* (www.stanfordreview.org/Archive/Volume_ XXXVI/Issue _9/Opinions/opinions6.shtml - 23k)

Olomenji (1984). *White Genocide, Black Obsolescence.* New Frontiers Limited Press.

Pew Research Center (November 2007). "Blacks See Growing Values Gap Between Poor and Middle Class." (http://pewsocialtrends.org/pubs/700/black-public-opinion)

Quarles, Benjamin (1987). *The Negro in the Making of America, Third Edition Revised.* New York: Macmillan Publishing Company.

Race, Richard W. (1965). "Analyzing ethnic education policymaking in England and Wales." (www.shef.ac.uk/socstudies/Shop/race_article.pdf -)

Richards, Dona M. (1990). "The Implications of African-American Spirituality," pp. 207-231 in Molefi K. Ashante and Kariamu Welsh-Ashante (eds.) *African Culture: The Rhythms of Unity.* Trenton, New Jersey: Africa World Press, Inc.

Rosaldo, Michelle Z. (1974). *Woman, Culture, and Society.* Palo Alto, California: Stanford University Press.

Rothstein, Richard (2007). "Are Black Cops Cut from the Same Cloth as Gay Republicans? A blog submitted to *The Daily Gotham.* (http://www.dailygotham.com/blog/richard_ rothstein/are_black_cops_cut_from_the _same)

Salmonson, Jessica A. (1991). *The Encyclopedia of Amazons.* St. Paul, Minnesota: Paragon House Publishers.

Scobie, Edward (1994). *Global African Presence.* Brooklyn, New York: A & B Books Publishers.

Shaw, Todd C. (June 2004). "Two Warring Ideals: Double Consciousness, Dialogue, and African American Patriotism Post-911," *Journal of African American Studies,* 8(1-2), pp. 20-37.

Speight, Suzette L., Elizabeth M. Vera, and Kennedy B. Derrickson, M.D. (1996). "Racial Self-Designation, Racial Identity, and Self-Esteem Revisited," *Journal of Black Psychology,* 22(1), pp. 37-52.

Stringer, Christopher and Robin McKie (1997). *African Exodus: The Origins of Modern Humanity.* New York: Henry Holt and Company.

Stewart, Julia (1997). *African Proverbs and Wisdom.* New York: Kensington Publishing Corp.

Thompson, Robert Farris (1984). *Flash of the Spirit: African and Afro-American Art and Philosophy.* New York: Vintage Books.

_____ (1974). *African Art in Motion.* California: U.C.L.A. Press.

Temple, Cristel N. (2006). "Strategies for Cultural Renewal in an American-Based Version of African Globalism," *Journal of Black Studies, Vol. 36*(3), pp. 301-317. (SAGE Publications)

Unsworth, Tim (2006). "Racism and Religion: Partners in Crime?" *Salt of the Earth.* Macau, China: Claretian Publications. (http://salt.claretianpubs.org/issues/racism unsworth.html).

Vanzant, Iyanla (1993). *Acts of Faith: Daily Meditations for People of Color.* New York: Simon & Schuster.

Wa Thiong'o, Ngugi (1987). *Decolonizing the Mind: The Politics of Language in African Literature.* Portsmouth, New Hampshire: Heinemann.

Washington, Margaret (2005). "Rachel Weeping for Her Children," *Black Women and the Abolition of Slavery.* History Now, American History Online, Issue 5. www.historynow.org/09_2005/historian3.html. Retrieved on 2/18/08.

Welsing, Frances Cress (1991). *The Isis (Yssis) Papers.* Chicago, Illinois: Third World Press.

Whittle, A.R. (1996). *Europe in the Neolithic: The Creation of New Worlds.* London: Cambridge University Press.

Wilde, Lyn Webster (2000). *On the Trail of Women Warriors: The Amazons in Myth and History.* Great Britain: Constable Company, Limited.

Williams, Chancellor (1972). *The Destruction of Black Civilization: Great Issues of a Race from 4500 B.C.E. to 2000 A.D.* Chicago, Illinois: Third World Press.

Wilson, Amos N. (1993). *The Falsification of Afrikan Consciousness: Eurocentric History, Psychology and the Policy of White Supremacy.* New York: Afrikan World Infosystems.

_____ (1990). *Black-On-Black Violence: The Psychodynamics of Black Self-Annihilation in Service of White Domination.* New York: Afrikan World Infosystems.

Wiredu, Kwasi (1980). *Philosophy and an African Culture.* London and New York: Cambridge University Press.

Wolf, Paul et. al. (2001). "COINTELPRO: The Untold American Story." Report presented to U.N. High Commissioner for Human Rights Mary Robinson at the World Conference Against Racism in Durban, South Africa by the members of the Congressional Black Caucus attending the conference.(http://www.icdc.com/~paulwolf/cointelpro/cointelpro/coinwcar.

Woodson, Carter G. (1977). *The Miseducation of the Negro.* Washington, D.C.: Associated Publishers. (First published 1933)

Wright, Bobby E (1989). *The Psychopathic Racial Personality.* Chicago, Illinois: Third World Press.

Yai, Olabiyi Babalola (October 2001). "Yoruba Religion and Globalization: Some Reflections." Paper presented at the University of Costa Rica, School of History.

(en.wikipedia.org/wiki/Mende_people). "Mende People."

(en.wikipedia.org/wiki/Moremi). "Moremi."

(en.wikipedia.org/wiki/Seh-Dong-Hong-Beh). "She-Dong-Hong-Beh."

(http://www.questia.com/library/ encyclopedia/ falashas.jsp). "Falashas," *Free Encyclopedia Articles at Questia.com Online Library.* Retrieved 2/28/08.

(http://www.geocities.com/jywanza1/AfrikanWarriors.html). "Afrikan Women Warriors."

African Origins of Science and Mathematics
Prepared by Ali B. Ali-Dinar,
African Studies Center
University of Pennsylvania

THE AFRICAN ORIGINS OF SCIENCE AND MATHEMATICS: A NEW PARADIGM FOR SCIENTIFIC THINKING; AN ANNOTATED BIBLIOGRAPHY

Last Update: February 1991 dt>Developed by: Kamau Beyete A. Sadiki, Hydropower Engineer, dt>Science & Mathematics Education Consultant dt>Co-Founder, Sirius Study Group, Western Region, ASCAC dt>PO Box 3791, Portland, OR 97208 dt>kamau@pwrip1.npd.usace.army.mil

This annotated bibliography is a compilation of books, papers and articles that can provide some insight into the accomplishments of early Africans and African-Americans in science and mathematics. It can be utilized for research purposes or just to expand the general reader's consciousness on the subject matter. It is by no means exhaustive or all inclusive. It merely reflects some of the materials that I have utilized in my own research.

1. Blacks in Science: Ancient and Modern, ed. by Ivan VanSertima, Transaction Books, New Brunswick, NJ, 1983

A compilation of very thoroughly researched papers that documents Africa's contributions to astronomy, agriculture, architecture, engineering, aeronautics, mathematics, medicine, metallurgy, physics and writing systems. Also included in this text are articles detailing the African-American's contributions to science and invention. Some of the papers that are worth special mention are John Pappademos' "An Outline of Africa's Role in the History of Physics", Dr.

Charles Finch's "The African Background of Medical Science", "Steel Making in Ancient Africa" by Debra Shore, "The Pyramids: Ancient Showcase of African Science and Technology" by Beatrice Lumpkin and John Henrik Clarke's "Lewis Latimer: Bringer of the Light".

2. Africa Counts, Claudia Zaslavsky, Prindle, Weber, and Schmidt, New Your, 1973

This is a pioneering work that is well written and documented. It details the early African mathematical practices found almost throughout Africa. A must reading for those interested in the African origins of mathematics.

3. Stolen Legacy, George G. M. James, Julian Richardson Associates, San Francisco, 1976

In this scholarly book, Professor James declares that Greek philosophy is a misnomer. He thoroughly documents the African origins of Grecian civilization and the study of Greek philosophers and mathematicians in Africa. Dr. James also puts forth an hypothesis based on the ancient Kemetic creation story as a metaphorical scientific explanation for the creation of the universe.

4. Journal of African Civilizations, Vol. 4, No. 1, ed. by Ivan VanSertima, Transaction Books, New Burnswick, NJ, 1982

This special issue of the scholarly journal edited by Dr. VanSertima deals exclusively with the African and African-American contributions to science and invention.

5. The African Origins of Civilization, Cheikh Anta Diop, Lawrence Hill Press, New York, 1974

Here we have the most thorough documentation of the African ethnicity of the ancient people who developed the mathematics and sciences upon which modern civilization is based (Ethiopians, so-called Egyptians, Nubians, Sudanese, Colchis, etc.). Excellent documentation regarding the origins of the scholarship of Greek philosophers, i.e., Herodotus, Diodorus, Plato, Plutarch, et. al.

6. An Introduction to the History of Mathematics, Howard Eves, Holt, Rinehart & Winston, New York, 3rd ed., 1969; History of Mathematics, Arthur Gittleman, Charles E. Merrill Press, Columbus, Ohio, 1975.

These two books are primarily devoted to the origin of mathematics in the ancient world, followed by subsequent European developments based upon these model: Kemetic number system, Ahmose (Rhind) Papyri, African surveyors, 3-4-5 triangle, truncated pyramid (seal of the US dollar bill), Kemetic algebra, etc.

7. The Pyramids, Ahmed Fakhry, University of Chicago Press, Chicago, IL, 1975

This book not only describes the structure and dimensions of the three best known pyramids at Giza, but furnishes the same information in respect to at least a dozen others, including the Step Pyramid at Saqqara.

8. The Rhind Mathematical Papyrus, Arnold Chase, National Council of Teachers of Mathematics, 1979

A thorough analysis of one of the ancient mathematical journal left by African mathematicians. Originally known as the Ahmose Mathematician Papyrus (Ahmose being the author), it documents the use of geometry, trigonometry, algebra (aha), arithmetic progression, proportionality, volume and area calculations, etc.

9. Mathematics in the Time of the Pharaohs, Richard Gillings, Cambridge MIT Press, 1972

Gillings thoroughly documents the extensive mathematical activity of the ancient Kemetic people. His work begins with the four basic arithmetic operations and continues with fractions, algebra, geometric and arithmetic progression, and finding areas and volumes of various geometric shapes.

10. Golden Legacy, Baylor Publishing Co. and Community Enterprise, Inc., Seattle, WA, 1983

Golden Legacy is a series of illustrated Black history magazines written in a "comic book" type format. Short biographical stories are developed around great personalities in Black history. Several volumes deals with scientists and inventors. Excellent for kindergarten and early elementary lesson planning on African-American science and mathematics.

11. A Young Genius in Old Egypt, Beatrice Lumpkin, DuSable Museum Press, Chicago, 1979

This is an excellent primer for early elementary school ages on the origins of mathematics. It tells the story of a young African growing up to become one of ancient Kemet's (Egypt's) greatest mathematicians. It is very well illustrated, also.

12. Seven Black American Scientists and Eight Black American Inventors, Robert Hayden, Addisonian Press, Reading, MA, 1970 & 1972, respectively; Black Inventors of America, McKinley Burt, Jr., National Book Co., Portland, OR, 1969

Excellent biographies on the lives of Black American scientists and inventors are detailed in these works. Each of them can easily be used to develop lessons using the "Great Personality" approach as suggested by Dr. John Henrik Clarke. Professor Burt's book goes a step further and offers a still timely analysis of how some of these Black innovator's invention tremendously affected the American and, in some instances, world industrial complex.

13. The Physicians of Pharaonic Egypt, Paul Ghalioungui, Verlan Phillip Von Zabern, Mainz, West Germany, 1983

In this work Dr. Ghaliougui provides us with a good look into the high level of development that was achieved by ancient African priest- physicians in the medical sciences. There were specialized physicians such as surgeons, veterinarians, therapists, pathologists, physicians of the eyes, stomach and teeth, etc. Dr. Ghaliougui also looks closely at the organization of the ancient medical profession and the personalities of some of the ancient priest-physicians.

14. A History of Science, George Sarton, Vol. 1, Harvard Press, Cambridge, MA, 1952

Although this volume deals with the Hellenistic sciences, it is mentioned here because chapter two is a thoroughly written exposition of the sciences of ancient Kemet. A position is taken by Sarton that the supposedly scientific activity of the ancient Kemetic people was indeed scientific and the priest-scientist of that time laid the foundation for later Greek and Wester science. "They were our first guides and our first teachers (in the sciences)", says Sarton.

15. "African Star Gazers: Why Doesn't Western Science Take Them Seriously?", Hunter H. Adams, III, Paper delivered at the 5th Annual Third World Conference, Chicago, IL, March, 1979

In this paper Mr. Adams clearly articulates the fundamental differences between the development and practice of African science and what later develops as Western science. He utilized the Dogon people West Africa and their astronomical knowledge, particularly their knowledge about the Sirius star system, to exemplify the differences. To understand the differences in the development of scientific knowledge in African and the West, this paper is highly recommended.

16. The Dawn of Astronomy, N. Lockyer, MacMillan and Co., New York, 1894

This is the most authoritative documentation on the advent of astronomy in Africa. Lockyer scholarly documents how the science of astronomy was an integral part of the ancient Kemetic people's lifeways, from religion to architecture.

17. Secrets of the Great Pyramid, Peter Tompkins, Harper & Row, New York, 1971

An intriguing but well documented look at the early scientific and mathematical investigations in the Great Pyramid of Khufu. An excellent and detailed description of the mathematics, astronomy, geodesics, and mensuration techniques developed form the configurations of the Great Pyramid. Tompkins emphatically states that the builders knew the precise circumference of the earth, the mean length of the earth's orbit, the value po pi and phi (know as the Golden Section during the recent "Age of Enlightenment" in Europe), the acceleration of Gravity, the speed of light, trigonometric values, and a host of other mathematical and scientific facts. He also offers evidence that such great Greek mathematicians and philosophers as Plato, Pythagoras, Solon, Thales, Diodorus, Herodotus, and others named Kemet as the birthplace of geometry, and the place in which many Greeks went to study.

18. Mathematics in the Making, Lancelot Hogben, Doubleday & Co., New York, 1960

This is an omnibus volume providing a thorough survey of developments in all areas of mathematics from Dynastic Kemet of the times of Newton and Gauss. Many illustrations and diagrams in color that lends themselves to lesson plans and class projects.

19. Africa: Mother of Western Civilizations, Yosef A. A. ben-Jochannan, Alkebu-lan Books, New York, 1971

20. The Healing Hand: Man and Wound in the Ancient World, Guido Majno, Harvard University Press, Cambridge, MA, 1975

21. The Edwin Smith Medical Papyrus, James Breasted, University of Chicago Press, Chicago, 1931

An in-depth analysis of what is probably the most detailed medical book written by ancient Africans. It has an illustration of a cross-section of the head with sections of the brain identified in Mdw Ntr (so-called hieroglyphics).

22. The House of Life (Per Ankh): Magic and Medical Science in Ancient Egypt, Paul Ghalioungui, B. M. Israel Press, Amsterdam, 1973

This text is a well written treatise on the medical profession in ancient Kemet. It documents the ancient African sacerdotal medical activity in such fields as surgery, physiopathology, gynecology, obstetrics pharmacology, ophthalmology, and dentistry. Ghalioungui also deals with the application "magic" in the healing arts of ancient Kemet.

23. The Mechanical Triumph of the Ancient Egyptians, F. Barber, Kegan, Paul, Trench, Trubner & Co., Ltd, London, 1900

This is a good early attempt to explain the engineering and mechanical achievements of the ancient Kemetic engineers without the use of some simple machines.

24. Destruction of Black Civilization, Chancellor Williams, Third World Press, Chicago, 1974

Dr. Williams offers the reader an explanation of the often neglected aspect of African history. i.e., how African civilizations were destroyed by hostile forces from Europe and Asia. He goes further and offers a plan on ho to reverse the harmful effects of the destruction of African civilization.

25. The African Presence in Ancient America: They Came Before Columbus, Ivan VanSertima, Random House, New York, 1976

In this book Dr. VanSertima draws upon his mastery of several academic disciplines to demonstrate that African made successful voyages to the American continent before Columbus. He further proves that the earliest civilization in America was influenced by these African visitors perhaps as early as 1000 B.C. (See also Before Columbus by Dr. Samuel D. Marble, A. S. Barnes & Co., New York, 1980; The Black Discovery of America by Michael Bradley, Personal Library Publishers, Toronto, Canada, 1981; and African and the Discovery of America by Leo Wiener, Innes and Sons, Philadelphia, 1920).

26. Scared Science: The King of Pharaonic Theocracy, R. A. Schwaller deLubicz, Inner Traditions International, New York, 1982

27. The Time Falling Bodies Take to Light: Mythology, Sexuality and the Origins of Culture, William I. Thompson, St. Martin's Press, New York, 1981.

28. Black Man of the Nile and His Family, Yosef A. A. ben-Jochannan, Alkebulan Books, New York, 1981

Dr. ben-Jochannan draws upon his varied experiences, talents and academic training to bring the reader a monumental work that shows convincingly that the original Kemetic people (so-called Egyptians) were Black people. He employs a multi-disciplinary approach that can leave no doubt in the mind of honest readers that the Nile Valley is the original home of African civilization.

29. World's Greatest Men of Color, Joel A. Rogers, Vols. I & II, MacMillan Press, New York, 1973

J. A. Rogers brilliantly recounts the individual achievements of African men and women around the world. Each biography is supported by a complete bibliography. This is a rare work that demonstrates that Africans have participated in all of the major cultures of the world.

30. Africa's Gift to America, Joel A. Rogers, Helga M. Rogers (publisher), New York, 1961

This is an easy to read introduction to great African Achievements form the African continent to America. Mr. Rogers offers complete references throughout the book.

31. Wretched of the Earth, Franz Fanon, Grove Press, New York, 1968

The author, a revolutionary and brilliant psychoanalyst, expertly explores the harmful aspects of colonization from the perspective of the colonized. This work has universal applications for all oppressed people in their struggles against foreign domination.

32. Introduction to African Civilizations, John G. Jackson, University Press, New York, 1970

With painstaking objectivity, and brilliant scholarship, Prof. Jackson obliterates the picture of African being backward and contributing nothing of significance to the evolution of civilization. This work challenges all of the standard approaches to African history and provides new insights into the subject that clearly show the development of civilization in Africa. Mr. Jackson provides the reader with an abundance of documentation and references that corroborates the contention of an African origin of civilization.

33. Early Hydraulic Civilization in Egypt: A Study in Cultural Ecology, Karl Butzer, University of Chicago Press, Chicago, 1976

Butzer has produced an excellent primer on the early hydraulic culture of Nile Valley civilization. It is revealing in that show some of the sophisticated hydraulic techniques used by ancient Africans in the Nile Valley which propel them into civilized societies.

34. Selections from the Husia: The Sacred Wisdom of Ancient Egypt, Maulana Karenga, Kawaida Publications, Los Angeles, 1984

Dr. Karenga meaningfully selected and beautifully retranslated several books ancient scared literature that clearly illustrates the high moral and ethical lifeways of the ancient Kemetic people. The Husia also provides literary insights into Kemetic pedagogy, religion, philosophy, and human behavior. A must reading for any student who seeks a rich and clear understanding of Kemetic literature and lifeways.

35. The Sirius Mystery, Robert K. G. Temple, St. Martin's Press, New York, 1976

Robert Temple attempts to shed some light on the extraordinary astronomical knowledge of the Dogon people of Mali, West Africa. The binary star system called Sirius A and B is central to the Dogon lifeway. After doing meticulous research on the Sirius question, Temple implies that the Dogon was instructed in their wisdom by extra- terrestrial visitors from outer space.

36. The Pyramids: An Enigma Solved, Joseph Davidovits and Margie Morris, Hippocrene Books, New York, 1988

Davidovits and Morris puts forth yet another theory on the construction of the pyramids. It provides new insights into the question because old data is not rehashed. Their thesis is that the stones used as building material is a cement aggregate that were casted in place and not quarried blocks of limestone as most pyramid construction theorist suggest. The critical piece of data for their thesis is the so-called Famine Stele found on the Shele Island that, according toe Davidovits' translation, has the alchemical process for producing the aggregate.

37. The Legacy of Egypt, S. R. K. Glanville, Oxford University Press, 1942

This is a compilation of several articles that discuss ancient Kemetic contributions from the calendar to modern Islam and Christianity. There are three excellent papers on mechanical and technical processes, materials, science, and medicine. Good primers on ancient Kemetic scientific achievements.

38. Egyptian Sacred Science in Islam, Rafiq Bilal & Thomas Goodwin, Bennu Publishers, San Francisco, 1985

Bilal and Goodwin are two young African-American scholars that are carrying on the tradition of cutting edge research among African scholars concerning ancient Kemet's impact on the major religions of today. This work documents the parallels in Kemetic lifeways and the Islamic religion. They also proposes an interesting hypothesis about the ancient Kemetic symbol for like, the ankh, being a symbol of the phenomena in nature known as the Hydrologic Cycle.

39. "Maat: The African Universe", Jacob Carruthers, Journal of Black Studies, Vol. 1, No. 1, San Francisco State University Black Studies Dept. San Francisco, 1982

Maat, in its simplest definition, is defined as truth, justice and righteousness. It was the supreme ethical paradigm which dictated the behavior of ancient Kemetic people and priest-scientist. In this article Dr. Carruthers explains the universality of the concept of Maat and how ethical behavior was a norm in Kemetic society.

40. Egyptian Mysteries: New Light on Ancient Spiritual Knowledge, Lucy Lamy, Crossroads Books, New York, 1981

Lamy studied very closely with the French Egyptologist Schwaller deLubiz at the Temple of Ipet Isut, in present day Luxor. This book provides a good interpretation of the transphysical aspects of the lifeways of ancient Kemetic people. With the exoterica removed, it also reveals a certain degree of scientific thinking that would be other wise obscure. A good reference in understanding the scientific-spiritual relationship in ancient Kemet.

41. Islamic Science: An Illustrated Study, Seyyed H. Nasr, Westerham Press, 1976

42. Le Temple de L'Homme (The Temple in Man), R. A. Schwaller deLubiz, Tome 1, Vol. 1, Apet Du

Sud a Lougsor, Caracteres 3, rue Haute Feuille, Paris 6, 1957 (1977 condensed translation available from Inner Traditions International, New York)

43. Symbol and the Symbolic: Ancient Egypt Science and the Evolution of Consciousness, R. A. Schwaller deLubicz, Inner Traditions International, New York, 1978 (Condensed translation of original volume published in France in 1949 entitled Symbol et Symbolique).

44. "The Shabaka Text (Memphite Theology)", Chapter VIII in Stolen Legacy by George G. M. James (#3 of bibliography). See Also The Dawn of Conscience, James H Breasted, Charles Scribner's Sons, New York, 1933, pages 29-42; and Ancient Egyptian Literature, Miriam Lichtheim, Vol. 1, University of California Press, Berkeley, 1973, pages 51-57

The Shabaka Text, known in European Egyptological circles as the Memphite Theology, is one of several ancient Kemetic texts that deal with the creation of the universe. George G. M. James contents that it can very well be a scientific thesis that explains the cosmology and physics at the first moment of creation and at incremental times thereafter. In light of insights being revealed by research in quantum mechanics and nonlinear sciences, The Shabaka Text and other ancient Kemetic creation text needs to be given renewed attention for their scientific detail.

45. The Afrocentric Idea, Molefi Kete Asante, Temple University Press, Philadelphia, 1987

Dr. Asante brilliantly asserts the need for an afrocentric paradigm that accurately articulates the experiences and life-ways of people of African descent. Furthermore, he maintains that this paradigm can only be developed by African scholars. He exposes the inadequacies of logic based Western scientific discoveries in their attempt to understand African cultural data. A must-read for those interested in a more intelligent context in which to understand African cultural dynamics.

46. Toward A Science of Consciousness, Kenneth R Pelletier, Celestial Arts, Berkeley, CA, 1985

47. Turbulent Mirror, John Briggs & F. David Peat, Harper & Row, New York, 1989

This text is the best published thus far that uses easily understandable metaphors to explain the "new" science of complexity, chaos and non-linearity. It offers some insights into how ancient African priest- scientist understood the universe as one and all phenomena within it as being inter-related. It also corroborates the ancient understanding that reality is infinite.

48. "African Consciousness and the Liberation Struggle: Implications for the Development and Construction of Scientific Paradigms", Wade Nobles, privately published paper, Oakland, CA, 1978

A very bold and courageous paper that attempts to articulate an African perspective on scientific inquiry. It offers an African-centered definition for science and formulates a scientific paradigm that is founded on the collective African experience.

49. Black Pioneers of Science & Invention, Louis Haber, Harcourts, Brace, & World, Inc., New York, 1970

This is another good publication that documents the creative genius and inventiveness of early African-American scientists and engineers. (See reference #12 for other sources on this subject)

50. "The Scar on the African's Arm", Hippocrates (magazine), March/ April 1989 issue

This article provides insights on the African origins of the immunization process for smallpox. Most western sources wrongly credits a Dr. Mather for the process but an African by the name of Onesimus revealed the secret of the process to him.

51. "From Celestial Flow to Terrestrial Flow: Ancient Hydraulic Developments in the Nile Valley", Kamau Beyete A. Sadiki, paper delivered at the Third Annual Conference of the Association for the Study of Classical African Civilizations, City College of New York, Harlem, NY, March, 1986

This paper details the origin and evolution of hydraulics system in the Nile Valley. It also shows how these hydraulic systems were developed in harmony with the annual inundation of the Nile and how the scientific thinking of ancient African scientists dealt with both physical and transphysical phenomena, synthesizing intuitive and analytical processes, simultaneously.

52. "The Peopling of Ancient Egypt", Chiekh Anta Diop, published paper in The General History of Africa: Ancient Civilizations, Vol. II, edit by K. Moktar, United Nation's Educational, Scientific and Cultural Organization (UNESCO), Paris, France, 1976.

This paper by Dr. Chiekh Anta Diop, author of The African Origins of Civilization, was delivered at the Cairo Symposium in Cairo, Egypt in 1974. Dr. Diop provided extensive linguistic, anthropological, and other scientific data that demonstrated the ethnic origins of the so- called ancient Egyptian people was from the south. His research along with that of Dr. Theophile Obenga was so thorough that the other scholars in attendance was not able to provide an adequate response to their thesis. This paper is one of the definitive, if not the most definitive, work on the question of the origins of the so-called ancient Egyptians.

53. The Dreams of Reason: The Computer and the Rise of Complexity, Heinz Pagels, Simon & Schuster, New York, 1988

An excellent layperson's resource on the recent emergence of the science of complexity and chaos. Well written by a respected physicist who uses good prose and metaphor to explain complexity and it's implication on how we view the universe.

54. Black Athena, Martin Bernal, Rutgers University Press, Rutgers, New Jersey, 1988

This text is a very scholarly attempt to continue the in-depth study of the thesis proposed by George G. M. James, Yosef ben-Jochannan and others. Bernal argues for an overthrow of the old historical paradigms he calls the "Ancient Model" and "Aryan Model" and replace them with his "Revised Ancient Model". The Revised Ancient Model discredits the Aryan Model as pure fabrication motivated by racism during the 17th through 19th centuries and proposes a new paradigm for historiography that show the tremendous "afroasiatic" influences on civilization.

55. Fascinating Fibonaccis: Mystery of Magic in Numbers, Trudi H. Garland, Dale Seymour Publications, 1987

This is an excellent reference for a lesson plan on the natural functions of mathematics. It gives a good overview of the so-called Fibonacci numbers. Most importantly, It documents the fact that ancient African mathematicians was cognizant of the transcendental function, know by the Greek letter phi, which equals 1.618.... It was called the golden ratio in Europe during its emergence from the Dark Ages.

56. American Black Scientists and Inventors, ed. by Edward Jenkins, National Science Teachers Association, Washington, D. C., 1975

57. At Last Recognition: A Reference Handbook of Unknown Black Inventors and Their Contributions to

America, James C. Wiliiams, B. C. A. Publishing Company, Chicago, IL, 1978

58. Banneker, The Afro-American Astronomer, ed. by Will W. Allen, Books for Libraries, Freeport, NY, 1969

59. Benjamin Banneker: Genius of Early America, Lillie Patterson, Abingdon, Nashville, TN, 1978

60. Black Apollo of Science: The Life of Ernest Everett Just, Kenneth R. Manning, Oxford Press, New York, 1983

61. Black Giants in Science, Paul J. Driver, VAntage Books, New York, 1973

62. Blacks in Science: Astrophysicist to Zoologist, Hattie Carwell, Exposition Books, Hicksville, NY, 1987

63. Black Mathematicians and Their Work, Virginia Newell, Dorrance and Company, Ardmore, PA, 1980

64. Dr. George Washington Carver, Scientist, Shirley Graham & George D. Lipscomb, WAshington Square Press, New York

65. George Washington Carver: The Story of A Great American, Ann Terry White, E. M. Hale, Eau Claire, WI, 1953

66. Life of Benjamin Banneker, Silvio A. Bendini, Little Brown Books, New York, 1954

67. Many Shades of Black, Stanton L. Wormley, and Lewis H. Fenderson, ed., Morrow Publishing Co., New York, 1969

68. The Negro In Science, Julius Taylor, ed., Morgan College Press, Baltimore, MD, 1955

69. "The Negro Benjamin Banneker, Astronomer and Mathematician, Plea for Universal Peace", by Phillip LePhillips, Records of the Columbian Historical Society, Vol. 20, Columbia, MD, pg 114-120

70. Negros Who Helped Build America, Madeline Stratton, Ginn & Co., Lexington, MA, 1965

71. Pocketful of Goobers: A Story About George Washington Carver, Barbara Mitchell, Carolrhoda Press, Minneapolis, MN, 1968

72. Shortchanged by History: America's Neglected Innovators, by Vernon Pizer, Putnam Books, New York, 1978

73. The Story of George Washington Carver, Arna Sontemps, Grosset & Dunlap, New York, 1954

74. They Showed the Way, Charlemae Rollins, Crowell Press, New York, 1964.

INDEX

(DSM-IV), 7
"inner head", 2
18th and early 19th centuries, 92
Abimbola, Wande, 44, 246-247, 248, 253, 320
Abiodun, 247, 249, 250, 251, 258, 259, 320
Aborigines of northern Australia, 176
Abraham, 70
accommodationists, 99
Adam, 12, 318
adaptation, 34, 56, 170, 172, 179, 180, 181, 183, 185; adaptive response, 56, 185
adolescents, 298, 319
adults: 14, 16, 77, 221, 298, 300, 314; males, 15
Africa centered approach, 3, 6, 21, 27, 45,-46,149, 154; arguments, 47; education, 285; philosophical theory, 44
Africa's classical period, 75
African American: 295, 308, 309; community, 23; elders, 307; history, 18, 19; mental disorders, 204; parents, 6; policemen, 108; preachers, 30; psychologists, 64; society, 4; studies, 69; theologians, 30, 168; women, 74
African Ancestors, 241, 304; parents of humanity, 304

African: behaviors, 45, 289; Christians, 3; consciousness, 33, 62, 73, 77, 81, 189, 303; double-consciousness, 84; dowry, 199
African contributions, 306, 155; cradle of civilization, 177; mathematics and science, 337
African Cultural Renaissance, 114
African culture, 44, 84, 168, 212, 213, 214, 215, 267, 277; osmology 214, 42
African deities, 224; Destiny, 287;
African Diaspora, 239, 240
African ethnic groups, 217, 220, 222, 239; African globalism, 82
African history, 35, 75, 76, 82, 228, 237, 306
African Independence Movement, 5, 261
African personality, 7, 64, 154
African: philosophy, 44; scientific aspect of, 42 276; worldview, 188
African religion, 24, 27, 113, 168, 221, 222, 224, 237, 238, 239, 240
African religious beliefs, 228; religious doctrines,

28
African scientific knowledge, 46, 47; spiritual worldview, 274, 279
African traditional: beliefs and values, 217, 306; culture, 254, 270; education, 285; philosophy, 35,60, 276; political systems, 214; religion, 187, 237, 249; institutions, 298; values, 306
African women, 155, 177, 198, 270; Afro-Brazilian, 237; female chieftainship, 198; African Eve, 12, 177; warriors, 176, 179, 180, 186, 190, 193, 273
Africoid, 168, 175, 176, 177
Afro-Asiatic, 150; Afro-Latin Americans, 113, 240
AIDS health services, 203; pandemic, 203
Akan, 277; Akans, 297
Akbar,Na'im, 77 203, 205, 206, 320
Ali, Muhammad, 92
American apartheid, 122; citizen groups, 117; citizens, 33, 91, 98, 208
American Friends Service Committee, 126
American history, 9, 75
American Indian Movement (AIM), 140
Americas, the, 5, 34, 64, 188, 212, 220, 226
ancestors, 5, 65, 76, 108, 148, 156, 167, 179, 197, 225, 231, 278

ancient Kush, 227, 232, 242
ancient African Model of History and Culture, 33, 146, 147, 148, 154, 155,157
Andah, Bassey 294, 296, 298
Anglo Americans, 17, 18, 19, 32,103, 114; belief and culture, 105; culture, 72; history, 227
Arabic invasion, 227; knowledge, 237; Arabs, 205, 228, 236
Arctic environments, 57
art for art's sake, 216; Aryan Model of History and Culture, 33, 146, 152, 155, 157, 161, 163, 165, 169
Asia, 159, 160, 175, 176, 192, 236, 332; Asians, 98, 126, 151, 158-159, 175-176, 207, 212;317
Asian Americans, 99, 126; Asiatic, 151, 159
assimilate, 103; assimilation, 4, 16, 32, 103, 104, 105, 164, 165
barbarians, 31, 153
beauty, 166, 167, 178, 202, 215, 216, 251, 277, 301
behavioral change, 51, 53, 183
belief system, 38, 65, 186, 246
ben-Jochannan, Yosef 151
Bernal, Martin 149, 150, 152, 153, 157, 323
Bible, 13, 40, 71, 230; biblical figures, 30; interpretation, 30;

sanction, 69
biological and cultural responses, 56
Birdsell, J.B.172, 175, 176, 177, 182, 323
Black: Activist Groups, 127; activists, 140; administrators, 21
Black Afro-Saxons, 165
Black: Americans, 19, 20, 103; collaborators, 99; colleges, 17; communities, 22, 87, 96, 100-101, 102; collective consciousness, 38, 73; economic base, 102
Black:: English, 64, 219, 266; females, 74; freedom., 124; homes and businesses, 102; inferiority, 101, 106; males, 73; mental illness, 203; mind, 205
Black Nationalism, 73, 89, 91; Black Panther Party, 92, 96, 121, 138
Black people, 74, 92, 93, 96, 103, 109, 123, 201, 204, 205, 208, 209; Black: progress, 83, 84, 315; rebellions, 119; seminarians, 29; teachers, 100; urban centers, 100; black women, 74;
Black Power, 29, 91, 99, 326
Black professionals, 21; psychiatrists and psychologists, 205
Black-American Indian" identity, 80
Borishade, Adetokunbo 64, 85, 86, 219, 220, 221, 222, 223, 224, 323
Bras, Mari, 137, 142
Brazil, 113, 237, 238, 239, 240
Campbell, Mary E., 80
Candace, Queen 198
Caribbean, the 5, 34, 64, 113, 188, 212, 238, 240
Carmichael, Stokely (aka Kwame Toure), 92, 130, 191 200
Cacuse, Larry, 141
Catholic beliefs and practices, 224; iconography, 224; saints, 224, 240
Caucasians, 8, 25-26, 27, 45-46, 48, 72, 104, 108, 144, 146, 156, 160, 162,165, 166, 167, 180, 195 200, 287, 308, 309; ; cultural norms, 208; nationalism, 152; personality, 8; social workers, 206;
Caucasoid, 175, 176
character, 7, 15, 20, 34, 35, 74, 100, 115, 124, 196, 199, 225, 243, 245, 246, 247, 248, 249, 250, 251, 252, 253, 256, 257, 261, 265, 274, 275, 279, 301, 302, 307
Chicanos, 98
childhood, 68, 253, 273, 280; childrearing, 6, 35, 202
Christian, 9, 30, 31, 40, 91, 111, 121, 131, 166, 168, 178, 215, 221, 224; churches, 9, 22, 40, 71, 87, 127, 156, 166, 201;

missionaries, 9, 178; theology, 30
Christianity, 30, 40, 69, 93, 151, 152, 161, 167, 168, 190, 239
CIA covert actions, 119 *(see FBI)*
civil rights, 32, 89, 91, 94, 108, 109, 118, 124, 125, 126, 132, 133, 134, 136, 164, 170; Civil Rights Act of 1964, 124; Civil Rights Movement, 4, 73, 88, 89, 94, 96, 100, 102, 154
Civil War, 122, 305, 328
Clarke, John Henrik 95, 94, 48-149, 150, 159, 229, 237, 233, 284, 326
Cleaver, Eldridge, 73, 130, 287
clinical therapists, 6
COINTELPRO, 32, 117, 118, 120, 121, 126, 127, 128, 129, 130, 132, 135, 138, 141, 144, 330, 342 *(see FBI)*
Commission on Decolonization, 142
Communist Party-USA, 126; Communists, 118, 131
communities, 5, 11, 23, 38, 56, 85, 88, 93, 96, 98, 102, 263, 286; community activism, 266; centers, 22, 128; leaders, 6, 298 program facilitators, 6; stake-holders, 22
Cone, James H. 29
Continent, 5, 87, 210, 212, 217, 221, 224, 296, 300, 309

Copeland, 123, 124
Cotton, Joel, 149
Council for Conservative Citizens, 134
Creole language, 63, 64, 219, 266
Cuffee, Paul, 92
cultural: assimilation, 32; beliefs, 68; confusion, 72; dissonance, 58
cultural elements, 58, 72, 217, 224, 241; features, 224
cultural: identity, 32, 59, 60-61, 63, 76, 224; nterests, 60; knowledge, 86; manipulations, 201; mission, 62; norms and interpretations; reality, 69; security, 115; similarities, 213; values, 85, 112, 276
cultural responses to the Arctic, 57
cultural cultural cultural cultural weapon, 62
culture-related illness, 10
cultures, 24, 28, 34, 37, 57, 60, 65, 68, 72, 152, 170, 193, 206, 212, 213, 268
curriculum, 21, 43, 75, 288, 289
curse, 69, 70, 310
customs, 64, 213, 243
Dark Ages, 9, 156, 305
Delaney, Martin, 92
Deloria, Vine, 5
democracy, 119, 121, 122, 123, 144
Derrickson, Kennedy B., 81, 339
Destiny, 2, 192, 258, 260
Developmental adaptation,

181
Diaspora, 63, 84, 188, 212, 241, 294, 297, 306, 321
Diasporan Africans, *(see African Americans*
Diop, Cheikh Anta, 55, 61-62, 64, 65, 69-70, 71, 148, 151, 158, 159, 179, 193, 195, 196, 197, 198, 199, 216, 217, 328
disaster capitalism, 25, 125, 285
discrimination, 89, 109, 137, 185, 285, 313, 315
dissimulation, 224
Divine Destiny, 2, 29, 265, 287; Divine Forces, 259, 261, 262, 263, 267, 271; Divine Mandate, 260; Divine Mission, 26, 29, 62, 90, 94, 117, 136, 228, 263, 264-265, 287; Divine Retribution, 309; Divine Rhythms of the Universe, 263; divine sanctioning, 37; divine scheme, 42; Divine Spirit, 188; Divine Transformative Power, 266
DNA evidence, 177
Dopamu, p. Ade, 245, 246, 333
Dorey, Shannon, 46
DSM-IV, 7, 8
DuBois, 17, 18, 19, 20, 90, 154, 321, 330
Ebonics, 64, 266, 325
Ecun, 218, 219, 220, 226
education, 14, 17, 19, 38, 43, 49, 63, 68, 89, 170, 178, 199, 201, 232, 233, 266, 285, 286, 288, 289, 290, 294, 298, 308, 337; and training, 223; institutions, 5; systems, 44, 49, 284
institutions of America, 69
educators, 6, 14, 21, 45
Egypt, 70, 71, 149, 150, 158, 159, 167, 197, 198, 227, 229, 234, 261, 269, 288, 325, 335
Egyptian: civilization, 159; history, 27, 160; knowledge, 152-153,;
Egyptian pyramids, 152, 270
Egyptians, 70, 71, 147, 151, 153, 154, 158, 160, 161, 234, 269
Egypto-Nubian antiquity, 63
eighteenth century, 31
elderly people, 13, 140
Electoral College, 123
Elizabeth M. Vera, 81, 339
enslaved, 26, 85, 169, 217, 220, 222, 237, 264, 284
environment, 56, 60, 65, 85, 101, 155, 175, 179, 180, 181, 183, 196, 197, 206, 299; Epistemology, 42
ethical behavior, 54, 275; concepts, 196; ethics, 41, 187, 214, 246, 267, 274, 282, 300
Ethiopia, 150, 180, 198, 227, 229, 261, 325
Eurasian: 176, 193, 195, 196, 197, 199; culture, 196; plains, 193, 195; Eurocentric, 44, 152, 160, 340; theory, 44
Europe, 7, 26, 43, 44, 48,

49, 108, 149, 156, 158, 176, 187, 199, 230, 231, 235, 284, 309, 337, 340
Europe's childhood, 156
European, 7, 29, 34, 85, 104, 105, 107, 108, 144, 149, 156, 157, 158, 163, 169, 192, 222, 226, 232, 308, 311, 321; intellectuals, 155; peninsula, 175; perspective, 69; philosophers, 29; religion, 149; European/American culture, 217
Europeans, 11, 18, 85, 104, 145, 146, 149, 156, 157, 158, 160, 163, 178, 199, 220, 227, 230, 231, 269, 305
Evers, Medgar, 91, 121, 209
evil, 25, 26, 39, 185, 247, 275, 277, 278
evolutionary period, 3, 55, 65, 229
experience, 11, 12, 13, 29, 56, 58, 59, 60, 191, 208, 245, 257, 298
Fanon, Frantz, 287
Farrakhan, Louis, 92
FBI, 32, 116, 117, 118, 119, 120, 121, 126, 127, 128, 129, 130, 131, 132, 133, 135, 136, 137, 138, 139, 140, 141, 142, 143, 144; *agents provocateurs*; 130, 139; Border Coverage Program, 128; Counter-intelligence Program, 117 . *(see COINTELPRO)*

female African scholars., 36; females, 12, 15, 166, 177
Forten, James, 90
Fourteen Principles, 252, 266
Fourteenth and Fifteenth Amendments, 122
Frances Cress Welsing, 73, 200
Frederick Douglass, 90, 154
Freire, Paulo, 286
Garnet, Henry Highland 92
Garvey, Marcus, 92, 94, 107, 168
genetic: ability; color inferiority, 8; genetics, 46, 155, 179, 224
genocide, 205
Genotype, 76
geographic locations, 24, 56
German, 31, 162
German National Socialism, 31, 162-163
Ghana, 218, 236, 276
Glick, Brian 118, 119, 120, 126, 330
God, 2, 3, 24, 26, 37, 39, 40, 42, 69, 70, 104, 161, 166, 170, 186, 187, 189, 191, 194, 197, 211, 214, 215, 239, 244, 251, 268, 273, 274, 275, 279, 289, 290, 291, 294, 297, 300, 310, 325, 332
godhood, 253, 273, 280, 297, 298, 301
Golden Ages of Africa: , 75, 237; First 148, 229; Second 231-232; Second 231, 232; Third,

236; Fourth, 237
Greco-Latin antiquity, 63; Greece, 147, 152, 157, 217, 230; Greek civilization, 154, 158 Greek culture, 45, 147, 150, 152
Greeks, 45, 147, 150, 151, 153, 156, 160, 163, 199, 233
Gregerson, Edgar, 218, 220
Griaule, Marcele, 46
group behaviors, 54, 68; group is manipulated, 60
Gyekye, 212-213, 221, 275, 276, 278, 330
Haisch, Bernard 189-191 191
Ham, 69, 70, 71
Hamer, Fanny Lou 91
Hare, Nathan 73, 74, 169, 330
Harlem Renaissance, 114
hatred and oppression, 10
Hatshepsut, 198
Hayes, Rutherford B., 122; Hayes betrayal, 122, 125
healing, 5, 6, 10, 24, 27, 35, 79, 87, 112, 115, 207, 254, 267, 288, 303, 306, 310; healing arts, 223
health, 8, 11, 12, 24, 28, 32, 34, 68, 72, 88, 128, 164, 182, 202, 205, 214, 241, 254, 279, 316
Hebrew: 69, 70, 159, 176, 230; literature, 70
Hebrews, 151
hegemony, 104, 105, 165-166
Herodotus, 150, 152

high priests, 46
higher education, 17, 18, 19, 170, 265
Hilliard, Asa 286, 296, 332
Hindu-Sanskritic India., 162
historiography, 160, 162
history of Africa, 229; of African Americans, 19; of humanity, 196
HIV/AIDS, 11, 12, 202
holistic belief system, 186
Holy City of Ile-Ife, 238
Hoover, J. Edgar, 118, 129, 131, 136,
Horney, Karen, 80
human: behavior, 206; human beings, 38, 42, 65, 111, 173, 183, 261, 263, 267, 268, 270, 273, 279, 300, 305; human condition, 267, 268; ecology, 181; expectations, 275; nature, 254; progress, 226
human rights, 89; human society, 278
humanistic outlook, 187
humanity, 2, 7, 10, 37, 42, 51, 148, 155, 164, 172, 177, 180, 196, 229, 264, 297
Hyksos, 71, 151, 232, 233
Ice Age, 193
ideals: 4, 19, 28, 29, 35, 37, 41, 49, 58, 68, 163, 167, 216, 241, 246, 263, 281, 303-304, 307; of peace, 216; of war, violence, crime and conquests, 217
identity, 16, 20, 27, 28, 32, 34, 37, 49, 59, 60, 61,

62, 63, 69, 73, 74, 76, 77, 80, 81, 82, 84, 87, 88, 107, 108, 112, 113, 115, 116, 186, 210, 225, 250, 263, 296, 298, 318; confusion, 84; crisis, 88, 164; loss of, 18
Idowu, E. Bolaji, 247, 251, 279, 332
imperialism, 93, 104, 105, 137, 144, 158, 160, 165-166, 104; imperialist, 48, 97, 123
Independence for Puerto Rico Activists, 128
Indian Sanskrit language, 162
Indians, 31, 141, 317
indigenous cultural features, 58
Indo-European languages, 162; Indo-European linguistic family, 220
inferiority of Blacks, 8
infinity, immortality, and eternity, 192
iinstitutional racism, 34, 73, 200, 201, 202
institutions, 9, 38, 39, 68, 93, 200, 201, 202, 213, 217, 222, 305, 328; integration, 16, 21, 122, 123, 124, 125, 133, 134, 164; integrationist, 89, 90, 91, 94, 95, 96, 127
intellectual: development, 266; oppression, 204
Islam, 96, 151, 152, 227, 239; Islamic extremists, 40; jihad, 236
Israelite persecution, 70; Israelites, 71
Jahn, Janheinz, 46

Jim Crow laws, 123
Judaism, 151, 152
justice, 21, 99, 109, 118, 122, 169, 196, 216, 244, 282, 303, 310, 313
Kemet, 70, 227, 229, 231, 232, 233, 234, 235, 242, 261, 288
Kennedy, John and Robert, 94, 209
King, Martin L., xxiv, 10, 90, 91, 95, 121, 130, 131, 135, 136, 208, 252
Kongo-Kordofanian languages, 218-219
Ku Klux Klan, 127, 132, 134
Kush, 70, 229, 231, 233, 235, 236, 261, 335; Kushite pyramids, 234; Kushites, 234
Lagosian Cultural Renaissance, 113, 237, 238
Latin America, 113; Latin Americans, 113, 239
Leakey, Louis S.B. 148
Malcolm X (aka El Hajj Malik El Shabazz), 92, 93, 95, 121, 128, 130, 185, 208, 287, 306
Mali, 107, 236
manhood, 16, 95, 301
March on Washington, 92, 94, 95
Massey, Gerald, 149, 150, 151, 333
material belief system, 187
materialism, 152, 197
mathematicians, 46, 270
matriarchal family system, 197, 216; matriarchy, 198, 328

Karenga, Maulana, 94, 154
McCarthy, Joseph 117
medicine, 38, 44, 46, 68, 100, 112, 148, 230, 232, 236, 305
mental: balance, 11, 252; enslavement, 28, 163; health, 34, 79, 204, 206, 211; mental health disorders, 8, 107, 306; oppression, 203
Meroe, 34, 234, 235, 335; Meroites, 235
Mesopotamian Semitic world, 159
Middle East, 176, 235, 236; Middle Eastern, 40, 212
Militancy, 93; militant, 93, 98, 130
miseducation, 2, 19, 284, 342
Mississippi Freedom Democratic Party, 126
Mitchell, Henry, 30
models of history and culture, 33
Asante, Molefi Kete, 154
Mongoloids, 175, 176
moral; behavior, 253, 274; character, 277; goodness, 275; discipline, 275; injunction, 214; values, 249
morality, 41, 51, 187, 214, 246, 251, 267, 274, 275, 276, 279,282
Moses, 70
Movimiento Pro-Independencia, 137
MtDna, 155
Muhammad, Elijah, 92, 94, 130; Fruit of Islam (FOI), 96

multinational corporations, 25, 125
multi-racial protests, 97, 98
music, 246, 271, 320
Muslim imams, 6; Muslims, 3, 121
mystical powers, 267, 273, 274, 301
mythology, 39, 161, 222
NAACP, 126, 315
Napata culture, 234
Nation of Islam, 92, 94;
National Committee for a SANE Nuclear Policy., 127
National Lawyers Guild, 126
Nationalist, 24, 89, 92, 94, 127, 129, 90, 93, 129, 162 *(see Black Nationalist)*
Native Americans, 28, 99, 107, 126, 139, 141, 175, 269
Near Eastern civilizations, 158
Negro, 19, 20, 22, 31, 94, 129, 131, 153, 196, 206, 284, 285, 327, 331, 333, 337, 342
Neolithic culture, 230, 231, 340
Neutralization, 121, 126
New Left Activists, 127
New World natives, 175
Newton, Huey, 92
Nigeria, 107, 113, 218, 237, 238, 320
Niger-Kongo, 64, 218, 219
Niger-Kongo grammatical structure, 219
Niger-Kongo languages, 64, 219-220

NileRiver Valley, 34, 63, 196, 227, 233, 234, 290; civilizations, 63
nomadism, 193, 197
non-violent passive resistance, 89, 91, 94, 95
northern cradle, 193, 196, 197, 199
Nubia, 227, 229, 231, 232, 233, 234, 242, 261, 325, 335
Nzinga,Queen, 198
Oglala nation, 140
Yai, Olabiyi B., 226
Olomenji, 204, 205
oppression, 2, 10, 35, 40, 45, 73, 86, 95, 97, 109, 116, 123, 164, 166, 183, 185, 203, 204, 206, 208, 225, 256; oppressive institutions, 204
Oreos, 99
Osiris, 152
Out-of-Africa" theorists, 177
Oyebade, Bayo 154
Palmer, R.R., 149
pathological, 7
patriarchy, 199, 328
patriotism in post-9/11, 81
pedagogy, 286, 330
people of color, 8, 18, 26, 28, 49, 145, 163, 186, 200
perception of reality, 38
personal advancement., 266
personal and spiritual growth, 257; 271
PEW Research Center, 83
pharonic era of Africa, 229; pharonic traditions, 235
philosophers, 31, 152, 155, 287; philosophical principles, 307; source material, 6
philosophy, 24, 27, 28, 29, 31, 35, 40, 41, 42, 43, 44, 49, 59, 60, 114, 215, 221, 236, 241, 267, 268, 286, 300, 302, 304, 305, 306, 323, 333, 335, 339, 341
physical environments, 56, 173
physical illness, 72
physical superiority, 48
physical traits, 57, 174
physiological adaptations, 180
political control, 7, 8, 9, 17, 24, 26, 41, 51, 81, 86, 97, 98, 117, 119, 120, 123, 135, 138, 145, 183, 185, 203, 223, 235, 256, 282, 284, 315; power, 25; rulers, 46
politicians, 22, 125, 135, 164, 166
politics, 17, 25, 68, 124, 125, 201, 314
positive change, 11, 36, 41, 302
prehistoric, 179, 181, 182, 196
principles of the universe, 268
prison value system, 7; prisoners, 98, 138
professors, 43, 69, 155
program facilitators, 6
progressive movement, 32, 33, 116, 126, 144
propaganda of self-destruction, 77
protest, 32, 98, 117, 119,

124, 127, 128, 141
psyche, 51, 104, 115
psychological, 27, 62, 64, 65, 72, 86, 105, 107, 12,135, 163, 165, 185; escape and denial, 73; psychological warfare, 205, 135
Ptahhotep, 288, 289, 290, 291, 292, 293, 300
Puerto Rican Socialist Party, 128; Puerto Ricans, 98, 128
race, 2, 3, 17, 19, 21, 22, 33, 70, 77, 80, 83, 84, 86, 145, 148, 153, 155, 164, 167, 172, 173, 174, 178, 182, 202, 228, 287, 306, 313, 314, 337; as adaptive group, 173
race consciousness, 21, 24, 33, 76, 77; pride, 33
Race, Richard R., 200
racial: destiny, 287; discrimination, 21, 91; identity, 61, 82, 112; oppression, 208, 307; racketeers, 22
racial segregation, 89; racial toadies, 22
racial types-variations, 28, 162 172
racism, 19, 34, 73, 100, 104, 105, 109, 110, 127, 137, 144, 155, 160, 165, 185, 200, 202, 209, 328, 340
Racism, 157, 165, 200, 328, 332, 340, 342; racist, 21, 26, 29, 43, 44, 46, 49, 87, 91, 93, 96, 109, 110, 123, 127, 132, 133, 134, 158, 186, 200, 201
racist barriers, 21; interests, 21; oppression, 116
racist practices, 200; school systems, 109, 288; social system, 109
Reconstruction Period, 122, 123, 334
Red Power, 99
Re-Education, 288
rehabilitate, 6, 94
reinforcement, 56
religion, 24, 25, 26, 28, 29, 31, 37,38, 39, 44, 59, 60,68, 69, 104, 113, 146, 149, 151, 152, 158, 160, 161, 166, 178, 190, 201, 214, 222, 238, 239, 240, 246, 251, 268, 308, 328, 333, 340, 342
religion of Ifa, 238, 239
religious beliefs, 12, 30, 45, 51, 65, 76, 191, 221, 223, 241
religious differences, 24
religious faith, 253, 265, 307
right-wing paramilitary groups, 139
rites, 35, 298
Temple, Robert, 46
Roman historians, 150; Romans, 199; Rome, 217
Rosa Parks, 91
Sankofa, 297, 323, 324
science, 27, 46, 83, 100, 148, 152, 155, 157, 188, 190, 207, 230, 232, 305
scientific beliefs, 51
scientific knowledge, 47, 153
SCLC, 91, 126, 131, 135,

136
Scranton, Laird, 46
sedentary lifestyle, 193
segregation, 19, 89, 123, 131, 133
self-alienation, 80, 86; self-dehumanization, 86
self-development, 265; self-discipline,, 41, 271; self-empowerment, 77, 265
self-hatred, 49, 79, 86, 87, 101, 106, 107, 109, 164, 167; loathing, 106, 109, 211, 308
self-identity, 79, 84, 87; Semites, 176, 230; Semitic blood, 163
sermons, 26, 30, 39, 40, 51, 71
Seven liberal arts, 266; seven Virtues, 261, 266
sexism, 104, 105, 165, 166
Sheba, Queen, 198
sheriff's office representatives, 22
sin, 215, 217, 247
slave population, 20; slave thinking, 28; slavery, 5, 9, 20, 40, 69, 70, 71, 74, 75, 77, 89, 112, 122, 158, 169, 201, 223; slaves, 28, 76, 169, 204, 221
Smith, T.H. 30
social: decline, 1, 34, 88, 164, 165, 211; expectations, 54, 280; fragmentation and decline, 224; social group, 17; harmony, 275; infrastructures, 35, 38, 294, 298; institutions, 47, 68, 77, 214, 223; interaction, 60; organization, 197, 199; stability, 38, 100, 114, 296, 300; values, 39, 214
social stresses, 73; structures, 41; 61, 260; transgression, 277
social uplift agencies, 22
Socialist League (LSP), 128; Socialist Workers Party, 128
socialization process, 68, 286, 294, 298
societies, 33, 41, 56, 58, 68, 195, 198, 210, 213, 220, 221, 222, 231, 266, 267, 276, 278, 298, 305
socio-political oppression, 77
Sojourner Truth, 90
Songhai, 236
Southern Christian Leadership Coalition (SCLC)., 91
southern cradle of civilization, 148, 193, 195, 196
southern ruling class, 123, 124
speech, 17, 51, 95, 121, 131, 141, 215, 290, 292
Speight, Suzette L., 81
spirit, 12, 40, 72, 85, 120, 161, 186, 188, 189, 196, 197, 207, 258, 268, 275, 279, 339
spiritual, 2, 3, 24, 27, 28, 36, 65, 72, 112, 164, 165, 186, 187, 192, 207, 214, 215, 223, 248, 251, 252, 256, 260, 261, 263, 264, 265, 268, 273, 274,

275, 280, 289, 297, 298, 300, 301, 302, 304, 307, 309, 310; spiritual advancement, 265; beauty, 253; development, 274, 278; growth, 265, 271; harmony, 271; spiritual head, 258; language, 207; spiritual person, 297; self, 79; self-destruction., 80; spiritual strength, 73
spiritual worldview, 187, 188, 189, 274
spirituality, 51, 190, 239, 253, 279
spoken word, 252, 257, 267, 273
STD, 12
students, 12, 14, 43, 44, 45, 46, 48, 98, 100, 103, 108, 121, 227, 236, 285, 289, 300
Sudan, 150, 196, 198, 227, 229, 236, 261, 335; Sudanic empires, 236; Sudanic universities, 236
superiority, 8, 9, 104, 156, 200
supernatural, 248, 275, 277; supernatural beings, 278; supernaturalism, 187, 276
Supreme Being, 189
Supreme Court, 123, 133, 169
survival, 14, 17, 32, 35, 49, 54, 55, 57, 59, 60, 72, 75, 86, 105, 113, 165, 169, 170, 180, 183, 185, 186, 190, 193, 196, 199,

206, 207, 211, 222, 241, 242, 263, 286, 297, 303, 307, 310
synchronization, 224
synchronized, 224
syncretization, 240
teachers, 22, 43, 50, 69, 100, 108, 133, 289, 291
teaching, 14, 18, 26, 29, 43, 44, 46, 49, 100, 161, 289, 290; teachings, 16, 45, 58, 94, 106, 113, 238, 261, 288, 292, 293, 300, 306, 307, 311
teen mothers, 14
Temple, Cristel N. 82
Thomas, Clarence 169
Todd C. Shaw, 81
total history, 28, 116, 228
Toure, Kwame Toure (aka Stokely Carmichael, 92
Traditional Oglalas, 140
traditions, 6, 13, 24, 28, 30, 33, 44, 65, 106, 113, 114, 161, 178, 199, 210, 223, 234, 235, 241, 297, 307, 308
transformation, 3, 30, 137, 295, 302
tropical environments, 57, 186
Turner, Nat, 92
U.S. activists, 118
U.S. Bureau of Education, 19; Congress, 91, 120; constitutional rights, 25; government, 32, 33, 100, 103, 117, 120, 140, 144, 285; government strategy, 100; intervention abroad, 98; State Department, 97
United Nations, 93, 97, 142

United Negro Improvement Association (UNIA)., 94
United States, 16, 17, 25, 82, 93, 96, 121, 125, 128, 144, 156, 186, 204, 227
universal balance and harmony, 187; Universal Circle of human existence, 255; Universal Laws, 253
universe, 41, 42, 51, 153, 161, 186, 188, 189, 248, 256, 259, 268, 269, 270
universities, 18, 22, 69, 200, 308; university researchers, 22
Urban Renewal, 102
V.Y. Mudimbe, 44
values, 4, 7, 9, 10, 13, 14, 16, 33, 34, 35, 37, 39, 41, 49, 51, 52, 53, 54, 58, 62, 64, 65, 68, 72, 83, 85, 88, 100, 104, 106, 112, 114, 164, 165, 166, 172, 186, 187, 204, 207, 210, 211, 214, 224, 225, 231, 241, 242, 248, 281, 286, 302, 303, 304, 308, 314, 323, 337
Vasant Kaiwar's, 157
Vietnam, 98, 119, 128, 129
Vietnam War, 98
violence, 73, 89, 93, 95, 96, 108, 123, 127, 130, 133, 134, 135, 138, 139, 140, 144, 164, 208, 209
vision, 20, 99, 114, 260, 287, 288
vocational schools, 17
W.E.B. DuBois, 90
war, 25, 40, 98, 118, 127, 137, 285, 305; in Iraq, 208
warriors, 46, 198
welfare mothers, 98
wellbeing, 7, 24, 32, 59, 72, 79, 90, 207, 214, 255, 263, 275, 279
West Africa, 218, 235, 236, 237
West Africans: 219, 226; ethnic groups, 226
West Africans, 219
Western, 4, 7, 9, 10, 26, 46, 49, 83, 85, 87, 104, 129, 147, 149, 152, 154, 157, 159, 175, 187, 190, 212, 213, 215, 216, 217, 226, 228, 299, 303, 307, 309, 318, 323, 325; capitalism, 85; civilization, 87, 150, 153, 227; culture, 7, 75, 147, 150, 188, 217, 304
Western Diaspora, 87
Western educational system, 63
Western hemisphere, 218, 219, 221, 224, 240; Western imperialism, 9, 69, 87; Western mind, 207; Western scientific know-ledge, 47
White 'ego ideals, 74
White females, 73
White hate groups, 127, 132
White New Left Movement, 98
White *status quo*, 21
White superiors, 21
White supremacists, 165; White supremacy, 43, 47, 48, 49, 101, 104, 163, 165, 169, 201, 211,

308, 320, 340
whites, 8, 31, 80, 84, 201, 313, 314, 315
Whites, 8, 17, 48, 69, 74, 75, 84, 89, 90, 91, 93, 96, 101, 109, 110, 121, 123, 178, 205, 208, 309, 317
Whites' deep-seated sense of inferiority, 200
wholeness, 32, 72
Wiredu, Kwasi, 44, 214, 276
wisdom, 9, 14, 16, 41, 214, 216, 252, 259, 261, 263, 265, 267, 281, 290, 292, 300, 302, 305, 307, 309
Wolf et.al, 119, 120, 129, 130, 132, 136, 137, 138, 139, 141, 142, 143, 144
women, 11, 12, 13, 15, 26, 45, 99, 105, 109, 112, 113, 121, 155, 166, 177, 180, 198, 199, 229, 245, 274, 278; Afro-Brazilian, 237
women's liberation struggle, 99
Women's Strike for Peace, 126
Woodson, Carter G. 19, 20, 21, 285, 342
world civilizations, 31, 44
world cultures, 24, 188, 191, 192
World cultures, 189
world history, 4
world peace, 24
worldview, 16, 30, 34, 42, 45, 65, 68, 75, 76, 186, 187, 207, 221
worldviews, 1, 37, 188, 192, 207

wrongdoing, 10, 30, 209, 277, 278
Yoruba, 2, 34, 35, 85, 113, 218, 225, 226, 227, 228, 236, 237-238, 242, 243, 245, 246, 247, 248, 249, 251, 252, 253, 258, 264, 265, 273, 274, 277, 279, 289, 292, 300, 303, 310, 320, 323, 325, 332, 333, 342; language, 240; literary corpus, 243, 245, 247, 249; mythology, 249; oral and written histories, 240; traditional philosophy, 249, 252; principles, 262; proverbs, 258; religion, 238, 240; worldwide religion, 25
Young Lords Party, 128
young people, 13, 256, 307
youth, 6, 14, 22, 23, 74, 111, 128, 130, 318

www.ingramcontent.com/pod-product-compliance
Ingram Content Group UK Ltd.
Pitfield, Milton Keynes, MK11 3LW, UK
UKHW021301180426
11947UKWH00015B/958